"**Mother Loyola's name** is becoming one that in itself is an endorsement of every book over which it appears...A careful use of Mother Loyola's work will be productive of the best results."   --Rosary Magazine, November 1901

About Mother Mary Loyola:

Most Catholics today who have heard the name Mother Mary Loyola know her as the author of *The King of the Golden City*, which has enjoyed a resurgence in popularity in recent years. But few know that she wrote over two dozen works, and that she was once a household name among Catholics of her era. What made her unique among Catholic authors was her ability to draw in her listeners with story after story—and not just any stories, but ones that incorporated current events and brand new inventions of the time. Despite the fact that those events are no longer current, and those inventions no longer brand new, her books scintillate with the appeal of an active mind that could find a moral in the most unusual places. And while the printed word lacks the animated facial expressions and vocal inflections which reveal a gifted storyteller, hers convey her enthusiasm so capably that the reader can easily imagine sitting at the feet of this wise old nun.

About *The Soldier of Christ*:

Any book on the sacrament of Confirmation can explain what Confirmation *is*, but this is the only book that explains, in the most original and engaging manner, what Confirmation *does*. It is both a dialogue and a travelogue, taking the reader on a journey from the Crusades to the Crimea; from medieval ceremonies of Knighthood to early modern methods of warfare.

What does it mean to be a Soldier of Christ? For the true child of God, life is a daily battle against a well-concealed foe—that is, our own flaws and failings—and Mother Mary Loyola proposes to arm young recruits adequately for this task, leaving no stone unturned in her quest to root out this 'enemy at home'. This is the sort of basic training no young Catholic should be without.

To learn more about Mother Mary Loyola, visit our website at
www.staugustineacademypress.com.

THE SOLDIER OF CHRIST

IGNATIUS OF LOYOLA EXCHANGING THE EARTHLY FOR
THE HEAVENLY WARFARE.

"O thou sword of the Lord, how long wilt thou not be quiet? Go into
thy scabbard, rest and be still.

"How shall it be quiet when the Lord hath given it a charge and hath
made an appointment for it?"   (JEREM. 47: 6, 7.)

The Soldier of Christ

Talks before Confirmation

By

Mother Mary Loyola

Edited by
Father Herbert Thurston, S.J.

"Labour as a good soldier of Christ Jesus."
(2 Tim. 2, 3.)

2011

St. Augustine Academy Press

Lisle, Illinois

This book is newly typeset based on the 1904 edition published by Burns & Oates. All editing strictly limited to the correction of errors in the original text, the addition of selected footnotes, and minor clarifications in punctuation or phrasing. Any remaining oddities of spelling or phrasing are as found in the original.

Nihil Obstat:
GEORGIUS TYRRELL, S.J.

Imprimatur:
HERBERTUS CARD. VAUGHAN.
Archiep. Westmonast.

This book was originally published in 1900 by Burns & Oates. This edition ©2010 by St. Augustine Academy Press. All editing by Lisa Bergman.
Second printing, Feb. 2016: errata corrected, some racial references softened.

ISBN: 978-1-64051-052-4
Library of Congress Control Number: 2011941816

Unless otherwise noted, all illustrations in this book, including the cover, are either the original illustrations as found in the book, or are public domain images.

To the Soldier of Christ

Who went forth from Loyola

To Wage War

First with Self and then with the World:

Who having given an Example

Of every Knightly Virtue

May say with St. Paul:

Be Ye Followers of Me

As I Am of Christ.

Editor's Note

I have endeavored in this new revised edition of Mother Mary Loyola's *The Soldier of Christ* to be as faithful as possible to the original text as printed in the 1904 edition by Burns and Oates. However, I have, in a few cases, judiciously corrected punctuation and spelling where the change significantly enhanced the clarity of the passage. I have also augmented the text with additional footnotes, in the hopes of shedding some light on personages and events which were well-known to readers at the time, but are no longer so. Therefore the reader should understand that though this text is considered revised due to these facts, the majority of the material found herein is exactly as it was written over 100 years ago.

The modern reader will no doubt find some of the ethnic references in this book to be awkward; however, it is my conviction that the value of this book *as a whole* is far greater than the idiosyncrasies of the particular cultural bias contained within—a bias which was quite normal for that time and place. Therefore, with a few exceptions, I felt it more appropriate to leave the reader and/or parent to treat these occasions as a learning experience, and to address any concerns on an individual basis, rather than changing or omitting such passages.

Lastly, I would point out that all Scriptural references found in this book are from the Catholic Douay-Rheims version, and thus they often do not align in chapter and verse with modern bibles, which conform more closely to the chapter and verse structure of the Protestant King James Version.

In Christ,
Lisa Bergman
St. Augustine Academy Press
April 2010

PREFACE

ENNODIUS of Pavia, an ecclesiastical writer of the fifth century, describes in a passage of his *Apologia pro Synodo*, how "the newly baptized in their white robes pass from the brink of the fountain to the Pope's portable chair, hard by the martyr-tomb of St. Peter, and there, while very joy forces streams of tears from their eyes, the gifts which God's goodness has just bestowed are forthwith renewed and doubled."[1] This "doubling of the gifts" by the administration of the Sacrament of Confirmation immediately after Baptism, was the universal practice down to the Middle Ages. Even to this day it is retained among the Eastern Churches, and it is alluded to by many early Fathers from St. Irenaus and Tertullian downwards. Very appropriately therefore has Mother Loyola followed up her book on Baptism with another kindred volume on the Sacrament of Confirmation. It was said in a review of the same author's *First Communion*, that her religious teaching was not only practical but practicable. This encomium will be found

---

1   "*Ecce nunc ad gestatoriam sellam apostolicae confessionis uda mittunt limina candidates et uberibus gaudio exactore fletibus collate Dei beneficio dona geminantur.*" (Ennodius, *Apologia pro Synodo*, Edit. Hartel, p. 328.) The chair to which reference is here made is that very *cathedra Petri*, now enclosed in the magnificent shrine build for it by Alexander VII, in the apse of St. Peter's.

to apply with not less force to the present book. Moreover, the apt and abundant illustration, the natural, chatty tone, the freshness of thought, the occasional lapse into dialogue, the details and enumerations which children love, the clever utilizing of the military spirit of the hour—all these are just what Mother Loyola's previous books have led us to expect. There will probably be few critics to dispute that in the present most useful volume, she also has "doubled her gifts."

I have called the volume most useful, because it seems to be a general complaint that in no branch of a child's religious training is there a greater dearth of suitable manuals then in this matter of confirmation. It may be that the subject is a difficult one to treat, but here again Mother Loyola appears to have struck altogether the right note in making the military idea the backbone of all her instruction. The gifts of the Holy Ghost have not been neglected, but they are not made prominent. It would seem to require (I speak with all deference for those who may hold a contrary opinion) much more mature minds than those the author is addressing to meditate profitably on the precise distinction between such abstractions as Wisdom and Understanding, Counsel and Knowledge. If the particular gift of Fortitude has been dwelt upon somewhat to the exclusion of the rest, the teaching of the Catechism may fairly be appealed to, which tells us, that the principal end of Confirmation, as indeed the very name imports, is "to make us strong and perfect Christians and soldiers of Jesus Christ."

In any case, we can hardly exaggerate the importance of courage for all beginners in the spiritual life. There was much good sense in the saying of the Anglican dignitary, spoken of by Mrs. Ewing in one of her books, who impressed it upon his hearers that the young men should be modest, and the maidens brave. And when they protested: "Surely, Reverend Father, you make a mistake, you mean that the young men should be brave and the maidens modest;" "No, no," he returned, "I meant what I said; it is the men who need the modesty and the maidens the fortitude." For the great bulk of children, at the age at which they are wont to receive Confirmation, let us hope that they are in the position of the maidens. We may take their modesty for granted yet a while. The more immediate need is the seriousness, the courage, and the self-discipline of the soldier. Perhaps Mother Loyola may someday be persuaded to give us a separate volume on the modesty of Our Lady's Knights, telling us how the little sodalists of Mary Immaculate should be Bayards[1] not only *sans peur* but also *sans reproche*.

It may be interesting in this connection to recall how Christians were prepared for Confirmation according to the traditions of the early Church. We have a document ready to hand in the twenty-first instruction given by St. Cyril of Jerusalem to his catechumens in A.D. 347. The military idea is there almost as prominent as it is in the pages which follow. St. Cyril points out first that after Christ our Lord had been baptized in the River Jordan, "and had imparted the fragrance of His Godhead to the waters," whereby they have acquired the power of cleansing from sin, He came up from the waters, and straightway there descended upon Him the Holy Ghost, in the likeness of a dove. "In the same manner," he says, "to you also after you have come up from the pool of the sacred streams, is given the one Unction, the antitype of that wherewith Christ our Lord was anointed."

"But," he goes on, "beware of supposing this to be plain chrism. For as the bread of the Eucharist, after the Invocation of the Holy Ghost, is mere bread no longer, but the Body of

---

1   A reference to Pierre Terrail LeVieux, the Chevalier du Bayard (1473-1524). He was famed for his chivalry, and has been lovingly called the 'fearless and faultless knight'— *'le chevalier sans peur and sans reproche'*.

Christ, so also this holy chrism, after the Invocation, is no more simple chrism, nor (so to say) common, but the gift of Christ; and by the presence of His Godhead, it worketh in us the Holy Ghost. It is symbolically applied to thy forehead and thy other senses; and while thy body is anointed with visible chrism, thy soul is sanctified by the Holy and life-giving Spirit.

"And ye were first anointed on your forehead, that ye might be delivered from the shame, which the first man, when he had transgressed, bore about with him everywhere; and that *with open face ye might behold as in a glass the glory of the Lord.* Then on your ears,[1] that ye might receive years quick to hear the Divine Mysteries of which Isaias has said: *The Lord wakened my ear that I might hear Him as a master;* and the Lord Jesus in the Gospels: *He that hath ears to hear let him hear.* Then on your nostrils, that receiving the sacred chrism ye may say: *we are the good odor of Christ unto God in them that are saved.* Then on your breast, that *having put on the breast-plate of justice ye may be able to stand against the deceits of the devil.* For as Christ after his baptism and the descent of the Holy Ghost went forth and vanquished the adversary, so likewise, having after Holy Baptism and the Mystical Chrism put on the whole armor of the Holy Ghost, do you stand against the power of the enemy and vanquish it, saying: *I can do all things in Christ who strengtheneth me.*"

Finally, St. Cyril concludes his instruction with these words: "Having been anointed therefore with this holy Chrism, keep it unspotted and unblemished in you, pressing forward by good works and becoming well pleasing to the Captain (τώ ἀρχήγώ) of your salvation, Christ Jesus, to Whom be glory for ever and ever. Amen."

1 In the time of St. Cyril, the Christians in receiving Confirmation were anointed not merely on the forehead, but on the ears, the eyes, the nostrils, the lips, the breast, and even the hands and feet. In all or nearly all the Eastern Churches, Confirmation is still administered in this way.

There are two objections which might, I conceive, be raised against the methods and language of Mother Loyola's new book. The first would question the advisability of familiarizing children with certain conceptions which are more usually reserved for times of retreat, such conceptions, for instance, as those of the Kingdom of Christ and the Two Standards, which St. Ignatius only introduces at the climax of his Spiritual Exercises, after carefully preparing the ground that the word may not fall on deaf or inattentive years. Even if a generous response were certain, it is a pity, such objectors might urge, to take the edge off these powerful instruments for good, at an age when their full significance cannot possibly be realized. That there is some weight in the objection it is hard to deny, but the sufficient response seems to be, that so long as the Church does not scruple to communicate the treasures of her Sacraments to children of ten and twelve years old, it is difficult to see why their teachers should exercise any "discipline of the secret," and economize that good seed which God provides so lavishly. We can hardly make too much of the Sacraments, and in the case of Confirmation more particularly, there is not even that danger to be feared which some have found in preparing children for the Holy Eucharist. It may be possible to magnify so much the importance of a child's first Communion, as to put a distinct obstacle in the way of his making a second or a third. But Confirmation is a Sacrament which is received but once during life, and in which the recipient will never be called upon to make the same effort again.

The other objection above referred to has already been advanced by one of the reviewers of Mother Loyola's last book, *Child of God*. The critic thinks that the language and range of ideas are apt to rise a little above the capacity of the younger children for whom it is professedly written. Without denying all foundation for such a criticism, I am inclined to think that here also Mother Loyola has not been ill-advised. I would submit that in addressing children, simplicity in the construction of sentences, and an abundance of concrete illustration, is much more important than the mere avoidance of words of many syllables. The long words are only names that can be picked up with very little effort, once the thing they represent has been carefully explained. Surely it is a fallacy to suppose that the imperfect vocabulary which children themselves use should alone be employed in addressing them. The delusion seems to me akin to that by which many persons assume that in order to teach a foreigner our language, it is necessary to speak to him in broken English.

The story of brave deeds and privations heroically borne which reaches us continually from South Africa will lend additional interest to many of the pages which follow. If Mother Loyola's book had not been completed before the war began, the incidents of the campaign would have supplied her with illustrations even more full of actuality than those which she has chosen. But even as things are, it is hoped that the reader will not find any serious blemish in what is said of modern military life. Mother Loyola desires to record her great obligations to Lord Wolseley's *Soldiers' Pocket Book*, from which much has been borrowed, and also to private friends, both gentle and simple, who have patiently answered her questions about soldiers and their ways.

For the regrettable delay in the appearance of this volume, which it is feared may have caused inconvenience to many, the writer of this Preface desires to say that he is alone responsible. He feels strongly that an apology is due to those who through his dilatoriness have been disappointed of the help which the book would otherwise have afforded them. The delay is the less excusable in that many of Mother Loyola's friends and fellow-religious, to whom a great debt of gratitude is owing, have contributed in every way in their power to expedite the progress of the work.

Of the illustrations contained in this volume, the frontispiece, representing the vigil of St. Ignatius at Montserrat, has been drawn for this book by Miss Josephine Padbury. The others are taken from older sources which need not here be particularized.

Herbert Thurston, S.J.

Feast of St. Thomas Aquinas, 1900.

Contents

Illustrations

PART THE FIRST.

I.

KNIGHTHOOD

Take this holy sword, a gift from God, wherewith thou shalt overcome the adversaries of My people.
(2 Mach. 15, 16)

Pax tecum. Some of you, all perhaps, have seen a Bishop administer the Sacrament of Confirmation. Did it strike you as strange that the new soldier of Christ should be dismissed with a blow? And that this again should be accompanied by the gentle words: *Pax tecum*—"Peace be with thee"? True, the blow is a very slight one and scarcely deserves the name. Still, that anything which professes to be a blow should be part, and a conspicuous part, of a joyous ceremony might seem, at first sight, strange.

To us perhaps, but certainly not to our forefathers. The boy of the Middle Ages looked forward eagerly to the day when a blow on the battlefield or beneath the arches of the cathedral would make him a knight. Further back still, hundreds of years before the coming of Christ, the young barbarian, wandering through the forests of Germany, longed for the blow which would make him one of the warriors of his tribe.

The great German or "Teutonic" family of which the Saxons were a branch, was a race of warriors. War was its chief occupation. To slay as many enemies as he might in this life, and after this life to drink ale out of their skulls—was the ambition and the happiness to which the child was taught to look forward from his earliest years. Great Wodin, the god of war, loved the brave, he was told, and would have none in his beautiful Valhalla after death but those who had wielded the sword and died by the sword. No wonder, then, that as years went on, and the solemn day drew near when he should be admitted to bear arms, his heart beat high. What cared he that the terrific blow accompanying the words, "Be brave!" would fell him to the earth? He knew that he would rise a soldier, privileged with sword and spear to follow his chief into the fight!

These barbarians were the ancestors of the knights of the Middle Ages, those heroes of chivalry whose gallant deeds are your delight. Do you see any resemblance between the fathers and the sons?

"Yes, plenty. The sons were brave and fond of fighting like their fathers, and they followed their chief faithfully and longed for battles, because if they did their duty there and killed a lot of the enemy, they had the chance of being made knights when the fight was over."

"But the old German fathers were barbarians, very rough and fierce, and the knights were polished and gentlemanly. Except, of course, just when they were fighting—they were gentle even to their enemies. Even if they were kings and princes, they waited upon them at table. And they were always kind to ladies and children, and to all who were weak and couldn't stand up for themselves. *I* don't see much likeness."

Well I think there *was* a resemblance, though the later knights had got rid of much of their rudeness and learned better manners. It would take us far out of our way to show you fully how the change came about. But to explain it all, I must use a word which comes to our minds whenever we think of the Middle Ages. That word is *chivalry*. It was the spirit of chivalry which raised our Teutonic forefathers from the hardness and brutality of barbarism and gradually brought them to that refinement of feeling and manner which you admire so much in your knights.

"What is chivalry?"

That question I knew must come. To give you anything like a clear idea of a very wide subject, is beyond my power. It will come gradually by your own reading. And yet I must try to say something, or we shall not understand what is coming. Let us see then.

You know what a change fireworks make in a scene; how Bengal lights transformed our little place into fairyland that night of Queen Victoria's Jubilee. The sky above us, the hills around, the church in the valley, the beech grove, old Susan's thatched cottage, the pond, the bridge—all the familiar objects that surround us in our every-day life, were suddenly lit up with a flood of rosy light that glorified them all.

"I remember, and I thought of enchanted gardens and wizards, and princesses waiting to be rescued, and lots of things like that."

You were carried away, you see, into the land of poetry and romance. Well, something like this rosy radiance was the light in which the nations of Europe were steeped for several centuries, from the eleventh to the fifteenth. Only it did not burst suddenly upon them like our Bengal fire.

"Where did it come from?"

That is not easy to say. Imperceptibly it stole up the sky, glowing gradually with richer colour till it attained its full glory. Then it faded away.

"I thought the night seemed darker and colder than ever when the light was gone. Was it like that when chivalry went out?"

In many respects it was. But we have to see one source, at least, from whence the light of chivalry came. In those German barbarians, fierce and self-willed as they were, we find many noble characteristics—love of freedom, of country and of home, of justice and truth and honour. They were remarkable too for their warm affections, their respect for women and their ready submission to the laws of their tribes. Obedience could not be wrung from them, but they submitted willingly and devoted themselves unreservedly to those whom they revered and loved. Their religion, such as it was, had a firm hold on their simple hearts. It was because he believed his laws had come to him from the gods that the German obeyed them; because his chief was their choice that he followed him even unto death.[1]

"If only they had been Christians, what good ones they would have made!"

Just what St. Gregory the Great said when he saw the fair-haired children in the marketplace of Rome. Their day of grace came. After many a tough struggle with the Roman legions, they broke over Europe in the fifth century after Christ and carried all before them. On and on they swept in countless numbers—Visigoths and Ostrogoths, Angles and Saxons and Franks. They destroyed the Europe over which Rome had ruled and made a new Europe for themselves. Then, in their turn, they were conquered. The church followed them into their distant homes, and for six centuries her missionaries went to and fro, converting and civilizing these barbarians of the north.

"And then did chivalry come and adventures and tournaments?"

"But what was it by itself, that's what *I* want to know?"

Chivalry is hardly one of those things that we can take to

1   Mrs. Hope, *Conversion of the Teutonic Race.*

pieces to find out what they are made of. You cannot analyze the perfume of the rose. You can see what electricity does, though you cannot tell what it *is*. So we can see what chivalry *did* better than we can define it. How it softened the ferocity, ennobled the warfare, and added poetry and grace to those stern times, we come to understand by reading such books as *The Talisman* and *Ivanhoe*. These give us a truer insight into its nature then we could get by any number of definitions. We have likened it to a glow overspreading the heavens, tinting everything with rosy light. And there was another illumination of that Jubilee time to which we might liken it.

You remember the huge bonfire we had on the hill—how it lit up the night; for how many miles its brightness was seen; to what a distance its heat was felt. Perhaps you remember too how quickly that fire was kindled. A vast amount of material had been collected and it was well prepared. No sooner then was the torch applied, than a pillar of light rose up into the sky. The pile was ablaze in no time. Swift as lightning, a bright line ran along the branches, twig after twig was caught, tongues of fire shot out on every side, till the black dead mass was turned into a sheet of living flame that illumined the country for miles around.

In some such fashion was the flame of chivalry kindled in those dark times. Its material was found in the simple hearts where, side by side with much that revolts us, were, as we have seen, many beautiful natural virtues. Only the touch of Religion was needed to make them bright with supernatural light, glorious in the eyes of men, and worthy of eternal life in the sight of God. The Church passed by with her torch—and there shot upwards towards Heaven, and far and wide over the lives of men, that flame which we call chivalry. For we must not suppose that in a Christian Knight, whom we may take as the embodiment of chivalry, there was nothing more than many of our story-books show us—valour and dexterity in arms, courtesy and generosity, the loyalty, the sense of honour, that won the admiration of men:

> The arm in battle bold,
> The courteous mien, the noble race,
> The stainless faith, the manly face.[1]

This there was, but much more than this. The true Knight was, before everything else, a true Christian, humble in mind, patient, mortified, charitable. It was from his faith and from the Sacraments that came the high sense of honour, the heroism, the contempt for riches, the truthfulness and the loyalty, the refinement and the delicacy of feeling that distinguished him. Of Godfrey de Bouillon[2], that Christian hero and true Knight, it was said that he united the wisdom, prudence, and valour of the most famous warriors of ancient times with the sweetness and humility of a monk.

"But were all knights like that?"

Alas! no. Some of them, very many perhaps, disgraced their order and their faith. Many, too, in the name of chivalry did foolish and extravagant things which deserve anything but admiration. But we are not now considering the extravagances of some, but the aim put before all. It was put before them by the Church, therefore it was a high one. And we may say in passing, that even in its extravagances the spirit of chivalry exhibited a generosity and an unselfishness very different from the spirit of later times.

The work of the Church is to take men as she finds them and train them for Heaven; to teach them to overcome what is bad in themselves; to draw out what is good; and to raise

---

1   Sir W. Scott.

2   Godfrey de Bouillon (c.1060-1100) was one of the leaders of the First Crusade and served as the first ruler of the liberated Jerusalem. He refused the title of King, as he claimed that title belonged to God alone. He was known instead as the Defender of the Holy Sepulchre.

and sanctify all the actions of their earthly life from the highest to the lowest, that all may deserve the rewards of the life to come. She is a mother who understands, and is at home with all her children, and knows how to deal with all. She took these races in hand. She taught them to curb their unruly passions, and turned their warlike ardour to account by sending them to fight the enemy of the faith in the East.

We shall have to speak later of the Crusades—that great contest between East and West, between the disciples of Christ and the followers of the false prophet Mahomet. What we have to notice here is the skill with which the Church directed to a good end the activity of her warlike children. Whilst striving by persuasion and by threats to put a stop to their quarrels at home, she pointed to a field in which their courage and enthusiasm would be well spent, and bade them draw their swords, not against each other, but for the recovery of the Holy Sepulchre and in defence of Christian lands. The Holy Wars called forth all that was noblest in Christian chivalry, and consecrated to religion the fiery energy of those fighting-loving Germans. Still they gloried in deeds of strength, still they loved the excitement of adventure and of battle. But the Christian faith put high and holy aims before them. Their wild passions were held in check by the grace that flowed from the Sacraments, and their natural virtues became supernaturalized and deserving of an eternal reward.

"Why couldn't their natural virtues have an eternal reward? I'm sure those Germans were a great deal better than some of us even when they were pagans?"

Let us see now why they could not. The marionettes that we saw the other day are very clever in their way. They move their heads and arms, and make a much better show than many of those who stand by admiring them. But can they see, or speak, or think? Could they, the cleverest of them, run a race, or write the papers for an Oxford Preliminary examination?

"Of course not, because they're not alive."

Just so. The springs that move them enable them to do many things. But there is no breath in these lifeless figures; they are incapable of the acts which require, for their performance, that living thing we call the soul. So it is with the soul itself. The grace of God, the breath of the Holy Spirit, must be within, if it is to be capable of moving a step towards Heaven, of doing the least act deserving an eternal reward. And therefore the greatest deeds of valour, or generosity, or heroism, when separated from this life-giving grace, cannot win any recompense in the world to come. They may have a reward here in the applause of men and other temporal goods. But nothing more. They have no force to go beyond the power of the spring that sets them in motion. For acts of natural virtue there are natural rewards. For supernatural rewards there must be supernatural acts springing from the grace of God in the soul. Do you understand this?

"Yes, and there's something else I want to ask. I know chivalry comes from '*cheval.*' But I can't see why they call it after the horses instead of the knights."

It would be truer to say that chivalry comes from *chevalier*, which means a horseman, that is, a knight; for the brave steeds were considered inseparable from the riders whom they bore into battle. But you are right in thinking that all the stirring ideas which arise in our minds with the word chivalry, centre in the knight.

So was it in olden times. Knighthood was the joyous hope throughout the baron's castle on the birth of a son. "In fifteen years," said the parents, "he will be a knight." "May he be a good knight like his father," cried the henchmen in the hall, "and to be dubbed on the field by our lord the King." The boy was brought up with the same aspiration. It entered into all his teaching. It was fostered by all that he saw or heard. Toy weapons were put into his baby hands as playthings. He was expected to manage a horse by the time he was seven. At ten or twelve he left his father's castle and, as a page, began his military training under some powerful baron, or even the King himself. A rough training it must have been, yet in France, the grand centre of chivalry, there was a tender word for bringing up these future knights. The word was *nourrir*, and the children were called *les nourris*. A sacred tie, like the bond between father and son, bound together *les nourris* and those who educated them. So much so, that "he brought me up and made me a knight," was throughout life one of a soldier's tenderest recollections.

The young noble had a long course of obedience before him when he began his apprenticeship as a page. Besides attending on his superiors, waiting at table, and learning the practice of arms, he had to lay his hands to hard, rough work, such as grooming horses and cleaning armour. When raised to the rank of an esquire and permitted to bear arms, he was still bound to close attendance on his lord. He had to carry his armour and keep it in order, and to follow him to battle. He did not fight, but kept by the side of his lord to receive his orders, warn him of danger, supply him with a fresh horse or weapons in case of need, take charge of his prisoners, and help him out of the battle if he were wounded. The fight over, many hours of hard labour followed, tending his master's horse and his own, and refurbishing arms.

Courage was the chief characteristic of the young aspirant to knighthood, and he was always eager for opportunities of displaying it, thus to attain more rapidly the object of all his desires. "When shall I be made a knight?" was the thought perpetually in his mind. "When shall I be able to sit at table with other knights; to enter a church in full armour; be entrusted with command; have a right to fight in the front ranks?" No wonder peril, pain—any chance—was welcomed that might bring the golden spurs within his reach!

"Were all boys caught up like that?"

Every youth of noble birth was early trained to military exercises with a view to knighthood, those excepted who were destined for the Church, and the sick or weakly who were incapable of the end of chivalry—*fighting*.

"And when were the knights made?"

Often on the battlefield, in the very heat of the fight; or in the hour of victory, when, after some deed of signal prowess, the soldier, pale, wounded, and covered with blood, was presented to the King or general in command. Two minutes sufficed for such dubbing on the field, the only essential part of the ceremony being the accolade or sword-stroke. Esquires thus knighted on the field, where the royal banner was displayed, were called knight-bannerets, and were considered of a higher order than others.

From the twelfth century, however, knights were generally consecrated by a Bishop, at Christmas, Easter, and Pentecost. Pentecost, in particular—the feast of the Church to whose defence their swords were to be dedicated—was a favourite time for conferring the long-desired honour. In a copy of the *Pontificale,* or Order of Episcopal Ceremonies, which perhaps belongs to the time of St. Louis of France, we find the *Benedictio novi militis,* or "blessing of the new knight," as we may translate it. *Miles* means soldier, but a man was not considered a finished soldier till knighted.

"Did they keep on giving that heavy blow after they became civilized, and did the Bishops give it too, in church?"

You take it for granted that the ceremonies by which knighthood were conferred grew out of those which, in earlier times, accompanied the delivery of arms to the young soldier.

Very possibly they did; any way the rough usages continued. Until the Church came in to consecrate the rite, the heavy blow with which the consecrator struck the candidate sufficed to fell him to the earth. It was now accompanied by a little exhortation in which he was admonished to be *preux*—"valiant."

But the church was not long in taking the new knight under her protection. She who is always blessing, who blesses not only things immediately connected with her sacraments and ceremonies—as salt, incense, candles—but all manner of things her children use—houses, cattle, bread, first-fruits, the earth, the sea—was not likely to leave unblessed the sword by which the enemies of the Faith were to be pursued and overthrown.

Before the young candidate for knighthood presented himself to her ministers, he was expected to go through a course of preparation and to carry out certain observances, each of which had its symbolical meaning.

On the eve, there was the solemn ceremony of watching the armour with which he was to be clad on the morrow. It was laid on the altar to show that it was to be used in defence of the Church and the Faith, as well as of country and of home, and that the wearer must be a champion of right against wrong—not merely a warrior of this world, but a Soldier of Christ.

It was, perhaps, in imitation of the solemn vigils or watchings, which once upon a time took place in all the churches of the Christian world on the eves of Easter and Pentecost, and which ended in the public baptism of the catechumens in their white robes, that the knight-elect passed the whole night preceding his consecration watching his armour before the altar. This watch began under the protection, and often before the altar, of the Mother of God. It followed upon a strict fast, and was long and severe. He was forbidden to sit for an instant. Standing or kneeling for ten hours—so was the vigil spent.

At last the great day came. In accordance with the general custom of hearing Mass before the reception of knighthood, the novice, as he was called, repaired to the church, accompanied by his joyous family and friends. He had made a general confession and received Holy Communion, and had taken a bath, emblematic of the purity becoming a Christian knight. Clad in a white tunic, in imitation of the white robes of neophytes in early times, he took his place before the altar, on which were laid his arms, to be sanctified by contact with the Divine Mysteries about to be celebrated. After the Gospel there was a sermon, in which the Creed was explained, for belief in all the Church's teaching, and a promise to keep her commandments, was required of a knight. Mass over, the novice, accompanied by knights, advanced towards the sanctuary, where the Bishop, surrounded by his attendants, awaited him.

We may see the solemnity attached by the Church to the ceremonies about to take place, not only from the special rite provided for the "Blessing of a new knight," but also from the fact of her appointing as consecrator a Bishop, who with his anointed hands fastened on the sword.

This was first blessed. A knight, kneeling, presented it to the Bishop, who, with head uncovered, pronounced over it these solemn words of benediction:

"Bless, O holy Lord, Almighty Father, Eternal God,...this sword with which Thy servant, by Thy mercy, is girt this day, that treading underfoot his visible enemies and completely victorious, he may be preserved from all danger. Through Christ our Lord. Amen."

"O holy Lord, Almighty Father, Eternal God...Who for the repression of wicked men and for the preservation of justice hast permitted the use of the sword,...we beseech Thy clemency that as Thou gavest strength to Thy servant David to overcome Goliath, and didst make Judas Machabeus to triumph over them that invoked not Thy holy Name, so Thou wouldst grant to this Thy servant, who has newly bowed his neck under the yoke of military service, strength and courage for the defence of faith and justice, and increase of faith, hope, and charity, and wouldst give to him Thy fear and Thy love, humility, perseverance, obedience, and patience...And as he is now promoted from a lesser grade to the honour of knighthood, so may he fear and rightly worship Thee, avoid the company of the wicked, show charity to his neighbour, obey those who are set over him, and faithfully fulfil all the duties of his state. Through Christ our Lord."

"That's a long prayer."

But a very beautiful one, and, as we shall want to come back upon it, I thought we must have it almost entire. At its close, the knights present fastened on the armour—the hauberk or coat of mail, the cuirass or breast-plate, the armlets, the gauntlets, the helmet, and the golden or gilded spurs, which were the special distinction of a knight. The shield was then attached to the arm of the candidate, and his lance was presented to him.

"If the armour was like what we see in the museum, it must have been awfully heavy and uncomfortable."

Yes, but comfort was about the last thing he would dream of. This hardiness is one of the chief virtues we expect to find in a soldier, as we shall see later.

And now the time so ardently desired was come. Taking the naked sword, the Bishop said: "Receive this sword in the name of the Father, and of the Son, and of the Holy Ghost, and use it in thy own defence, in defence of the Holy Church of God, and for the confusion of the enemies of the Cross of Christ; and so far as human frailty will permit, hurt no man with it unjustly...Amen."

He then replaced it in its scabbard, and—this was the solemn moment—girded with it the soldier kneeling before him. The new knight rose to his feet, unsheathed his sword, brandished it thrice, wiped it as if it were already covered with the blood of the enemies of the Faith, and replaced it in its scabbard.

"And then did the blow come?"

Yes—and no. A light touch thrice on the shoulder with the flat of the sword replaced the savage blow of barbarous times, and instead of the charge, "Be brave," the Bishop said, "Be a peaceful soldier, diligent, faithful, and vowed to God." He then gave the new knight a gentle blow on the cheek, after which he kissed him, with the words *Pax tecum*. The ceremony ended, in the words of the Roman Pontifical, by the knight "departing in peace."

Yet so loth, it seems, were the men of those days to give up the old blow, that when the dubbing was by a layman, as on the field of Crecy, where the Black Prince was knighted by his father, the consecrator came down with all his might on the neck of the novice, who was often so stunned that he had to be told when all was over. And embrace followed, showing that the blow was symbolical only, and not given in enmity.

"Do you know, I have been thinking that all this is like Confirmation. The blow and the *Pax tecum* are like, and we are like the knights. Not quite like, of course, if we were *quite* like, we should have *to be* knights, shouldn't we?"

Exactly, which is more than could be expected. I am glad you have seen the likeness for yourselves. There is a curious and close resemblance between the two ceremonies in the Roman Pontifical. So close, indeed, that the Church perhaps borrowed part of her ritual for Confirmation from the consecration of a knight.

"How could that be? because our Lord made all the sacraments long before there were any knights to be made?"

True, but many of the ceremonies now used in the

administration of the sacraments were added by the Church later, and we know that the blow in Confirmation is of comparatively recent date. But however that may be, it is interesting to see how the Church Militant concerned herself with the making of a new knight.

"But isn't fighting a dreadful thing? And isn't it strange to bless a sword? I heard those people in the train yesterday talking about the Arbitration Treaty between England and the United States. They said war is very wrong, and ought to be stopped. And that the nations of Europe are watching one another like wild beasts of the jungle, all trying to see which can be best prepared for war."

War is an evil so terrible that we may well ask how the Church could bless so freely the dread preparations. Is she not the lover of peace? Did she not establish the Truce of God to lessen the bloodshed of those fierce feudal times?[1] Yes, throughout all time the Church has raised her voice to stop the strife between Christian nations. Her prayer is always, "Give peace, O Lord, in our days," "From plague, famine, and war, O Lord, deliver us." The acolytes at the altar removed the swords and spurs of knights who came to her services without having first laid aside their arms. She is, by choice, a peacemaker. But war may be a necessity. If there is no other way of repressing wrong and injustice, of guarding our religion, our country, our homes, the rights we are bound to guard—then war is permitted by God, and Christians may lawfully become soldiers. And so when the faith of Christendom was threatened, when infidels were overrunning Christian lands and forcing into apostasy or into slavery the followers of Christ, the Church called out her knights and blessed their swords, and bid them go forth with words of benediction.

---

1   Around the tenth century, the Church used her influence to limit infighting between local lords and to protect noncombatants from violence.

A mother sits among her children at their play. She seems busily engaged with her own work, but her eye and her thoughts are with them always. She does not interfere unduly with their game, but throws in a suggestion now and again, acts as arbiter when appealed to, and shows a loving interest at all times. Occasionally she has to rise from her seat, and interfere actively when the play gets rough, but her general business is to watch the direction their ideas are taking, and skilfully guide them to high and noble ends.

This was the work of the Church in those ages of Faith when she sat enthroned among her children—the guide and umpire and sanctifier of Christian nations. Occasionally the play was very rough indeed, and, alas! her own representatives sometimes joined in it. And she came in with her Truce of God to mitigate the horrors of civil war. But her great work was to watch over the safety of Europe by keeping off the foe that was ever hovering on its frontiers. Again and again, she armed the nations for their own defence quite as much as for that Holy Sepulchre which was their war-cry. Taking advantage of the order of things brought in by chivalry, she took it under her protection, and blessed and girded the new knight for what was universally regarded as a high and holy mission.

But—and this is what specially concerns *us*—if she showed solicitude for soldiers engaged in an earthly warfare with *men*, who, however much they hated the Cross of Christ, were still redeemed with His Blood and bore God's image in their souls, how anxious will she be to equip for the fight those whose "wrestling is not with flesh and blood," as St. Paul says, but with the "*spirits of wickedness*," the declared and eternal enemies of God!

The Middle Ages have passed away, and chivalry with them. The foe of those times is no longer a danger to

Christendom. But he who stood behind the false Prophet and urged on the Mahometan arms is at work still. He is in deadly conflict with everyone who, by Baptism, is ranged under the banner of Christ. Therefore there is war still, all the world over, and the Church still strengthens and blesses in her Sacrament of Confirmation the young knight as he enters the fight.

"I read in the Introit on Christmas Day, 'He shall be called the Prince of Peace.'[1] But in our Scripture lesson it says, 'I came not to send peace, but the sword.'[2]

Our Lord brought peace to the earth as the Angels sang over Bethlehem on Christmas night. His special gift to His followers is peace. *Peace I leave with you, My peace I give unto you.*[3] *In Me you may have peace.*[4] But His peace is to be the fruit of victory. It is not to be had by folding our hands and doing nothing. We have to fight for it. It *must* be so with us now. Adam and Eve, with all their children, were turned out of Paradise on to a battlefield. Around us and within us are fierce and restless foes: the devil, the world, bad inclinations, bad habits. All these must be fought and conquered if we expect security and peace.

Yet there is a peace for our Lord's true soldiers, even in the midst of this warfare. "*My* peace," He calls it, because, unlike that of the world, it can live on through the fiercest fight. It is the joy of knowing that they are on His side Who can never be beaten, Who will stand by them to the end and give them victory.

Fitly, then, does the Church unite the "*Pax*" and the blow in the consecration of her young knights, sending them forth to conflict indeed, but strong in the strength of Him Who says to them by her lips, "*Pax tecum.*"

1   Isaias 9.
2   St. Matt. 10.
3   St. John 14.
4   St. John 16.

II.

The First Crusaders

Who is this that he should defy the armies of the Living God!
(I Kings 7, 26.)

MANY centuries ago there was a proclamation made in the name of Christ our Lord to all the nations of Europe. We know it well. But it will help us to refresh the memory of it, and to consider how His subjects of those days received it.

The various families of the German race—Anglo-Saxons, Visigoths, Franks, had settled down in the lands they had wrested from the Roman Emperor, and one by one were receiving the Christian faith, when a fresh danger threatened Europe from the East. The false prophet Mahomet appeared in Arabia, and began to preach a religion of his own invention. It spread with fearful rapidity, not so much because men believed what was as foul as it was foolish, but rather because of the promises and the threats with which the new teaching came to them. Plunder and pleasure in this life, and a martyr's crown in Paradise to all who died in battle—this was what Mahomet offered to the "true believers;" but to those who would not believe in him—death. His religion was to be propagated by the sword. He therefore put this bloody instrument of conversion into the hands of his followers, and started them on their road of conquest.

It is easy to see that these infidels from the East, who hated the Christian name, were a far greater danger to Europe than the races of the North, who had never heard of our Blessed Lord. For nearly one thousand years they were the terror of Christendom, and had it not armed again and again to keep them out of Europe, we should have been now among the miserable races that lie in oppression and slavery under Mahometan rule.

Some knowledge of the enemy the Christian nations had to encounter is necessary to our present purpose, so you must not think we are going out of our track if we follow the Mahometans rapidly along their road of victory. It will take us a little time, and a little trouble, no doubt: we must give the time and take the trouble, please. I say we will follow them rapidly, for we must move swiftly to keep up with them, they go so fast; their progress is a flight rather than a march. Get out your map of the Eastern Hemisphere, and with your finger on Arabia, whence they started, see how they swept everything before them. Under Omar, the second Caliph, or vicar of the Prophet, they captured innumerable cities and strongholds, destroyed four thousand Christian churches, and erected one thousand mosques for Mahometan worship. In less than a century their dominion reached from India to the Atlantic. They had conquered Persia, Syria, Palestine, Egypt, the north of Africa, and Spain, and were advancing into the heart of France, when Charles Martel, "the hammerer," at the head of the Franks, met them near Poitiers. The Christianity and civilization of Europe were both at stake that October morning when the tall, fair-haired sons of the North and the dark-faced Saracens met. The Christian army conquered; the mighty host of infidels was driven back by the hammering they got that day, and never again were their white turbans and loose robes, their scimitars and small fleet horses seen on this side of the Pyrenees. But they had taken Palestine, and held it still, and it was sad for Christian pilgrims to find in the hands of infidels the Holy Places they went so far to visit.

You know that from the day our Blessed Saviour ascended into Heaven, leaving on Mount Olivet the prints of His Feet, the Holy Places sanctified by His Presence became spots of loving veneration for His followers. As soon as the age of persecutions terminated by the conversion of Constantine, churches were built at Bethlehem, at Nazareth, and at Jerusalem. On the spot where our Lord was crucified, a basilica was raised which, because it covered the place where He was buried, as well as the site of the Crucifixion, was called the Church of the Holy Sepulchre.

Pilgrims from all parts of Christendom flocked to these Holy Places, whilst they formed part of the Eastern Empire. Even after the Saracens had wrested them from the weak grasp of the Eastern Emperor, pilgrims came and went unharmed. But about the time of our Norman Conquest, Jerusalem fell into the hands of the Seljukian Turks, a wild tribe of Mahometans from Tartary. They hated Christianity more than the Saracens had done, and barbarously ill-treated the pilgrims. Then the scheme was formed of arming Europe for the recovery of the Holy Land.

At the Council of Clermont, Pope Urban II appealed to all Christian rulers and to the chivalry of Europe in its behalf. He spoke of the desecration of the Places where man's redemption was accomplished, of the barbarity of the Mussulman tyrants, and of the necessity of arresting their march in order to protect the Christianity of the West.

"Soldiers," he said, "since you are eager for war, behold a war worthy of your valour. Become the soldiers of the living

God. Christ died for you, do you go forth to die for Him. For the love of Christ and the love of Christians, arm, and recover Jerusalem. Let every one take on his breast the sign of the Cross, as it is written: 'He that taketh not up his cross cannot be My disciple.'"

Few words since the world began have had a more extraordinary effect upon the minds of men than these words of Pope Urban. They were received by the princes and people assembled at Clermont as a proclamation of Christ our Lord Himself by the lips of His Vicar. The cry, "God wills it! God wills it!" arose as from one man. Enthusiasm spread. By thousands and tens of thousands men took the cross. On every side were heard the preparations for war. Within the moated castle, the smith was busy day and night hammering into shape the cumbersome armour for knights and men-at-arms and horses, and forging weapons of all kinds.

"What did he make?"

For princes and knights, coats-of-mail, round bucklers, and helmets; long shields for the foot-soldiers; swords, lances, pikes, spears, daggers, the mace, or spiked club, the battle-axe, and the terrible cross-bow.

But it was not princes and knights and men-at-arms alone who went forth to deliver Jerusalem. Men of all ranks and callings were suddenly transformed into soldiers; the merchant left his shop, the student his books, the workmen his tools; even robbers forsook the highway to atone for their crimes by joining the army of the Cross. The roads were too narrow for the hosts that poured out to the East—six millions, the old chroniclers tell us, obeying Urban's call.

"Nobody would give the robbers any arms."

They would take their own. Those who could not procure proper weapons, took anything they could get. The artisan would carry a heavy hammer, the peasant an axe or a spade.

To strong arms and willing hearts nothing came amiss with which a blow might be struck for Jerusalem.

Thus variously equipped, the crusading force set out. Forces we should say, for there were two hosts. In that headed by Godfrey de Bouillon were to be seen the most famous knights of Christendom, surrounded by their followers, splendidly mounted, and clad in linked mail from head to foot. Side by side as brothers-in-arms rode Edgar Atheling[1] and Duke Robert of Normandy[2]—around them, stretching as far as the eye could see, lances, helmets, shields—a tossing, glittering sea of steel—with here and there a banner bearing the painted figure of beast or bird to serve as a rallying-point for the soldiers of the various princes. For no fewer than six armies were gathered together under the leadership of the Duke of Lorraine[3].

The other host, led by Peter the Hermit, consisted of a vast multitude of men, women, and children, some in carts drawn by oxen or the heavy farm-horses, some on foot. This unwieldy mass—army we cannot call it—rolled slowly towards the Bosphorus, where it was to embark, growing continually in bulk as fresh recruits came flocking in from every part of France. Here, headed by its parish priest, was a whole village of simple folk, bringing with them their cattle, their provisions, their household goods. And on the breast or shoulder of each one there, from the old man to the little child, was the red

---

1 Edgar Ætheling (c. 1051-c. 1126) was heir to the throne after the death of Edward the Confessor, but was passed over in favor of Harold II, who died at the Battle of Hastings. Edgar was then proclaimed king, but William of Normandy took the throne before he could be crowned. Edgar was also the brother of St. Margaret of Scotland.

2 Robert Curthose, Duke of Normandy (c. 1054-1134) was the eldest son of William of Normandy "The Conqueror". His claim to the throne was usurped by his younger brother Henry before he could return from the Crusades.

3 One of the titles of Godfrey de Bouillon.

cross, marking all as Crusaders, soldiers of Christ. A hundred thousand men, and women and children innumerable, followed the Hermit, leaving behind them home and country and all they had, with little hope of ever seeing them again, ready for hardships and privations of which, in these days, we can form no idea. One hope in every heart—to see the City where our Lord had died for them. So that when the walls of distant towns became visible against the sky, they would press eagerly forward with the question, "Is this Jerusalem?"

"Did they do any good when they got there?"

Alas, few, if any, were so fortunate as to see the walls of the Holy City. Great numbers perished before reaching the European coast, and those who crossed the Bosphorus were cut to pieces almost immediately on the plains of Nicea by Sultan Solyman.

"But Jerusalem *was* taken."

By the army that followed. And not Jerusalem only, but Nicea and Antioch. Godfrey de Bouillon was elected King of Jerusalem. He refused to wear a crown of gold in the City where his Redeemer had been crowned with thorns. But he took upon himself the government of the little kingdom, and left it at his death to his brother Baldwin, who founded another principality, that of Edessa in Mesopotamia. It was the capture of Edessa by the infidels that called forth the second Crusade. But this did not prevent the fall of Jerusalem, which was taken soon after by Saladin. The five Crusades that followed all failed to attain their object, and the Holy City has never again been in Christian hands.

On the failure of the fifth, another was earnestly desired by the Christians of Syria. But the enthusiasm of the first Crusaders had long since died away, and the princes of Christendom were too much occupied with their own selfish quarrels to attend to the growing danger in the East, so the cry of distress went by

THE CHILDREN'S CRUSADE

From an engraving by Gustave Doré.

unheeded. Suddenly all Europe was startled by hearing that fifty thousand children had almost simultaneously enlisted in France and Germany.

"Children!"

Yes, they would have a Crusade of their own. For them, they maintained, God had reserved the honour of recovering Jerusalem. They were to succeed where kings and warriors had failed. Out from cities and country hamlets they streamed forth, flying their banners and filling the air with their hymns. When people asked them where they were going, the joyous answer was always the same: "To Jerusalem; we are going to deliver the Holy Sepulchre."

"And did they? Or at least, do they do any good at all, or gain any battle?"

Alas, poor little Crusaders, what could they do? Without food or shelter, cold, wet, and weary, many sickened on the march, and died. Others, unable to keep up, fell behind, and trying to find their way home, were lost, and never heard of again. A large number, it seems, reached Marseilles, but only to meet with bitter disappointment. Instead of the vessels waiting to take them on board, as they expected, they found only busy merchants, too full of their own affairs to listen to their earnest entreaties for a free passage to Palestine. All they got were angry threats, and orders to leave the city, and return at once to their parents. Sad and disheartened, they wandered disconsolately along the shore, or stood gazing over the blue Mediterranean, now and again imploring the captain of some vessel leaving port to find room for them in his ship. It was only after days of fruitless entreaty that the greater number gave up their cherished enterprise, and taking leave of their companions, began to make the best of their way back to their own country. Of the German children, many, we are told, succeeded in reaching their homes. But the French children never saw home again.

"And none of them got to Palestine? What a sad story."

The saddest part is yet to come. One or two merchants at length came forward and offered the starving children a free passage to the Holy Land. Joyfully the offer was accepted, and as they swarmed onto the deck, the spirits of the little Crusaders rose again. Once more their cry was heard: "The Holy Sepulchre! We are going to deliver Jerusalem!"

But the Holy City they were never to see. The vessels were steered straight to Alexandria, and there the Christian children were sold as slaves by the vile traders who had deceived them. Their infidel masters used every effort to make them forsake Christ for Mahomet, with what success we are not told, but twelve at least stood firm to their faith and suffered martyrdom.

"I think that is the sorrowfulest story I ever heard."

"I don't, the twelve martyrs were better off in Heaven than if they had gone to Jerusalem, and all the others who died or were lost on their way home would be counted as martyrs, I should think."

When Pope Innocent III heard of the Children's Crusade, he is said to have exclaimed: "Whilst we are asleep, these children are watching."

The Holy Wars extended over a period of nearly two hundred years, during which time eight Crusades were undertaken. The first, as we have said, was the only one that attained its object. Jerusalem was recovered. But after being held by Christian Kings for about ninety years, it fell again into the hands of the infidels, and there it remains to this day.

"So the Crusades were no good, and all those soldiers died for nothing!"

Had we lived then we should not have said so. Such was not the feeling of our Catholic forefathers. They thought it intolerable that the Land where our Blessed Lord had lived and died should be under the rule of the unbelieving Saracen. And if at the cost of pain and peril, of life itself, there could be even a chance of its restoration to Christian hands, they were ready to pay the price. This outburst of faith and devotion to the Passion of Christ was one of the grandest sights the world has ever seen.

You will say it was a pity, at least, that those who could not fight joined in the wars; they must have been sadly in the way and no good at all. Perhaps you are right, and it is certain the Church did not sanction the Children's Crusade. But it would have been no easy task to hold back the women and the children. They wanted to see with their own eyes the Land their Saviour had trod, the Hill on which He hung in death, the Grave where the Lord lay. They felt that to help in the recovery of the Holy City or to die in the attempt, was a worthier and a happier lot than to stay at home in ease and comfort. Love is slow to see that it is sadly in the way and no good at all. It thinks it can do all things: *Tell me where you have laid Him and I will take Him away,*" said Magdalen as she stood weeping at the Sepulchre. Love was strong in those Ages of Faith. It carried all before it—warriors, weak women, priests, peasants, little children—and cast them all upon the shores of Palestine.

The Countess of Richmond, mother of Henry VII, could never think without indignation of Jerusalem abandoned to infidel rule. "Would to God," she used to say, "that the princes of Christendom would combine as of old and the march against the Turk; gladly would I wait upon them and be the washer-woman of their camp!"

But the Ages of Faith passed away. Protestantism chilled the hearts of men, and then it became the fashion to sneer at the Crusades. What wonder! How should they love the Cross of Christ who had rejected His Real Presence in their midst, and revolted against His Vicar, and reviled His Church! In our days, however, there is another change. Men are beginning to see what the Church has done for the world and for Western nations in particular. How the Popes of the Middle Ages were the guardians of Europe. How they stood like watchmen on a tower noting all the movements of the enemy that was for ever hovering round the walls of Constantinople. How again and again they sounded the note of alarm and called the sovereigns of Europe to arms.

For the Crusades had a two-fold object, as we have seen. The war of the Cross against the Crescent was not simply an act of devotion—it was a necessity. If Christian soldiers had not poured over to Syria for the recovery of the Holy Sepulchre, they must have gone in defence of their homes. Charles Martel had saved Europe from the infidel hordes of the South. But they were always pressing on it from the East, always ready to pounce down upon Constantinople and sweep westward over Christian lands, making martyrs of all who would not become apostates. The Crusades kept them back for two hundred years. When the Holy Wars ceased with the two disastrous Crusades of St. Louis, the Turks knew that the fall of Constantinople was only a question of time. During another two hundred years they were slowly creeping towards it like the tide that surrounds a man before he has noticed its approach. At last the hour was come, and they closed round the city, an army of 250,000 men. What could its brave defenders do? They fought with desperate courage, but they were only 9,000—and it fell. The tidings of its fall dropped like a thunder-bolt upon Europe. Constantinople was the barrier to which nations of the West looked for protection. The barrier was broken down—who could tell where the enemy would stop? Every capital trembled as nearer and nearer each year drew those dreaded hosts. We may form some idea of their numbers from the fact that they once covered a plain with an army of 400,000 fighting men. And now the danger was renewed on the South. For all over the Mediterranean roved their corsair fleets. Rhodes fell, and Cyprus, and then the Crescent was seen under the very walls of Marseilles.

You have read, perhaps, how at Rhodes and Malta the gallant Knights of St. John defied the whole of the Turkish fleet. To fight against these enemies of the Christian name, was in those days to fight for God and for the Faith. So we can understand how even women and children helped in the warfare, defending breaches, hurling stones on the besiegers, working the guns. Wherever the Christian armies made a stand, they felt that on their swords depended the safety of the Christian world. The men who defied the whole Turkish fleet at Rhodes, and Malta, and Cyprus, fought not so much for their fair homes in the Mediterranean, as for the Faith and freedom of Europe. It was this that made them fight like heroes, and die with the fortitude of martyrs.

The danger on the South was great, but it was greater still on the East. The fall of Constantinople had opened the way to further conquests, and again and again the huge armies of the Sultan were let loose upon Europe. Terrible beyond the power of words to describe, were the scenes that marked the progress of the Turkish arms—towns pillaged and given up to the flames; churches profaned; women and babes slaughtered wholesale, without pity and without shame; old men and little children piled one upon another in a market-place and burnt alive; the brave defenders of Christendom put to death amid tortures as horrible as any we read of in the days of the general persecutions, or the annals of China and Japan.

It seemed as if the hour were come for Christian Europe to fall before her deadly foe. But "man's extremity is God's opportunity." Just when all seemed lost, the cry going up in countless

Rosaries "Holy Mary, Mother of God, pray for us," was heard in Heaven, and the Help of Christians came to the rescue.

Take a map of Greece and find Lepanto. The battle fought there on the 7th of October, 1571, was one of the most terrible conflicts the world has ever seen. The Turkish fleet never recovered the defeat of that day, and was never after a danger to Christendom. A hundred years later, the rout of the huge Turkish army before the walls of Vienna broke the power of the infidels for ever, and before the seventeenth century was out, all danger to Europe from the enemy that had harassed it for nearly a thousand years was over.

"But what have the Crusades to do *with us?* They were all over long ago and there is no Holy War now."

"And there's no Proclamation *to us.*"

No Holy War now! And you a soldier of Christ, or preparing to be one. What can you be thinking about! Are we not all signed with the Cross as Crusaders—signed in Baptism, signed again in Confirmation! Are we not bound to fight the battles of our King and Leader, against our enemies and His! This Holy War goes on age after age, taken up by all the followers of the King as they succeed one another upon the field. Not till we see Him coming in the eastern sky will the fight be over. Our warfare, like that of the Crusaders, is a necessity. We have no choice but to fight. For foes bent on our destruction surround us on all sides. Like the followers of Mahomet they grant us no quarter. It is a question of victory or death.

"But *our* enemies cannot be seen!"

They can be *felt*, and to meet them resolutely and perseveringly requires a heart as brave as that which faced the Turks on the plains of Syria. Courage, generosity, self-denial, a devoted love of our Blessed Lord—things excellently taught by the Crusaders—are very necessary to us in the warfare we have in hand. The thought of the Holy Wars, then, is one very much to our purpose, and we shall find as we go on, that those who took the Cross long ago—soldiers, peasants, old men, women, children—have left many a noble and useful lesson to the Crusaders of our own times.

You say there is no Proclamation *to us*. But here you are mistaken. On a memorable day, at Cæsarea Philippi, the King made a Proclamation, not only to the great multitude gathered together to hear Him, but to all His followers unto the end of time. Each and every one He had distinctly before Him. He knew the way in which each one would hear His words, and the answer each heart would make.

"What was the Proclamation?"

We are scarcely ready to hear it yet. Let us wait awhile. The King's words are very solemn. They are spoken *to you and to me*. Our life here and our eternal life hereafter depend on the way we listen to them. We must prepare ourselves, then, to hear them as we ought, with a reverent mind and a ready heart.

The struggle of Christian nations with the Turks has a few more helpful thoughts for us, and we must grudge neither time nor labour that may prepare us to hear the King's words when the time comes. So far we have been looking at the armies of the Cross. Let us turn our eyes now to a leader, and see what the greatest of Crusading heroes will do for us.

III.

LEADERS

We have chosen Thee to be our prince to fight our battles.
(I Mach. 9, 30.)

OF all the disappointing people in the world—ourselves, of course, excepted—few perhaps are more disappointing than kings. In state robes and on state occasions they look well enough; but when the royal pageant is over and their crowns are laid aside, how unkingly too many of them appear! Perhaps we require too much of them. In form, in feature, and, what is far more important, in tastes, motives, character, we expect them to be faultless. If they have any pretensions to be good at all, then they ought to be perfect. So it is just the good kings that disappoint us most. They forget that they are made of ordinary clay, and when we find them acting in ordinary fashion, we feel something like the little Protestant lads who ran themselves out of breath to see to live nuns, and, after peering cautiously beneath the black veils, exclaimed: "Why, they're only women!" We are too exacting no doubt, but still it is disappointing to see how few kings history can show who in every way come up to our expectations of what a king ought to be.

But there is a king who disappoints no one. If we want a hero, valiant in war like Godfrey de Bouillon or Cœur de Lion, a father to his people like St. Stephen of Hungary or

St. Edward the Confessor, a great ruler and law-giver like Charlemagne or Alfred the Great, and, like them, a friend of learning and learned men; if we look for a sovereign revered and trusted by his fellow-sovereigns, and passionately loved by his own subjects; if, above all, we seek for a perfect follower of Christ—all this we find in St. Louis of France. As Cyrus stands out nobly among heathen rulers, so does St. Louis among Christian kings. In him are united all the various excellencies be found singly in them. Every page in his history is grand, every picture of him is beautiful. Whether we look at him passing judgment in the quarrel between Henry III and his barons, and confirming Magna Charta; or, seated beneath the oak at Vincennes, listening tenderly to the troubles of the poor and punishing the nobles who oppressed them; or writing the code of law that goes by his name; or, seated at the table between St. Thomas Aquinas and St. Bonaventure, playfully offering to divide himself between the two Orders he loved so well; or refusing, in the firmness of his faith, to see a miracle at Mass by which the Real Presence was confirmed; or praying before the Holy Crown of Thorns in the *Sainte Chapelle* which he had built to enshrine it; whether we note his lowliness in the day of prosperity when neighbouring princes sought his alliance and referred their quarrels to him, or his greatness of soul in the very presence of torture and death, which made the very infidels exclaim in admiration, "Never saw we so proud a Christian!"—on whatever side, at whatever time we look at St. Louis, our ideal of a King is satisfied.

A soul like his could not but be stirred to its depths by the tales of cruelty and desecration that, from the time he was a little boy at his mother's knee, had poured in from the East. As he knelt at the altar, assisting at the unbloody Sacrifice of Calvary, it was an intolerable pain to him to think of the Calvary where we were redeemed, in infidel hands, and he longed to draw

his sword for its freedom. He longed to see the Holy Land a
Christian land again, to extend there that Kingdom of which
we are taught to say, "Thy Kingdom come!" And so he took the
Cross. God accepted his desires we may be sure. But his two
Crusades were unsuccessful. This will not surprise us when
we remember that six armies, headed by the most renowned
leaders of Christendom, combined to wrest Jerusalem from the
infidel in the first Crusade. In the seventh and eighth Crusades
there was but one.

If, instead of being so unfavourable to St. Louis,
circumstances had been as we will imagine them, would the
result have been different? Let us see.

We will suppose this great and good King to be chosen
by God Himself for supreme rule, a rule such as the world has
never seen before. His kingdom is the whole of Christendom.
Wherever the Name of Christ has reached, he is honoured and
obeyed. All Christian princes are subject to him, bound as
vassals to do him homage, and in time of war to follow him
into the field with all the soldiers under their command.

One day a summons goes forth from this mighty King.
His prince vassals in all parts of the kingdom are to assemble in
the capital, there to hear from him the purpose for which they
are called together. Not one may absent himself—no excuse
will be accepted. The matter in hand is of such weight, that
all other business must give place to it. The royal edict speeds
from one end of Europe to the other. For the King—

> Has named a trysting day
> And bidden messengers ride forth
> East and west, and south and north,
> To summon his array.
>
> East and west, and south and north,
> The messengers ride fast,
> And tower, and town, and cottage
> Have heard the trumpets' blast.

The day arrives, and we see them in the hall of audience, standing in glittering armour round the throne. It is a noble gathering. England and Scotland, Germany, Spain, and Portugal are represented by their Sovereigns, the military Religious Orders by their Grand Masters, the merchant princes of Venice by her Doge. Earls, barons, knights, fill the hall to overflowing. Without, stand a vast number of esquires and men-at-arms from every State in Europe.

What must the King be whom all these reverence and obey, the King who is to preside worthily in such an assembly! He does so with the dignity and grace of one who is immeasurably the superior of all around him. "Never saw I so noble a knight," says Joinville[1], "for he towered above them all from the shoulders upwards. On his head was a gilded helmet, and a sword of Germany in his hand." Nor is there another like him in valour and all chivalrous virtues. No wonder that his soldiers look up to him with an intense admiration, and serve him with a passionate loyalty worthy of the soldiers of David. He is a leader to draw the eyes and the hearts of all to himself. Men follow him and obey him on his personal account, not only for what he *does,* but for what he *is.* It is the blending in him of majesty and gentleness that makes him so attractive, and so idolised by his troops that they will follow him to the ends of the earth.

This is the King who now comes forward to address his subjects. From the dais where he stands, he surveys them all. Every eye is turned to him, every ear waits for his first word. It is a note of war. He is going forth to do battle against the enemies of God in the East. God Himself has given him the charge and promised to be with him and give him victory. He has called

---

1   Jean de Joinville (1224-1317) was counsellor and confidant to King Louis IX, and testified in the inquest for his canonization. He later wrote a biography of St. Louis.

them together to tell them of his commission and of his resolve, and to invite them and their subjects to join him in his war.

It is a necessary war. Unless the infidels are checked in their westward course they will overrun Europe. They will overthrow all that Christians hold sacred, and set up the hateful creed of their false prophet in place of "the faith once delivered to the saints." Will Christian warriors suffer a wrong like this? Will they wait quietly to see their homes and their wives and their children given up to fire and sword?

Look at the King. His habitual expression is one of bright serenity, imparting, like a tranquil sunset, a sense of security and peace. But his eye flashes as he speaks of Jerusalem in bondage, the Cross dishonoured, Christian blood shed by infidel hands.

Look around. See interest, ardour, enthusiasm, kindling on every side and increasing as, echoing the words of Urban, the King goes on:

"Soldiers! since you are eager for war, behold a war worthy of your valour. Become the soldiers of the living God. Go forth and fight for Him Who died for you. I will go with you. I will be at your head always. In every perilous enterprise I will lead the way. There will be the usual hardships of war—hunger, thirst, cold, fatigue; for the campaign will be a hard one. We must look forward to wounds and, it may be, death. But whatever you have to suffer shall be in my company. No man shall be asked to do anything he has not seen me do, or to bear anything he has not seen me bear. We will march together, carry burdens together, sleep on the ground together side by side. If there is only coarse food and poor shelter to be had, we will share it. I will work with you during the day and stand sentry at night. In battle, the post of danger shall be mine always, and on me the heaviest blows shall fall. Who will come with me? It is volunteers I want. Victory is assured to me. But I invite the willing service of my soldiers, that by sharing the labour they may share also the triumph that is to come."

How is the King's proclamation received? Is he heard patiently to the end, or has he been interrupted by cheer upon cheer? If enthusiasm has not carried his hearers away, if they have restrained themselves thus far, with what a burst of applause with his appeal be welcomed now! How will princes, lords, and knights flock round him and offer themselves to fight under his standard? With what eagerness will they demand the Cross?

"Oh, if I had been there, wouldn't I have cheered!"

"I wouldn't have stopped at that. I would have asked to be his esquire, or armour-bearer, or something, so that I could be always near him in battle to defend him. And I wouldn't have minded wounds and that sort of thing, if I could have got them instead of him. But there never was such a king as that to fight for, so it's no use talking about it."

The King having dismissed the assembly, it breaks up. Glittering armour melts away in the distance. Princes, barons, knights, go off to make their arrangements for the coming campaign. The King is left alone. No, not quite. See how one here and there lingers behind when the rest have gone. And now this little band crowd round him as if they would take him by storm. They have done what, as loyal vassals, they were bound to do, what others have done. But they are not satisfied yet. They want to show special loyalty and affection. They offer, not themselves only, but all they have, all they can bring for the King's service. They bespeak the most painful duties, the posts of special danger. They ask to be near him always. They offer not only to repel the enemy when he attacks, but to pursue him and give him battle wherever they find him.

"Just what I thought. I should have been one of those. I only wonder a lot more didn't stay and offer themselves to him, to be a kind of body-guard, you know."

It is a wonder, for the hearts of all must be aglow. And yet—I am mistaken perhaps. There may be some who do not care to join in the war. They think the terms hard. Or they are afraid of being killed or hurt. At any rate, they prefer to remain at home in safety and comfort.

"Then they must be a precious set of sneaks, that is all I can say, if they let the King go and do all the fighting by himself."

"And cowards too, and fools, who ought to be kicked out of the army. If there was to be trouble and pain, it would not last long, and they could have their comfort when they got home again, and a lot of glory too."

"I don't believe there would be such muffs anywhere. What is the good of a soldier who is afraid of a little pain! And what do men enlist for, if they never mean to fight!"

What, indeed! By the way, do any of you elder ones happen to have paper and pencil about you? Some of our reflections are noteworthy, and it is just possible they may be of use later. Please, jot them down one of you, as we go on.

The muffs we will not stop to consider, for we have none of us common patience with them. Our business is with those who undertake the campaign. Do you think there can be any difference among these followers of the King?

"I don't see how; if they go, they go."

Yes, but there are different ways of going and different degrees of following, as we saw just now. Let us look at three kinds of men in army. There is the so-called soldier, whose service begins with his putting on the uniform—and ends there. He cannot be said to *serve* in the noblest acceptation of the word. He has not the sense to be proud of his profession, still less has he the manliness to prove himself worthy of it. Such a disgrace to the service we might pass by unnoticed, were it not that we shall find him in the highest of services, where his presence is more disgraceful still.

Then there is the man who says to himself: "I will do my duty, keep my arms and kit in order, stand sentry, march, attack the enemy, or stay with the baggage as I am ordered. I won't shirk work. I'll take my share of fatigue-duty. No one shall say I'm not a good soldier. But I'm not going to do more than I'm obliged. I don't believe in volunteering."

Lastly, there is the soldier who burns with the desire to distinguish himself; he is always ready to volunteer for services of special danger or requiring more than ordinary courage. He sets personal comfort on one side, and for the love of country, the honor of the Sovereign, and safety of others, is prepared at any time to expose his life. Deeds of noble daring have an attraction for him. When a hazardous enterprise is on foot he does not stop to consider whether he is bound to join it, but jumps at the chance.

Among the heroes of the Peninsular War[1] was one Robert Elley. He served under Sir John Moore and had to cover the retreat to Corunna. This man's military career was a series of heroic deeds and hairbreadth escapes. He never seemed to think of himself. His own comfort, position, safety, counted for nothing where the service was concerned. What he *could* do, not what he was *bound* to do, was the thought ever in his mind. On one occasion, seeing his men wavering, he dismounted and fought beside them on foot. Whilst leading a charge at Salamanca, he had two horses killed under him. A French shot struck the first full in the chest, and Elley fell heavily to the ground. But as the cry of dismay broke from his men, their gallant leader reassured them by leaping to his feet and mounting another horse. "Come on, gentlemen! Don't let us miss the fun!" he exclaimed, as he rode again into the thick of

1   The Peninsular War was the name given to the fight for control of Spain when Napoleon invaded in 1808. The British helped the Spanish to drive out the French.

the fray. An hour later he was dragged out unconscious, not only severely wounded by a bayonet, but seriously injured by his dead charger having fallen upon him. He pulled through, however, and at Vittoria and other battles distinguished himself again. But it was at Waterloo that the irrepressible spirit of the man showed itself most strikingly. His gallantry had won for him well-deserved promotion. Step by step he had risen from the ranks, and on that memorable June morning he reined in his horse by the side of Wellington's to watch the conflict on which hung the fate of Europe. Owing to his high position on the head-quarter staff, he ought not to have taken any active part in the battle. But his patriotism got the better of his prudence, and no sooner did the guns begin to boom than, without even asking permission, he dashed down the hill and into the fight. When all was over he was sent for and severely censured by the old Duke for so flagrant a breach of discipline.

"What do you mean, sir, by riding at a French square in that harebrained fashion? You ought not to have done it."

"Ought not to have done it, my lord," replied Elley, saluting. "I fancy that is just what the French thought when I laid about 'em an hour ago."

What could the great General say? He rode away laughing.

In every army there are two kinds of soldiers, three perhaps, but the bad ones are not worth noticing. Which kind do you admire, the easy-going or the Elley? There is no doubt as to the opinion of their commanders. Whatever the Iron Duke might say, there is no doubt what he thought of that brave, eager soldier of his staff. Lord Wolseley[1], our late Commander-in-Chief, cannot do at all with the first sort. We shall hear presently what he has to say about them. But before considering what he expects in a soldier, we must see what he looks for in a commander.

1   Field Marshal Garnet Joseph Wolseley was Commander-in-Chief of the British army from 1895-1900.

When an army is to go out to battle, the first question at the War Office is: "Who is to be the leader?" Why? "*Because war is managed by due ordering,*"[1] Solomon tells us. It is to the leader that the country looks to uphold the honour of its arms, and to bring it out of the struggle, not safely only, but gloriously. The men may be splendid soldiers, splendidly drilled, splendidly equipped, and full of military ardour, but if they are badly led, they are simply going to the slaughter. They know this, and so the successful or disastrous result of a campaign depends a great deal on the army's opinion of the Commander-in-Chief.

Those who do not believe in the heavenly mission of Joan of Arc, ascribe her marvellous victories to the faith her troops had in her, and the enthusiasm with which they fought wherever her white standard floated. On fields where Napoleon commanded in person, his armies believed that defeat for the French flag was simply an impossibility. At Marengo, Austerlitz, Jena, they followed him like men assured of victory, and swept all before them. Belief in a leader is the secret of success.

Napoleon did not care for the men who followed him so devotedly, except in so far as they were useful to him, and helped him to gratify his ruling passion—ambition. His one idea was to exalt himself, to turn Europe into one big France. This could not be done without armies and a frightful sacrifice of life. He must raise armies then—army after army—till France had no more young lives to sacrifice. The picture of him prancing on his splendid charger over the Great St. Bernard may perhaps tempt some of us to admire the leader who could take men through hardship and danger like that. But if the painter had widened the scene a little and shown us the poor soldiers being blown like snow-flakes over those icy heights and dashed to pieces in the chasms below, we should have a truer knowledge of the chief they were serving, and be moved to indignation rather than admiration.

---

1   Prov. 24.

NAPOLEON CROSSING THE ALPS.

From the picture by David.

There was a fascination about Napoleon that blinded his men and drew them after him, as it were, in spite of themselves. They knew he had brought mourning and desolation into their homes throughout the land, yet such was their pride in "*Notre Empereur*," their trust in his marvellous genius as a commander, and the enthusiasm aroused by his victories, that on his escape from Elba they rushed to his standard once more, and the troops sent against him went over to his side.

Soon after the Battle of Waterloo, a young English lady visited the military hospital in Paris that housed the men wounded in that bloody field and those who had survived the horrors of the retreat from Moscow. Many of these poor fellows were frightfully mutilated, and the rest crippled for life. There was one, a mere boy, who had had both legs shot off. Full of pity, the girl went up to him, and after a few kind words was beginning some speech about "the selfishness of the men who had brought such suff..."—when he sprang up in bed, and turning upon her with flashing eyes exclaimed: "*Mademoiselle, c'est ainsi que vous parlez de mon Empereur!*"[1] Then at the top of his voice and waving both arms, he cried out, "*Vive l'Empereur! Vive l'Empereur!*" As if at a given signal the cry was taken up by the whole ward, and went out through the open windows over the city. Up came the nuns in consternation. Paris would think a revolution had broken out, the house would get into trouble. "*La bonne Mère*" hurried from bed to bed, now scolding, now quieting "*les mauvais garçons*," but it was some time before the uproar subsided.

Lord Wolseley tells us that we have never yet had an English commander who succeeded in calling forth a great enthusiasm for himself or his cause. Wellington was a great general, and it would be ungenerous as well as ungrateful

1   "Miss, it is thus that you speak of my Emperor!"

to seek to lessen in any way the reputation of the great Duke. Yet, as we read the history of his wars, we cannot help picturing to ourselves what he might have done if his soldiers had had for him the enthusiastic attachment that the French had for their Emperor. Napoleon studied men closely. He knew the passions and feelings that moved them. He knew how the spirit of Frenchmen is roused by stirring proclamations and appeals to their love of glory. He knew how a little condescension, a word of praise, a look of approbation on the part of their commander, enchants them and attaches them to his person. It was easy for him, therefore, to fire his troops with enthusiasm, and get from them all they were capable of.

As Commander-in-Chief, Lord Wolseley ought to know what a commander should be if he is to stir, and captivate, and lead men. In his advice to officers he says: "Study to be familiar without being vulgar, and habit, if not instinct, will soon enable you to be gracious and intimate with your men without any loss of dignity. In all regiments some officers are immense favourites with their men and others the reverse. This is especially the case on active service, where community of danger and constant association create comradeship unknown in peace...You must be intimate with your men before they will love you, and they must love you before you can hope to get the most out of them. The officers should learn their individual characters, take a lively interest in their amusements, sympathize with their likes and dislikes, their pleasures and annoyances, being ready at all times to listen attentively to their grievances, be they supposed or real, until at last they regard him as one of themselves, a companion and a friend. For and with such a man they will brave any danger or endure any amount of privation.

"Upon all occasions appeal to their honour and chivalrous feelings. It is not true that Englishmen are utterly devoid of such high sentiments...Let any general arise who knows how to appeal to them, and a new era of victory will be arrived at in British history. No man can respond with greater alacrity than the British soldier will, when an officer who understands him makes an appeal to his honour, his love of country, and his loyalty! Among the questions to be asked of prisoners in order to ascertain the strength of the enemy, ask, 'Is the general officer commanding popular? Have they a high opinion of him?'

"During the siege of Sebastopol,[1] I verily believe that a large proportion of our men did not know the name of the general officer commanding. They seldom saw him, he did not live amongst them; if he had feelings in common with them, they did not know it. No touching appeals were made to their feelings of honour and patriotism. The consequences were we never got much out of our men." "Employ officers," he says in another place, "to superintend all large fatigues, and associate them with the men in all their work. Often have I blushed for my profession when I have seen officers sitting down under some shelter reading a book, whilst their men were working, or rather, I should say, supposed to be working; for after a little time, when the men see that their officers do not take an interest in what is going on, they soon follow suit.

"It is humbug for an officer to lecture men about drinking, advising them against the use of spirits, and then go to his tent to be merry over a bottle of sherry. He ought cheerfully to go without his luxuries, when he compels those under his orders to forego theirs; the feeling that his conduct is for the good of

---

1   Sebastopol is a Russian port on the Black Sea. During the Crimean War, the British, French, Sardinian and Turkish troops lay siege to it for eleven months.

the service should amply compensate him for the privation."

Earl Roberts of Kandahar would say the same: "What's good enough for my men is good enough for me," he remarked quite simply to some railway official who expressed surprise on seeing him step out of a third-class carriage.

We are told of Nelson that even as a baby he did not know what it was to be afraid. "I wonder, child, that fear did not drive you home," said his grandmother, as he walked in one dark night after people had been scouring the country in search of him. "Fear, grandma, who is he? I never saw him," was the answer. Yet in after years, the great seaman could feel for poor little middies, who are often overcome with terror on their first attempt to ascend the rigging. He never laughed at them or scolded them, but gave them confidence by showing them he would not ask anything of them that he was not ready to do himself. "Come, sir," he would say, "I'm going a trip to the mast-head, and beg I may meet you there." To such an invitation there could be but one answer, and the poor fellow immediately began his climb. His companion made no remark on the slow, trembling ascent, but on meeting him at the top, spoke cheerily of the task they had accomplished, saying what a pity it was people should fancy there was anything dangerous, or even disagreeable about it. What example had shown to be possible, practice soon made easy, and a lad was often seen leading a companion in the same way, repeating his captain's words.

A leader need not be in an army. One of the most prominent that England has known in our times was the old man who died in the quiet village of Hawarden, in the May of 1898, and was buried with regal pomp in Westminster Abbey. Young as you are, you have heard of Mr. Gladstone,[1] the great

---

1   William Ewart Gladstone served four separate terms as Prime Minister of England between 1868 and 1894. Aside from his political career, he is

statesman, whose life of eighty-nine years was passed amid scenes as shifting and as stirring as those of a battlefield. You have heard how men hung on his words, how the telegraph flashed them continually to all parts of the earth, how they swayed the minds and hearts of millions. What gave him this wonderful influence? It was the power of feeling the keenest, intensest interest in the affairs of his fellow-men, of entering into their views and their feelings—what they value and strive for, what they account grievances. He was able to adapt himself to every company in which he found himself, to come down to the level of all. Whether he was speaking in the House of Commons, or addressing a crowd of 20,000 at Leeds, or discussing the price of leather with his cobbler, or sitting down in the kitchen of the little coffee-house at Hawarden to talk to its mistress, or chatting about school with the child, whom he relieved of her heavy pail, as they went up the hill together— the effect produced upon his hearers was the same. All felt that, great man as he was, they were not beneath his notice and his kindly interest. They were at home with him—he was one of themselves.

This was what made their "grand old man" as dear to the simple folk of his own village as he was idolised by thousands in the great world outside. It was this large-hearted fellow-feeling and his wonderful earnestness in expressing what he felt, that gave him his power as an orator and made him one of the greatest leaders of men that our country has ever seen.

But to return to the army.

In the spring of 1898 England discovered that she had another great general in the man who had led the British and Egyptian forces against the Dervishes at Atbara.

best known for his tireless efforts to help rehabilitate fallen women, finding them respectable jobs and homes.

"I know, the Sirdar.[1] And at Cambridge they made a bonfire for him of wheelbarrows and shutters and shavings. And they had crackers, and rockets, and Roman candles and bombs going off all night. And they drew his carriage for him instead of horses, and when it broke they kept the bits for relics. I have just been reading about it all."

You are evidently well up in University methods of fêting a hero. The country gave, and rightly gave, an enthusiastic welcome to the man whose victories will, in all probability, make a greater difference in the history of Africa than any that have been won upon its soil. In years to come children will learn what great things came of the Egyptian campaign, which, opening with the Atbara fight, closed with the momentous victory of Omdurman. We may surely hope that, freed from "the most cruel tyranny the world has ever known," to use the Sirdar's words, the immense population of the Soudan will be brought to the voluntary and sweet service of our Lord Jesus Christ, and that by means of larger and larger bands of Catholic missionaries, the whole of the vast continent which has so sadly deserved the name of "*Dark*," will have its day of grace.

Had we time to follow the Sirdar's campaign a little carefully, we should discover in him those qualities which, as we have seen, are found in every great leader.

He was sent, or rather he volunteered, to go to a land where the people groaned under a heavy tyranny, which for want of proper leadership they were unable to throw off. Their untrained soldiers, timid even to cowardice, knew not how to fight, and when they did make a show of resistance, they were beaten.

1   A *sirdar* was the name given to the British Commander-in-Chief of the 19th century Egyptian army. In this case, the title refers to Horatio Herbert Kitchener, who rose through the ranks to eventually become Lord Kitchener. A famous poster used for recruitment during the First World War featured his face, and served as an inspiration for a similar well-known American recruitment poster of "Uncle Sam" saying, "I want YOU!"

THE SIRDAR

Lord Horatio Herbert Kitchener

From a famous recruitment poster from World War I.

The Sirdar resolved to amend this state of things. How did he set to work? He went freely in and out amongst the enslaved and dispirited race. He learned their language, made himself familiar with their character, their habits and customs, their weak and their strong points. By degrees friendliness sprang up, then confidence. He made acquaintance with many of the Sheikhs, and was the guest of honour everywhere.

"He used to *salaam* when he went into an Arab tent, and say 'Salaam aleikoum,' which means 'peace be with you,' and he used to smoke a cigar they call Turkish Delight."

He seems to adapt himself to all kinds and classes of people, and—though severe in discipline—to be popular with his troops, especially with the black Soudanese, who style him "The Deliverer." Of his marvellous success in transforming abject slaves into soldiers, fit to fight side by side with the flower of the English army, we shall have to speak later. He is said to be the kindest officer in the army to the private soldier. In spite of the enormous difficulties of the Egyptian campaign, in which his troops were one thousand miles distant from their base of operations, they never wanted a meal. Never were the wounded so well cared for; never were the peculiar needs of a campaign so thoughtfully met. Think of his having strong gloves provided before the fight of Atbara for the soldiers who were to tear down the *zareba*, or thorny fence, behind which the enemy was entrenched! Think of his laying down over five hundred miles of railway line upon the desert sands! Of that wonderful march to Omdurman—25,000 men, white, yellow, black, with horses, mules, donkeys, camels, oxen, sheep, and goats—all supplied with food punctually and sufficiently, there in the heart of the desert! What wonder that the General who could plan and carry through so vast an enterprise should possess the full confidence of his troops. "When the columns move out of camp in the evening to march all night through the dark, they know not whither, and fight at dawn with an enemy they have never seen, every man goes forth with a tranquil mind. He may personally come back, or he may not; but about the general result there is not a doubt... 'The Sirdar knows: he wouldn't fight if he weren't going to win.' Other generals have been better loved; none was ever better trusted."[1]

And when the great work was accomplished, when the native soldiers had shown themselves worthy of their training, how hearty was the Sirdar's praise of his troops, how liberally he shared with them the glory of the triumph!

We have looked at a few of the world's famous chiefs—a king, a soldier, a sailor, a statesman—in order to gain something like a clear idea of what a leader of men should be. And now we turn away from the leaders of this world to fix our gaze on One in Whom we find all we look for in a leader, carried to a height that has been reached once, and once only, in the world's history.

1   G. W. Steevens, *With Kitchener to Khartoum.*

IV.

THE TRUE LEADER

Abide thou with Me, fear not... With Me thou shalt be safe.
(I Kings 22, 23.)

The True Leader! The youngest of us knows His Name, knows Who it was that volunteered to go to a land where the people groaned under a cruel tyranny, which for want of proper leadership they could not throw off; Who turned dispirited slaves into soldiers able to cope with their powerful enemy and overcome him.

How He did this we have now to learn.

Whenever we see an effect of any kind, we know for certain there has been a cause to bring it about. That some lights twinkle above us in the midnight sky while others do not; that thousands of sea-gulls have made themselves at home in St. James' Park, London, where five years ago there was not one; that my mind has quite veered round from the opinion I held last night; that the results of my brother's examination are different from what we expected—all these effects have been brought about by something going before, which has produced the effect, just as light produces colour. Whether it be in Heaven above or in the earth beneath, in my own soul or in the lives of others, "*nothing is done without a cause.*"[1] And a

1 Job 5.

sufficient cause. If the effect is very startling, a great cause has been at work.

Let us apply this to the most extraordinary effects that have ever been seen upon this earth of ours. Nineteen hundred years ago a Man passed through this world, one among millions that were born and lived and died with Him. It was a short passage, thirty-three years only, a mere point in the world's history. But that Life of His has changed the face of the earth and the lives of all men. The world was at its darkest when He came. Alas! it is dark enough now, but only where it shuts out His light. No one can shut it out quite. For St. John tells us, "*The Life*"—that is, the Life of the Word made Flesh, "*was the light of men;...the true light which enlightens every man that cometh into this world.*"[1] This he says of our Lord at the beginning of his Gospel. At the end he tells us that if all the "things which Jesus did were written every one, the world itself would not be able to contain the books that should be written." Certainly there never could be written all the effects of that one Divine Life upon the lives of men.

We are not going to consider now the effect produced after He had left this world, but only to catch a glimpse of it during those three out of the thirty years that were lived before the eyes of His fellow-countrymen, the Jews of Palestine.

"I often wonder when we say the *Angelus* why our Lord is called the Word, because a word, you know, is something we say to express ourselves, but it isn't anything of itself."

The Word is indeed one of our Lord's most mysterious names. Yet if we think a little, we shall find we can understand something, at least, of its meaning. Our Lord has come to help us to understand, as far as we can, the Incomprehensible God. God dwelt by Himself in light inaccessible from all eternity. We could not reach Him there, we could not see Him in that

1   St. John 1.

blinding light. We could not know Him unless He in some way expressed Himself. We express ourselves by our words. So does God. From all eternity He has been uttering His inmost thought. That thought is His Word. And His Word is God, the second Person of the ever Blessed Trinity. This is a mystery. Yet that name of our Lord, "*the Word of God,*"[1] teaches us many things. We look up into the face of another and try to guess what he is thinking. We are in doubt, perhaps, whether he cares for us, whether we can trust him, whether, if he be rich, he will give us what we need. We wait for his word to learn all this. By His Word God reveals Himself to us. When the Word was made Flesh and lay in the Crib, when He spoke tenderly to the poor, and to sinners and to little children, when He cured all manner of diseases and infirmity, when He forgave His crucifiers, when He comforted His Mother and His friends, it was the compassion, the patience, the love of God expressing itself in a way we could perceive and understand. And so to know what our Heavenly Father is like, what He thinks of us, what He is ready to do for us, we have only to listen to His Word, as He told us on the Mount of Transfiguration—"This is My beloved Son, hear ye Him."

God, Who made us to know, love, and enjoy Him, longs to make Himself known to us. And because, in His Divine Nature, He was too far above our reach for us to draw near to Him, He made Himself like to us and came amongst us. He went about this world, and men could see Him. His Feet trod the streets of their towns, and the winding paths among the corn, and the white, shingly shore. His Eyes looked up into the face of a human Mother, and out on to the Lake in the flowery slopes of the hills that shut in His village home. His Lips spoke the common words of daily life by which we tell our needs, our plans, our little joys and troubles. He handled our tools and rested when His day's work was done. He ate of our bread; He

1   Apoc. 19.

was clothed with the wool of the flocks; He drank the water of the well. He was homeless and footsore. He lay asleep in the rocking boat because He was tired. He listened for words of kindness; He spoke words of gentleness. He showed a tender interest in all that touched the people among whom His lot was cast—in their poor and their sick and their little children; in their feasts and in their house of mourning; in their sorrow for sin; in their desire for better things and for the life of the world to come. He knew the needs, the joys, the sorrows of human life, for He was truly man.

And He knew as no other man could know. "*He knew what was in man,*"—*all* that is in man, for He was God. And as He understood better than any other, so He felt for His fellow-men as no other could feel, for His Heart was the Heart of God. What wonder, then, that during the three years of His Public Ministry, when He "went about all the cities and towns, teaching in their synagogues and healing every sickness and every disease," the multitudes flocked after Him through the streets, along the dusty roads, out into desert places where He had sought a little rest!

The Evangelists, so sparing in superlatives, speak of "very great multitudes" following our Lord. "Great multitudes stood about Him, so that they trod one upon another."[1]

"They went after Him for what they could get! It's a wonder He cared for such love as that. I shouldn't."

It *was* "because of the loaves," as He Himself told them. Yet the love that drew them after Him was not all cupboard love. It was the spell that hung about Him, the sweet majesty of His beautiful Face, the indescribable charm of His voice, His tender words and ways that drew them all after Him, that attracted *all*. The reaper threw aside his sickle, the carpenter his saw. The scribe left his parchment, the fishermen his nets, the child its

1   St. Luke 12.

shells on the sea-shore. Women laid down their distaff, mothers caught up their babes and hurried forth to join the crowd that was gone after Jesus of Nazareth into the desert.

"And it would be the same now," said a mother of our days, as she spoke of the wonderful attractiveness of our Blessed Lord to the little tribe that clustered round her knee. "If now He were to pass through this room, my poor Scripture lesson would have no chance. You would set off after Him, every one of you, as fast as you could run—big ones and little ones, Baby and all. I should be left alone."

"No you wouldn't, Mother," cried Baby, "cos you'd run too."

"I wonder if I should have gone after our Lord like the rest. I am so funny. I don't like people that others like, though they are very good and kind and all that. I ought to like them, I suppose, but somehow I don't, and I can't make myself. It would have been dreadful not to have gone after our Lord. Did everyone except His enemies love Him, love Him *really*, I mean, not because they got things from Him, nor because they knew they *ought*, but because they *couldn't help?*"

What a pity you cannot ask that question of Mary Magdalen, or of the Twelve. They would have answered by sending you to our Blessed Lord, as St. John the Baptist sent his disciples, or by keeping you with them for a day, to see and hear Him through one round of twenty-four hours. Though twenty-four hours would not be necessary. One night for Nicodemus, one word for Matthew, one look for Peter, was enough to fill their hearts with lifelong loyalty and love. But let us examine your difficulty.

You think because you are hard to satisfy, because you do not readily make friends, our Lord might have failed to attract *you*. You need not fear. In His beautiful Human Nature is all the excellence that your mind and heart can long for. He is just the One you would love for a Leader, the One to attract *you*. True, He has very different requirements to meet. No two of us are drawn precisely in the same way or by the same qualities. What one likes, another dislikes; what charms you, may repel me. Our Lord has all hearts to win by attracting all. Is this easy? Impossible to any but Himself. Can He do it? Yes, for He is God. All that each heart longs for, He can give. To each one of us He shows Himself as the Leader after our own heart.

When men seek to account for the force which attracted so many to the Stuarts and made them the object of such devoted loyalty, they set it down to the immense charm which a kingly bearing, beauty, and grace of manner exercises over the minds of men. Our Leader is "beautiful above the sons of men," satisfying thus the craving of the human heart to find in the object of its love all the qualities that attract. Who shall tell what was the expectation of His Mother, who knew the glorious things spoken of Him by His prophets, who knew Him to be the Son of the Most High! If kings and prophets longed to see His day; if, as the time drew near, the whole nation—nay, the whole world—was "expecting, expecting;" if the Angels desired to look upon His Face, what was the longing of the young Mother's heart! She saw that Face in Bethlehem on Christmas night, and prostrated herself before It. It had surpassed all her expectation: "*O my Son and my God,*" she said, "*the word is true which I heard,...scarce one half hath been told me. Thou hast exceeded Thy fame.*"[1]

> Thou hast waited, Child of David!
>   And thy waiting now is o'er,
> Thou hast seen Him, Blessed Mother!
>   And wilt see Him evermore.
> O, His Human Face and Features,
>   They were passing sweet to see.
> Thou beholdest them this moment;
>   Mother, show them now to me![2]

If He filled to overflowing the expecting heart of His Mother,

1   2 Paral. 9.
2   Faber.

it was little for our Lord to satisfy every other. The simple shepherds came, and charmed by the winning grace of that little Face, went away glorifying and praising God, "for all the things that they had heard and seen."[1] The Magi expected great things in the Infant King, Whose star in the heavens was sent to lead them to His Feet. It led them to a weak Babe lying in the lap of a girlish Mother. Could there be a mistake? Oh, no. They looked upon His Face, and more than rewarded for their long search, more than satisfied, "falling down they adored Him."

He grew older. The tender grace of childhood gave place to something more attractive still. To the eyes of Mary and Joseph, He grew sweeter day by day. "Jesus advanced in wisdom, and age and grace with God and men."[2] *And men*—not, therefore, with the loving ones only that knew Who He was. Even the dull-sighted Nazarenes could not but stand still to watch the Boy that came, morning and evening, to fetch water from the well. He stirred their hearts and drew them to Him by a secret force, for which they could not account. In their troubles—so a tradition tells us—He was their refuge. "Let us go," they said, "and have a talk with the Son of Mary."

St. John saw our Lord as King going forth "*conquering that He might conquer.*"[3] What other leader ever drew men to his standard by simply looking at them, or saying as he passed them, busy at their occupations: "Follow Me." Two words were enough. Apostle after Apostle immediately left all. Left it unreservedly, left it for ever, without a hankering look afterwards on what he had left, without a single thought of regret for father, mother, wife, brethren, left behind. He had seen that Face, he had heard that Voice—henceforth Jesus was all in all to him.

---

1   St. Luke 2.
2   St. Luke 2.
3   Apoc. 6.

What attracted Peter was not precisely what attracted John, or Mary Magdalen, the man of refinement and education, or the crowd. Learned men like Nicodemus hung upon His words, charmed and carried away by the force and the persuasiveness of His teaching. So were the simple and the poor. The little children loved to be near Him, to look up into His Face, to play and prattle beside His Knee, to be taken up into His Arms and embraced, to feel His Hands laid in blessing on their heads. Happy with a deeper happiness, their mothers stood around, content to brave the threats of Pharisees and scribes and priests, so they might be near Him as He preached, and feed their souls with words such as had never been spoken by man before.

We may judge of a cause by its effects, as we have seen. How irresistible, then, must have been the attractiveness of our Blessed Savior, thus to rivet the attention and draw the hearts of all who approached Him.

All. Some people are more impressed by strength, others by sweetness. What must it have been when these were blended in perfect harmony, as they were in our Lord!

Stung to madness one day, the Pharisees sent officers to apprehend Him, and bring Him prisoner before them. The men set off, and came upon one of the great crowds that continually surrounded Him. It was no easy task to force a passage, but at last they had elbowed their way through the throng. They came within sight of His Face and sound of His Voice. His words fell upon their ears, and the fetters dropped from their hands. An hour they stood there spell-bound. Then empty-handed they returned to their masters.

"Why have you not brought Him?" was the angry question.

"Never man spake like this man," they replied. And the Pharisees turned away to mutter in their rage, "Behold the whole world is gone after Him."[1]

1 St. John 12.

"Why didn't they go themselves, they must have known He was God?"

They were proud, ambitious men. If He had come to bring them honour and dignity, they would have welcomed Him gladly. But they did not want His Blessed teaching, because they did not mean to correct their faults. And they were enraged beyond measure to find that He knew the secrets of their hearts, and that He warned the people to beware of them. They were jealous of Him too, because the people flocked after Him and listened more attentively to Him than to them.

Another day—it was just before the Passion—some Gentiles went to Philip saying, "Sir, we would see Jesus." Philip told Andrew, and the two went to our Lord and told Him. Everyone in Jerusalem was talking about Him at this time. Many followed Him eagerly, and many loved Him. Those who had become His disciples wanted everybody else to know Him. They pressed their friends to go and see Him as He was teaching in the synagogue, or from a boat on the lake. And as they hurried them forward to secure a good places in the crowd, they kept telling them that nothing that was said of His beauty or His attractiveness came near the truth. He is *beautiful above the sons of men,*[1] they said. *"Never man spake like this man."*[2] Expectation then ran high. Was it ever disappointed? Never. No one ever drew near to Jesus and went away disappointed. Many went away angry, and some who had not courage to do what He asked them went away sad. But disappointed, after looking upon that Face and listening to that Voice—there was not one.

And He has satisfied every heart since then. Those who have raised their expectations highest, whom it takes most to content, say as they look up into His Face, *"the report is true*

1   Psalm 44.
2   St. John 7.

which I heard. I did not believe them that told me till I came myself and saw with my own eyes and have found that the half hath not been told me.[1] *Thou hast exceeded Thy fame.*"[2]

We might be sure it would be so. When God designs anyone for a special work, He gives him the qualities that are needed to carry it out. He has done this for all His servants from the beginning down to our own days. What, then, did He do for His own Son? We have no words to tell it, no thoughts to imagine it. This we know—that all the treasures of His omnipotence and wisdom were poured out by the Father upon "*the Son of His love.*" An artist's grandest work is called his masterpiece. The Soul of our Blessed Lord was the masterpiece of God; and to His Sacred Body, grace, beauty, every perfection was given that it might be the worthy companion and dwelling-place of that glorious Soul.

There is everything, then, in the Person of our King to attract and charm us. Now about His character and His actions.

We love a hero-king. Cœur de Lion has won the heart of every English child that has heard his name. He was not a good king. A renowned warrior, a gallant leader, a generous foe—all this he was, but he was not a good king. Yet for all that, he is probably our favourite in the long line from Egbert to Edward VII. Why? Because we do so love to find a hero in our King. If a prince has done no glorious deeds in battle, we may admire him, reverence him even, but our hearts do not glow at the sound of his name. It is a natural longing this, for one who will set our hearts aglow.

Is "*Christ the Prince*"[3] a Hero-King? Has He glorious deeds to show? Is His war a useful one, bringing happiness to His subjects? Has He shown wisdom in planning His campaign,

1 3 Kings 10.
2 2 Paral. 10.
3 Daniel 9.

and perseverance in carrying it through? Has He been valiant and self-sacrificing in battle, brave in hardships, in suffering, in death?

Holy Scripture tells us: "*the Lord is as a man of war.*"[1] "Do not think," says Christ our Lord, "that I came to send peace upon earth. I came not to send peace but the sword."[2] He came amongst us, not to free one nation from a tyranny that would end with this life, but to deliver our whole race, every man, woman, and child, from a cruel and everlasting slavery. And this He did single-handed. He fought and conquered, not as the world's heroes by spilling the blood of others, but by pouring out His own, even to the last drop.

We know the enemies He had to fight—the devil and sin. We know when and how He gave them battle. He fought them in Bethlehem and at Nazareth, as well as in the desert. He fought them in His teaching, in His prayer, and His every action. He fought them in every stage of His bitter Passion—in the Garden, in the Praetorium, on Calvary. He fought them unshrinkingly, perseveringly, unto death.

But besides a hero, we want to find a leader in our King; one going before us, showing the way; not valiant only, but gracious and familiar. And above all compassionate; who will remember that too many of us are but sorry soldiers. Unlike the knights of olden times that were eager to fight in the front ranks, we are frightened to fight at all, afraid of a little pain, ready to cry out at the least smart, like the child that runs with every scratch to its mother. Will He, Who was so valiant, despise us in our shrinking and our fears, or will He condescend to be like us and encourage us by His example?

What are we told of Him when He was entering into that battle in which He was to be "wounded for our iniquities and

---

1   Exodus 15.
2   St. Matt. 10.

bruised for our sins,"[1] "from the sole of the foot unto the top of the head,...covered with wounds and bruises and swelling sores"?[2] What are we told of Him then? That *"He began to be sorrowful and to be sad."*[3] *"He began to fear and to be heavy,... His Soul was sorrowful even unto death,...and He prayed that, if it might be, the hour might pass from Him."*[4]

Why was this? That He might be like us in all things. That we might be able to run in our troubles to One Who has "felt as we have felt, and knelt as we have knelt," Who has shrunk as we shrink from pain and cruelty and shame.

A famous General, hearing on the eve of an engagement that a young fellow in the Army, a mere boy, was beside himself with terror at the thought of the morrow, when he was to see fire for the first time, sent for him, encouraged him, and made him sleep near him that night. Our Leader does more than encourage us with His words. He shares our fears, that He may know from His own experience how to pity and how to comfort. *"All shall answer and say to Thee: Thou also art wounded as well as we, Thou art become like unto us."*[5] Like, yet how unlike. For who was ever like that "Man of sorrows," that "worm and no man"? *"There hath been no one like Thee before Thee, nor shall arise after Thee."*[6] *"O Lord, my God, there is no one like to Thee."*[7] In trying to be like us and to go with us, O dearest Lord, You have outstripped us and left us far behind.

Not only would He suffer in ordinary ways, and be hungry and thirsty, cold, homeless, footsore, weary, poor and in labours from His youth; but He would endure from the cruelty of men torture of body, the very thought of which makes us tremble—

1   Isaias 53.
2   Isaias 1.
3   St. Matt. 26.
4   St. Mark 14.
5   Isaias 14.
6   3 Kings 3.
7   Psalm 34.

whips and thorns, kicks, blows, spitting. And pain of mind more fearful still—the bitterness of ingratitude and unrequited love, rejection by His people, betrayal and desertion by His friends, calumny, mocking, contempt. And, most terrible of all to His loving, sensitive Heart, the hiding of the Father's Face, that one intolerable drop in His chalice which wrung from Him the cry, "My God, My God, why hast Thou forsaken Me!"

> Cur igitur non amem Te
> O Jesu amantissime!

O children, *we must, we must* love our Lord Jesus Christ, for indeed He has loved us!

Our Leader, then, can feel for us in our weakness and our fears. But we need more than this. In olden times the esquire followed his lord closely wherever he went. He kept near him in battle to supply him with a fresh horse or arms if he lost his own, and to help him out of the battle if he were wounded. We, on the contrary, want our Leader to follow *us* about closely, to keep near *us* always, to make good all our losses, to cure all our wounds. Will He do all this for us? Let us hear His own words: "*Fear not, for the Lord your God will fight for you.*"[1] "*Do manfully and be of good heart, for the Lord thy God Himself is thy Leader. He will not leave thee nor forsake thee.*"[2] "*Take courage and be very valiant.... I will show thee what thou art to do.*"[3]

And He Who promises so much is the "Faithful and True," Who cannot fail anyone that trusts in Him. David says, "*It is good to trust in the Lord. Being pushed, I was overturned that I might fall, but the Lord supported me. The Lord is my strength.*"[4]

---

1   Deut. 3.
2   Deut. 31.
3   1 Kings 16.
4   Psalm 117.

"I didn't know Almighty God said kind things like that. I can't help being afraid of Him because He sends such dreadful punishments. He made the earth swallow up Core, Dathan, and Abiron[1]. And He struck Oza dead[2]. And made bears come and eat the boys that mocked Eliseus."

All that is true. It is one half of the story. But you have forgotten the other half. What is surprising, almost beyond belief in the history of God's dealings with the Jews, is not the terrible punishments they drew down upon themselves from time to time, but the perversity and ingratitude of that stiff-necked people, of which He complains so lovingly: *"All the day I have spread forth My Hands to an unbelieving people,...a people that continually provoke Me to anger before My Face."*[3] He punished them sometimes when their wickedness had "grown up even unto heaven." But at the first sign of repentance He forgave them and treated them as if they had never offended Him. And this over and over again, with an untiring patience. He even called upon them in tender words to return to Him. *"Return, O rebellious Israel, and I will not turn away My Face from you and I will not be angry for ever...Return, you rebellious children, and I will heal your rebellion."*[4] *"The Lord thy God hath carried thee, as a man is wont to carry his little son."*[5] *"Can a woman forget her child... and if she should forget, yet will I not forget thee."*[6] *"As one whom the mother caresseth so will I comfort you."*[7] Can you think of words more loving than these? They were said by Almighty God in the Old Law. They are said with a fuller meaning to His people now. They are said to each one of us, to you and me.

---

1   Leaders of a revolt against Moses and Aaron in Num. 16.
2   For touching the Ark of the Covenant. See 2 Samuel 6.
3   Isaias 65.
4   Jerem. 3.
5   Deut. 1.
6   Isaias 49.
7   Isaias 66.

"But not by our Lord Himself, are they? I thought you said our Leader said them to us."

What! have we to come back to the first question of the Catechism: "Are there more Gods than one?" Jesus our Leader is God. All that God says, He says. His Life, remember, did not begin when He came into this world. His human Life did. But He is from everlasting. He was living His eternal Life before the world was made. As she prostrated herself before her little One an hour old, His Mother said to Him, "Wast Thou not from the beginning, O Lord, my God, my Holy One!"[1] Thus His love for us did not begin when He stretched out His little arms to us from the manger straw. It never began at all.

The love of God is like the sun, from whose light and heat no one can hide himself. The effects of the sun's rays are the same always, but they are not always the same *to us.* To us, his light and heat increase as he mounts in the heavens. So it is with the Incarnation, the Passion, the Eucharist, the revelation of the Sacred Heart. In the sweet and tender mysteries in which "*the goodness and kindness of God our Saviour appeared,*"[2] we see the love of our God mounting and ever mounting, brightening and ever brightening, till it reaches its meridian height. But it is the same love that has loved us from the beginning; it is the same Lover, "*Jesus, yesterday, to-day, and for ever.*"[3]

A sad silence fell on the little group round our Lord that day, when the rich young man, having received His invitation, went away sorrowful, not having the courage to leave the pleasant things of this world for the treasure in Heaven that was promised him. The silence was broken by Peter saying with his usual impulsiveness: "Behold, *we* have left all things and followed Thee, what therefore shall we have?"

1   Habacuc 1.
2   Titus 3.
3   Hebrews 13.

"How bold of him!"

"And how unfeeling! To want pay for being our Lord's Apostle!"

Notice this: our Lord, Who never hesitated to rebuke Peter, because he took rebuke so well, had no rebuke for him here. Neither did He show Himself hurt, as we might have supposed. He did not say, "O Peter, surely, to follow Me as My intimate companion and friend should be reward enough!" No, He seemed pleased with the child-like question, and at once told Peter what he and others who followed Him should have as their reward. As Lord and Master, He could require us to follow Him without promise of recompense. But His way is to invite, rather than to exact. He draws us after Him with cheery words. He holds a crown above us, as the gilded spurs were held before the future knight: "*Be thou faithful unto death, and I will give thee the crown of life.*"[1] The prospect of reward makes effort easy, and pain welcome, and long waiting momentary and light. It is so with us, and therefore—how sweet this is of Him!—it shall be so with Him. He, too, will look to a reward. "*Having joy set before Him*"—the joy of saving those whom He loves—He will endure the cross, despising the shame. He goes to meet His cross. He takes it up bravely, and, looking round upon His soldiers who are following in His steps, He bids them do as He does: "I have given you an example that as I have done, so you do also."[2] "If you suffer with Me, you shall be glorified with Me."

What He promises He will give. For "*He is faithful Who hath called you,*"[3] says St. Paul. If there is one thing more than another on which—might we reverently say it—our God prides Himself, it is His fidelity. "*Thou shalt know that the Lord thy*

---

1   Apoc. 2.

2   St. John 13.

3   Thess. 5.

God is a strong and faithful God."[1] All His servants from the beginning bear delighted testimony to His fidelity. *"The Lord is faithful in all His words,"* said King David. *"There is a faithful reward,"* says Solomon. *"God is faithful, God is faithful,"* St. Paul is never tired of telling us. *"Faithful and true"* is the name by which our Leader loves to be known. "Faithful and True!" is the cry of all His Redeemed, when, the battle over, they fall in a transport of joy at His Feet.

He has proved Himself the *"Friend that loveth at all times."*[2] *"A steadfast Friend,...a strong defence,...a faithful Friend,"*[3] *"more friendly than a brother."*[4] *Faithful and true* through all the varying fortunes of war, through all the dangers now so clearly seen. Faithful to succour us when we called upon Him; to raise us when we fell; to tend us when we were wounded; to ransom us when, through our own fault, we were made captives. Faithful when *we* were faithless, when we abandoned His Standard and went over to the enemy, and fought against Him, and wounded those He loved. Faithful to cheer us when we were downhearted, to warn us when we were rash; standing by us always, supplying our losses, putting up with our cowardice, never failing us, never weary, faithful at all times, faithful unto death. "O, Faithful and True!" we shall say to Him in a transport of love, "the word is true which I heard... I did not believe them that told me until I came, and my eyes had seen, and I had proved that scarce one half had been told me. Thou hast exceeded Thy fame."[5]

And faithful now, to reward our poor services with joys which *"eye hath not seen, nor ear heard, nor the heart of man*

---

1   Deut. 7.
2   Prov. 17.
3   Ecclus. 6.
4   Prov. 18.
5   2 Paral. 9.

conceived."[1] "*His reward is with Him.*"[2] Nay, this is not enough. His reward is Himself: "*I will be thy Reward exceeding great.*"[3]

Such is our Leader. Does He satisfy us? Is He all that was promised us, all we should *like* Him to be? Do we desire anything more? Not till we see Him in His glory, "*King of kings and Lord of lords,*"[4] shall we understand Who it was we had for our Leader on earth. Yet, even now, we can see some little of His beauty—even here we must cry out in admiration: "*Lord who is like Thee!*"[5] "*There hath been no one like Thee before Thee nor shall arise after Thee.*"[6] "*Happy are Thy servants who stand always before Thee...Because God loveth Israel hath He made Thee King over them.*"[7]

Shall we not love such a Leader and be ready to take the Law from His Lips when He makes His Proclamation now!

1   1 Cor. 2.
2   Isaias 62.
3   Genesis 15.
4   Apoc. 19.
5   Psalm 34.
6   3 Kings 3.
7   2 Paral. 9.

V.

THE PROCLAMATION

Ask...if it hath been known at any time, that the people should hear the voice of God speaking...as thou hast heard.
(Deut. 4, 32.)

LET us join this vast throng moving slowly northward—a very great multitude, growing in bulk continually, as from hamlet and highway, country parts and crowded cities, smaller crowds come up and mingle with it.

The people have heard that Jesus of Nazareth is at Cæsarea Philippi and they are on their way to Him. Twice lately He has multiplied loaves in a marvellous way to feed the thousands that followed Him into the desert. Enthusiasm is at its height. If they could, they would take Him by force and make Him King, for will the Messiah—when He comes—do greater things than He has done?

Get onto this grey boulder and look around. On every side the people are coming up the incline—the sick carried carefully and tenderly, yet not without difficulty and pain, for the bearers have come far, and the poor invalids are weary with the jolting on the uneven ground, the cramped posture, the heat and the noise. But each heart is kept up by its joyful expectation. *"I am travelling in a path by which I shall not return.*[1] In a few hours

1   Job 16.

at most I shall be laid at His feet. His Hands will touch me. I shall rise up and walk."

Here is a set of men evidently well-to-do in the world. Yet they walk apart as if shunned by the crowd and beneath the companionship of the poorest. Even those boys yonder point to them scornfully, and we catch the word "Publicans!" "They have gone over to Rome; they are tax-gatherers and in her pay, aye, and grow rich upon it. What right have they among the people of God, whom the Messiah is going to free for ever from the foreign yoke!" The young scoffer and his three companions are "sons of the law" who have begged their master, a learned scribe, to take them to hear the new rabbi. On the road they have been plying him with questions: Who is this Jesus of Nazareth? Elias that is to come, the people say, or John the Baptist, Jeremias, or one of the prophets risen again. What does their master think of the poor Carpenter Who is teaching without having received His key and tablets as a scribe, and has silenced the Pharisees and Sadducees and Herodians?

What a motley crowd it is! Here, holding themselves carefully aloof from some Gentile strangers near them, stalk a party of Pharisees, scarcely deigning to acknowledge the reverent salutations of the multitude. There, side by side, are field labourers, fishermen, vine-dressers, traders from the bazaars, a sprinkling of Roman soldiers even—all talking eagerly of the young Prophet. And here, with a chattering tribe of little ones about their feet, come a whole crowd of those daughters of Israel who will earn for themselves the glory of having never approached our Lord except to minister to Him, to glorify Him, and to soothe the sorrows of His Heart. When the teachers of the Law seek to catch Him in His speech, when His priests are contriving His Death; when Apostles betray or desert Him, *they* will be true to Him always. Yet not they only—Hebrews, women of His own race—Pagans also, like the

Syro-Phœnician and the wife of Pilate, revealing a faith and courage that would have done honour to Apostles, fearlessly hail Him as the Son of David, or, in the very teeth of His raging enemies, defend Him.

And where is He Whom all these are seeking? Let us see. Not long after the second multiplication of the loaves in the wild highlands to the east of the Lake of Genesareth, our Lord went northward with His disciples till He reached the highest mountain in Palestine, Hermon, whose summit, overtopping all the surrounding peaks, is covered with glittering snow. On a natural terrace of this mountain stands the capital of the district, Cæsarea Philippi, which Philip the tetrarch, son of Herod the Great, has enlarged and called after the reigning Emperor, Tiberius Cæsar, adding his own name to distinguish it from the other Cæsarea on the sea-coast. It is a splendid city, interesting to us as being the most northerly point reached by our Lord in His journeyings, and more especially for two events which—occurring in its neighbourhood—have made it for ever memorable in the history of the Church.

Leaving it now on His left, our Lord passes with His disciples into the "quarters" beyond, and seeks, as is His wont, a retired spot for prayer. The steep side of Hermon here descends into a wide tract of open country, uneven ground thinly covered with prickly oak, wild olive, thickets of oleander, the hawthorn, so familiar to us, and jungles of evergreen shrubs, all fed by numberless brooks, the watersprings of the Jordan. Here and there, embedded in the soil, are huge masses of grey rock which give an air of savage grandeur to the scene. Wild and desolate it all is, but it will secure Him a quiet time for prayer, before the multitude, which can already be seen making its way across the upland plain, has time to reach Him.

We are taught to notice that before the most important actions of His Public Life, our Lord prayed. He prayed before entering on the great conflict with Satan in the desert. Before choosing His Apostles and beginning His teaching, He prayed. Before teaching us to pray, He prayed. Before the Transfiguration "He went up into a mountain to pray."[1] In the supper-room, before instituting the Blessed Sacrament, He prayed. "And Jesus took bread, and blessing broke and gave to them...And having taken the chalice, giving thanks He gave to them."[2] On the Cross, before consummating His sacrifice, He prayed. His whole life was prayer, but it is important to notice what the Evangelists plainly mean us to notice, that before certain events of special importance, He, *to Whom is given all power in Heaven and on earth,* prayed. An important day, this day at Cæsarea Philippi, will be for every follower of His until the end of time. He must pray.

It is the third year of His ministry; the years of miracles are drawn to a close. His work of teaching the people and training the Twelve is nearly done. Henceforth, His labour for the souls of men is to be carried on by His Church.

His Church! that name so dear to His Heart, has not as yet passed His Lips. But the hour has now come for Him to speak openly of what He has so often called His Kingdom, and to point out the signs by which His church may be known from all others that will usurp her name and her office. Looking around Him on this rocky scene, He thinks of Peter. He thinks of the storms that, so long as time shall last, will beat upon that Rock. He prays that the faith of Peter may never fail, and that, himself confirmed, he may confirm his brethren to the end.

An hour has passed since our Lord knelt down to pray, and still the disciples, untired, stand around Him in silent reverence, their eyes riveted upon His Face. Never, it seems to them, does He look at once more human and more divine

1   St. Luke 9.
2   St. Mark 14.

than when His Soul is pouring itself forth in prayer. No mere man, seeing no further than the things of this world, could pray "with a strong cry and tears" like His. But for whom or for what can He be praying now? Never have they seen the vehemence of His supplication so intense. What name is being breathed by those Divine Lips? What love lights up His Face with that unwonted glow? Motionless they stand around Him, and join their prayer with His—the Foundation-stones and the Rock offering themselves unconsciously to the Hand of the Builder Whose time has come.

Rising from His knees and looking towards the multitude that, awed by the majesty of His countenance, keeps silence before Him, Jesus says to the Twelve:

"Whom do men say that I am?" Altogether they answer:

"Some John the Baptist, and other some Elias, and others Jeremias, or one of the prophets." He says to them:

"But whom do you say that I am?" What a chance for Peter! Instantly the words leap from his heart to his lips:

"Thou art Christ, the Son of the living God." Jesus says to him:

"Blessed art thou, Simon Bar-Jona; because flesh and blood hath not revealed it to thee, but My Father Who is in Heaven. And I Say to Thee: That thou art Peter and upon this rock I will build My Church, and the gates of Hell shall not prevail against it. And I will give to thee the keys of the Kingdom of Heaven. And whatsoever thou shalt bind upon earth, it shall be bound also in Heaven; and whatsoever thou shalt loose on earth, it shall be loosed also in Heaven."[1]

The thought of our Lord goes out over the whole world and over all time, to every soul which, clinging to that Rock and admitted by those keys, is to reach in safety that Heavenly Kingdom. But the price has yet to be paid, and the price is

1   St. Matt. 16.

Calvary. The time has come for Him to speak to the Twelve and to all who call themselves His disciples, of the path by which the Leader first, and then all His followers after Him, are to enter into His glory.

"The Son of Man," He goes on to say, "must suffer many things, and be rejected by the ancients and chief priests and scribes, and be killed, and the third day rise again."

This is more than Peter can stand. His loyal heart is up in a moment. His cheek burns. He comes forward boldly, and leading our Lord aside, he says:

"Lord, be it far from Thee, this shall not be unto Thee."

The Lord turning looks on Peter:

"Go behind Me, Satan," He says, "thou art a scandal unto Me, because thou savourest not the things that are of God, but the things that are of man."

It is the flash and the thunder-clap from a bright sky suddenly overcast. Poor Peter's eyes fall before that wrathful glance; his hand, which in his eagerness had grasped his Master's wrist drops; he staggers back among the terrified disciples. Our Lord means them to be frightened by such terrible words—means them to see what it is for even the most beloved to dare to stand between Him and that dear Baptism of Blood, with which He is to redeem the world. He means to dispel, once for all, their illusion that He is going to be a great temporal prince whom neither sorrow nor disgrace shall touch. And what we have to notice specially—He means to impress upon them, and upon us all, that as "the servant is not above his Master," so our lot must be the same.

Passing before the group of trembling disciples, our Lord stands before the multitude. Above Him, the rugged heights of Hermon towering to the skies: behind, His chosen Twelve: in front and all around, as far as the eye can reach, a vast concourse turning to Him as with one uplifted face—this is the scene.

From the ledge of rock on which He stands, His eye ranges over that multitude of all ages, ranks, and callings who have made their way to His Feet to learn of Him. It represents His followers to the end of time. *We* are there, standing out clear and distinct before Him, you and I. What He says to these, He says to you and to me. We are told most emphatically that He speaks *to all:*

IF ANY MAN WILL COME AFTER ME, LET HIM DENY HIMSELF, AND TAKE UP HIS CROSS DAILY, AND FOLLOW ME. *For whosoever will save his life, shall lose it; for he that shall lose his life for My sake shall save it. For what is a man advantaged, if he gain the whole world, and lose himself and cast away himself? For he that shall be ashamed of Me and of My words—of him the Son of Man shall be ashamed when He shall come in His majesty, and that of His Father, and of the holy Angels.*[1]

This is the King's Proclamation. His words go out into the world beyond Judea, beyond the days in which He lived, for they are words for all time. They have reached the four quarters of the globe, and been heard by the men, women, and children of every age. They are heard now, in England and Ireland, in France and Germany, in the busy cities of the New World, in poor dark Africa, in Australia, and in the islands of the Pacific: "Their sound has gone forth into all the earth."[2] "*If any man will come after Me, let him deny himself.*"

We must not hear hurriedly what the King proclaims so solemnly. The various circumstances of time, place, and manner mentioned by the Evangelists we must note carefully, that we may come to understand the tremendous importance of those words spoken *to all.*

Mark, in the first place, how the King has no sooner laid the foundation of His Kingdom, than He raises His

1   St. Luke 9.
2   Psalm 18

Standard, and summons beneath it all who would enter that Kingdom: "*I will build My Church*" is followed by: "*If any man will come after Me, let him deny himself, and take up his cross daily, and follow Me.*" It is to the Church Militant, or *fighting,* that He calls His followers first; only through this can they pass to the Church Triumphant. To be a Catholic, then, is to undertake to fight. I am no true Catholic unless I thoroughly understand this. Unless at my Baptism the promise had been made in my name, that as soon as I was able I would fight the King's enemies, I should never have been admitted into His Kingdom on earth. "If any man will follow Me, he must follow Me *fighting,*" says our King. These are His terms. This is what He calls *losing our life here for His sake that we may find it* in the eternal Kingdom to which He is leading us. If I refuse His terms, if I want to save my life here, I shall lose it. I shall lose myself. I shall cast away myself. For I shall have been ashamed of my King and of His words. And He in His turn will be ashamed of such a faithless follower, when He shall come in His majesty and that of His Father and of the holy Angels.

"*Me and My words.*" How solemn this Proclamation is! Spoken in the silence that followed our Lord's stern rebuke to Peter, who would have dissuaded Him from raising His standard of the Cross, it evidently made on the Twelve the deepest impression, an impression which from them passed to the Evangelists, who have recorded for us the events of that memorable day at Cæsarea Philippi.

Three out of four give it. St. Mark, who will have had the account direct from St. Peter, tells us that our Lord "turning about and seeing His disciples, threatened Peter, saying: Go behind Me, Satan, thou art a *scandal* to Me," that is, a hindrance, a disgrace. *Threatened* Peter. See what displeasure there is in every look and word and gesture. Threatened him, because he who ought to have known better than the others, and encouraged them to follow their Master, carrying their cross, was giving them bad example. Threatened, nay, stunned him with that tremendous word, "*Satan.*" It was the same as saying "adversary, enemy." And that to *Peter!* Foolish things Peter would say later, and our Lord would bear them patiently. But He was indignant that His Standard-bearer, who was to carry the cross so nobly and to die in its embrace, should be ashamed of it now.

It was not cowardice or fear of pain in following His Master that made Peter speak so boldly. It was no want of love, but the very vehemence of love that made him rise up in indignation at the thought of the Passion. This our Lord knew well. He knew that in a little while, he would be crying out in the Supper Room: "Why cannot I follow Thee now—I will lay down my life for Thee!" But it was a mistaken love, and so our Lord rebuked with such severity him He loved so dearly, to teach him, and to teach us all, that true love is shown, as Peter showed it later, by following in our Master's footsteps and bearing our cross bravely after Him till death.

St. Mark notices also that before the Proclamation, our Lord drew His own around Him to hear His words. "And calling the multitude together with His disciples He said to them, *If any man will come after Me, let him deny himself.*" As if He Who would have gathered together the children of Jerusalem "as the hen gathers her chicks under her wings," would say, " Come to Me, all you who desire to follow after Me, that I may tell you tenderly, yet frankly, what you must be prepared to do and to suffer if you mean to be My disciples. It will not be enough merely to believe in Me and what My Church will tell you; you must be ready to live up to what you believe, and to suffer for your belief. Not everyone that saith to Me, Lord, Lord, shall enter into the Kingdom of Heaven, but he that doth the will of My Father Who is in Heaven, he shall enter into the Kingdom of Heaven.[1]

It will cost, it will hurt, to overcome in yourselves those faults and those habits which are contrary to His will and cannot be brought into His Kingdom. You must be ready to pay the price, to make the effort, to bear the pain. This is the cross that you must take up, and take up *daily*. Unless you follow Me like this, you are only pretending to be My disciples. You are ashamed of your Master, and I shall be ashamed of you, when I come in the glory of My Father with the holy Angels."

Solemn words! They show us that to be baptized and confirmed, to hear Mass on Sundays and abstain on Fridays is not by any means all we have to do to get to Heaven. Only our Lord's true disciples enter there. And He will own as His disciples those only who follow Him *seriously*, that is, in the daily struggle with self, which He calls carrying our cross.

Notice, too, how earnestly the Evangelists impress upon us that He spoke *to all*: "Calling the multitude together He said to *all*: If *any* man will come after Me, let him deny himself, for *whosoever* will save his life"—that is, keep out of his life all that is painful or uncomfortable—"shall lose it." *Whosoever.* I speak to you, rich and poor, learned and ignorant; I speak to you, fathers and mothers; I speak to you, young men and maidens; I speak to you, little children; I speak to you babes— "if *any one* will come after Me, let him deny himself."

St. Luke tells us that later on, when His Passion was close at hand, our Lord took advantage of another occasion when an immense concourse was gathered together, to repeat His solemn Proclamation: "And there went great multitudes with Him, and turning, He said to them: *Whosoever doth not carry his cross and come after Me cannot be My disciple.*"[2]

---

1   St. Matt. 7.
2   St. Luke 14.

80

Our King and Leader knows His soldiers well. He knows that we are afraid of pain and labour and that the Cross is a heavy Standard to put into the hands of the little and the weak. Yet He bids us all come to Him and take it from His Hands without fear. "*Come to Me all. Take up My yoke upon you and you shall find rest to your souls, for My yoke is sweet and My burden light*"[1]

How is this? It is because of the help He gives us in His grace, His example, and His promises. In His grace which supports us; in His example which encourages us; in His promised reward, which is magnificent beyond anything we can conceive. Our King is not one of those who say we ought to do our duty simply because it *is* our duty, without thought of reward. We are distinctly told that it was because of the "*joy set before Him*" that He endured the Cross despising the shame.[2] The joy of satisfying the Father, of bringing into eternal joy those whom He loved, this was the noble joy of the Sacred Heart, the reward our Lord kept steadily before His Eyes all through His cruel Passion. And here, as everywhere, He says to us, "Learn of Me. Think of Heaven. You do not think of it half enough. Think of eternal rest when effort has to be made. Think of everlasting joy and reward when pain has to be borne. Think, when you are mourning, of the hour when God will wipe away all tears from your eyes."

The three Evangelists who give us the stern words of the Proclamation, go on at once to speak of the glory of the Transfiguration, and take care to tell us that this wonderful event took place almost immediately after. "After six days," say St. Matthew and St. Mark; "About eight days *after these words*," says St. Luke. "Jesus taketh unto Him Peter and James and John his brother, and bringeth them up into a high mountain apart.

1   St. Matt. 11.
2   Hebrews 12.

And He was transfigured before them. And His Face did shine as the sun, and His garments became white as snow." St. Luke adds "and glittering." "And a bright cloud overshadowed them. And a voice out of the cloud saying: This is My beloved Son, in Whom I am well pleased; hear ye Him."[1]

Transported out of themselves with exceeding joy, the three desired to remain on the Mount, that they might drink in for ever the glorious beauty of that sight. "Lord," cried out the impetuous Peter, "it is good for us to be here." It was to encourage them, and all who are to come after them, to bear the cross bravely after our Lord, that there was given to these favoured three this glimpse of the glory to come—a glory which the members are to share with their Head. For St. Paul tells us that, "the body of our lowness He will make like to the Body of His glory."[2] And St. John says, "We know that we shall be like Him."[3]

What should I have felt, if our Lord coming down from the rocky ledge where He had been standing that day at Cæsarea Philippi, and seeking me out in the crowd had said to me:

"Well, child, you have heard the Proclamation at last. You know what My terms are; what I want of My soldiers; what I am ready to do for them now, and to give them presently when the time for reward comes. What has your heart got to say to Me? You are old enough to understand that, in receiving you under My Standard at Confirmation and ranking you among My soldiers, I expect you to fight My enemies—not in infidel lands, but *in your own heart*. What these enemies are you know in part and you shall know more clearly by-and-by. Are you ready? Will you make efforts? Will you be My ensign-bearer, carrying My Cross? Will you come?

1   St. Matt. 17.
2   Philipp. 3.
3   I St. John 3.

VI.

THE TRUE SOLDIER

Labour as a true soldier of Christ Jesus. (2 Tim. 2, 3.)

HERE is the King's Proclamation. What answer will His followers make? *His followers*, mind, for every baptized soul is enlisted in His army and bound to follow Him into the field. We are not to decide whether we will be on His side or no. That question was settled at the font long ago, when we were made the children of God. What, then, does the King's call mean to us? Let us see.

Children have to grow up. The child loses his baby ways and gains muscle and strength, and knowledge, and power of will. A few years more and he must choose his profession. So it is with us. Our life as children of God began at the font. But it must not stop there. We are not to remain for ever "as new-born babes," to use St. Peter's words; "needing milk and not solid food," as St. Paul says. We must grow up and gain strength by using and increasing the grace we have received. As to our profession, it is chosen for us, as we have seen. It is not a matter of liking; every one who has been made a Christian and child of God by Baptism, must begin his training as a soldier on coming to the use of reason. *Then* the Church calls upon us to answer for ourselves and make good our engagements. After this, the Sacrament of Confirmation renders us strong and perfect Christians and soldiers of Jesus Christ; our uniform is handed to us, and we take our place in the regular army. The character made on our soul that day stands out as clearly before God and His Heavenly Court, yes, and before the enemy too, as the bright scarlet of our troops does before us. It marks us, and through all eternity will mark us as *soldiers of Christ.*

The only point, then, is what *kind* of soldiers we mean to be. The Heavenly King, like the leaders of this world, has all sorts of men in His army. The Proclamation is a test, and shows the stuff they are made of.

Before going further, we must make it quite clear to ourselves that His call is no *make believe.* As truly as He has redeemed us and prepared a place in Heaven for us, so truly does He summon us to follow Him that He may lead us thither. He calls us, every one. Women and children have no place in the armies of this world, but they occupy a very important position in our Lord's service. They have distinguished themselves and reflected as much credit on the colours as any. The army-list has no names more glorious than theirs.

The call, then, is to all, and to each one in particular. The King looks lovingly at each one. He looks lovingly *at me.* He holds out His Hand to me and says: "Will you come?" I am just going to spring forward, to throw myself at His Feet and offer myself eagerly, when He says: "Remember, whoever wishes to follow Me will have to do what is hard and to bear what hurts. He will have to follow Me in pain, that he may afterwards follow Me in glory. Are you ready for this?"

Before giving my own answer, let me look at the response His call is drawing from those around me. I might think, perhaps, there could be one only. But just as there were different kinds of soldiers in the service of the earthly King, so are there in our Lord's army. Some draw back when they hear the going is to cost them something. Some promise to go later on when they get older; it is too much trouble and would cost too much to think about it now. And some, though they know it will cost, look up into His Face and meet His smile with another, and hold out their arms to Him and say, "Lord, I will follow Thee whithersoever Thou goest."

There is nothing more to be said about the first set. If we belong to it, this is the place for us to close our book and go off to something more to our taste. All that follows concerns those who go, and cannot interest the stay-at-homes. Let carpet-knights who never expect to see any real fighting, lay aside the King's uniform and take service in a Church Dormant. They have no business in the Church Militant.

St. Paul was very earnest in impressing upon his converts that they came into the Church, not to saunter quietly towards Heaven, but to fight their way thither. He speaks to the Philippians of Epaphroditus "*my fellow-soldier.*"[1] And he tells the Hebrews that "*Jesus, the Captain of our salvation,* for the suffering of death was crowned with glory and honour."[2]

We are told of the people of God under the Old Law that, "The Lord spoke to Moses in the desert of Sinai...the first day of the second month, the second year of their going out of Egypt, saying: Take the sum of all the congregations of the children of Israel by their families, and houses, and the names of every one from twenty years old and upwards *of all the men of Israel fit for war*...And they were numbered in the desert of Sinai. Of Reuben...all from twenty years old and upward, *that were able to go forth to war,* were 46,500. Of the sons of Simeon *that were able to go forth to war* 59,300. Of the sons of Juda *all that were able to go forth to war* 74,600. Of the sons of Issachar *all that could go forth to war* 54,400." And so the list goes on through the twelve tribes. "And the whole number of the children of

1   Philipp. 2.
2   Hebrews 2.

Israel that were able to go to war was 603,550."[1]   No account, you see, is taken of any others.

"They hadn't to fight till they were twenty?"

No. And here, please to notice a difference. In our Lord's service even baby hands may handle weapons, and all take their appointed place in the ranks at Confirmation.

St. Paul tells us, *"No man is crowned except he strive."*[2]   And even to get just inside Heaven we must have crowns. None but crowned heads are there. The *levées*[3] of Napoleon I, when he was at the height of his glory, are described as something gorgeous. Members of royal families elbowed each other in such numbers, as they came to do him honour and secure his favour, that the courtiers had to shout: "Mind that King there, you are treading on his toes." Think of the numbers in the Heavenly Court. "Thousands of thousands ministered to Him and ten thousand times a hundred thousand stood before Him."[4] And all crowned. Why? Because *they fought manfully.*[5] You see, there is no getting out of it—"if we refuse to fight we refuse to be crowned."

Moses was the meekest of men, but occasionally we find him thoroughly roused. One of those times was when he had brought the people at last up to the borders of the Promised Land and was giving them directions as to its conquest. Two of the tribes, Reuben and Gad, came up and asked to have the land on which they stood for their portion. They did not care to cross the Jordan with the rest. "And Moses answered them: *'What, shall your brethren go to fight, and will you sit here!'* "[6]

---

1   Numbers 2.

2   2 Timothy 2.

3   King Louis XIV instituted this formal court ceremony. When the King rose in the morning, the entire court was present. The most privileged could actually be in the room with the King while he dressed, giving them the opportunity to have a private word with the King, and curry his favor.

4   Daniel 7.

5   Mach. 6.

6   Numbers 32.

So our Leader says to us: "Do you expect to enter without pain or trouble into that Promised Land that others have laid down their lives to win? Children no older than you are there in multitudes, young boys and timid girls, but there is not one without a crown."

Surely, however, these reproaches are not needed. You called by such an ugly name the vassals of the earthly King, who let him go out alone to fight his enemies, that pure shame would prevent you being "sneaks" like them.

We make up our mind, then, to follow our Leader and to fight. Let us look now at three sorts of soldiers who follow Him into the field.

There is the class that serve only because they are afraid not to serve, who do no more than they are obliged, and do that grumbling. When they have to fight, they fight feebly. Temptation comes, and they are content to keep just out of mortal sin. As to venial sin, they never trouble themselves about it. Soldiers of this class not only do no good in the army, but they do an incalculable amount of harm by their bad example, the way they talk of the officers, the way they despise regulations and shirk work, and the way they ridicule those who possess more soldierly qualities than themselves.

"I am seeing who these are all the time."

All right. Only don't put caps on to other people. If they fit your own head, well and good; if they do not, let them alone. Soldiers such as these do not deserve their name, and when we have said they do not actually desert, we have said about all we can in their favour. The Leader puts up with them—but oh, when He remembers what He has done for them; that He has given them a place under His Standard, in preference to so many others who would have served Him loyally; that He had such a reward in store for them—how sad His Heart is!

Then there are the ordinary, good, common-sense soldiers, who give themselves honestly to the work they have undertaken. They do not go in for extra labours and hardships, but when these come they take their share. They are not looking out for posts of honour, but they are faithful in their own. No one can say they are not good soldiers, but it does not seem to be in their line to aim at distinction. What concerns their own work and the movements of their own corps is enough for them. As to volunteering for a hazardous enterprise or following the King closely, these are things they never dream of. No daily Mass for such as these. Why? Our Lord is offering Himself on the altar for them, and His faithful ones are round Him there. Yes, but it costs too much trouble to get up in time, and in winter it is so much more comfortable to lie snug and warm in bed. Frequent Confession and Communion are not to be thought of for a moment. Why? The sacraments would give them a wonderful strength against the enemy and make them ever so much more useful in the service. True, but there is no *obligation*, and no one can say they ought to take all that trouble when they are not bound. These soldiers never tackle the enemy thoroughly. They never get a decided advantage over him. And thus they are often found, after many years in the army, as self-willed and selfish, as churlish and disagreeable to their comrades as when they entered the service years ago.

Lastly, there are those who have given themselves heart and soul to the King and His cause. No half-measures, no reserves for them. All they have is little enough for such a One as He—they are not going to offer Him anything less. Such as these are ready for any work their Leader gives them, and they do it heartily. The fortunes of the whole army, the interests of the King in every part of the field are their affair. They love Him with a deep personal love, and so they take to their hearts whatever has a place in His. "What can I do for Him?"—this is their thought. They will take up tiresome tasks that others shirk, and toil on steadily at daily duties after the freshness has worn off. No work comes amiss to them, so long as it is work for Him; or seems too difficult when He goes on before and shows the way. To be near Him, to be like Him, to show their love by doing and bearing hard things for His sake—this is their desire. Blows and bruises, aye, and sharp wounds may come, so long as it is all in His company and He will turn round and smile to see them at His Side.

So the Apostles rejoiced *that they were accounted worthy to suffer reproach for the Name of Jesus,*[1] and St. Paul exceedingly abounded with joy in all his tribulation. St. Agnes smiled when they fettered her little wrists, and St. Laurence and Blessed Thomas More made merry in the midst of torments and death. So multitudes in this country have borne, for the name of Jesus, the loss of all they held dear—father and mother, and children, and home.

Everywhere, thank God, the King has these devoted followers of whom it can be said: "*Thou also wast with Jesus of Nazareth*"[2] The world may know nothing of them, and their nearest friends but little. Their work is done quietly, and their pain borne silently in their Leader's company with none but His Eye to see. But oh! what a reward awaits them when the day of reward comes! It is of them especially that St. Paul says: "When Christ shall appear Who is your life, then you also shall appear with Him in glory."[3] And their Lord Himself says: "Father, I will that where I am, they also whom Thou hast given Me may be with Me."[4]

---

1   Acts 5.
2   St. Mark 14.
3   Coloss. 3.
4   St. John 17.

I have to make up my mind then—not *whether* I will follow the King, but *how closely*; not *if* I will fight, but *in what class*. As to following, one may saunter, walk briskly, or run. As to fighting, it may be like the coward or the half-hearted; like the ordinary soldier, or like the hero who wins the Victoria Cross.

Of course, it is quite clear what we mean by following our Lord. The Catechism tells us it is to "walk in His footsteps, by imitating His virtues." What do we do when we are going to walk in any one's footsteps? We get behind our leader and watch him closely. Where he goes, we go; what he does, we do; and this, whether we like it or not; liking has nothing to do with it. The first thing, then, that we have to do is to watch our Blessed Lord, *to study Him*. Now, there is no use denying that some of us, many of us indeed, find this uninteresting work.

Many who read the Gospel are very little affected by it, the *Imitation of Christ* tells us. Is not this strange? For what is the Gospel? The Life of a God-Man—of *the* God-Man—there has never been but one. Only one life, out of the countless lives that have been lived on this earth, has been more than a human life. But that one is the Life of *God*, the God Who made Heaven and earth.

His Life ought to be intensely interesting. How is it, then, that so few read it, and that fewer still see anything delightful and attractive about it? One reason is they read carelessly, they will not stop *to think* about what they read. They scamper over the most wonderful mysteries, the most stupendous miracles, as if they were things that happen every day. No wonder they are not affected—the wonder would be if they were. The natural remedy for this state of things is *not* to read carelessly, not to rush on at such a rate.

When your ferns have been neglected and are drooping in the dry parched earth, you water them slowly, waiting patiently for the poor thirsty things to drink in a first draught, before you give them a second. Only a baby would deluge them with a whole canful at once.

Our hearts are hard and dry—perhaps they have been a bit neglected too. They will soften little by little, but we must give them a fair chance. When we read, two thoughts must have time to sink in—*It was God* Who did all this. And He did it *for me.* The remembrance of this makes all the difference. It makes the Life of our Lord not only wonderfully interesting in itself, but wonderfully interesting *to me. It was God* Whose little Feet followed Mary about the house, holding on by her finger or her dress; *God* Whom she put to bed, and woke, and dressed, and fed; *God* Who left His play when He was told, and helped to keep the cottage tidy, and ran errands, and washed plates, and worked at a rough hard trade.

And He did it *for me*—to teach me, so that if I think it hard and beneath me to work heartily and obey cheerfully, and do tiresome disagreeable little things in order to help others, I may have the example of my God before me to encourage and help me on.

To follow Him. Have I ever thought what my name of Christian means? I am to be a *follower* of Christ, not merely a *believer* in Him. Can anyone with common sense suppose that to sit down, close your eyes, fold your hands and believe in Christ will get you to Heaven? No, we must be "up and doing." To believe in a doctor is to have confidence in him, and if he is *my* doctor, to be prepared to do as he tells me. Believing in Christ means learning from Him, copying Him, obeying Him. If, then, we want to follow our Lord at all seriously, we must take some trouble.

He has done all He can to make His lessons easy for us. But He cannot do everything. We must do something for ourselves. We must attend, look thoughtfully, listen carefully, and make some effort. Every one who has seen a class with its teacher, knows that there are two kinds of watchers and listeners. Not every one who watched our Lord watched to any purpose. Herod watched Him when He was brought before him. But it was not to learn and to copy. So when he found there was nothing to satisfy his curiosity, nothing to amuse him, he turned away. The soldiers on guard at the Crucifixion *sat and watched Him.* Yet not one of them, as far as we know, turned that three hours' study to profit. But there were others who looked up to the Cross and learned the lesson He hung there to teach. "There stood by the Cross of Jesus, His Mother and His Mother's sister, Mary of Cleophas, and Mary Magdalen."[1] They watched, and the good thief watched from his cross. Nothing escaped them, not a word, not a sigh, not a movement of Hand, or Eyes or Lips. They taught us there how to study our crucifix. "And all the multitude of them that were come together to that sight, returned striking their breasts."[2] *That sight*—oh, that we could watch and learn from it, as they did!

When a good teacher puts a drawing before the class to be copied, he takes care to secure two things, first, that the children are interested in their work; secondly, that they can see the blackboard easily. The light must be good, but not too strong.

"Can you all see the board?" he asks. And he moves it this way and that till all are satisfied.

God is a good Teacher. He knows that what we need is a good model—a perfect model—therefore Himself. But who could see Him in the blinding light of His glory? "No man hath seen God at any time," St. John tells us. What, then, did He do? He moved out of the light; He shaded His glory with the veil of His beautiful Human Nature, and so He came amongst us.

1   St. John 19.
2   St. Luke 23.

"And we saw Him the only-begotten of the Father, full of grace and truth."[1]

One thing He has secured. He has come near to us; we can see our Model. And the other thing—our interest—is that wanting? Look round the world and see. Are men and women and children making it their chief business to copy Him? If not, it is because He does not interest them. Does He interest *me?* Am I trying to study and to imitate His humility, His gentleness, His obedience? If not, it is because He has failed as yet to arouse my interest. He has not made Himself attractive enough. O Sacred Heart, and You have tried so hard! You have done so much to win me to the study of Yourself before You say: "*Learn of Me.*"

One after another, our Lord puts the scenes of His Life on earth before us and bids us look and learn. Bethlehem, Egypt, Nazareth, and Calvary are the different classes in His School. The highest class, where the most difficult lessons are taught, is Mount Calvary. And yet, so wonderful and so necessary for every one of us is that Divine *Pattern on the Mount,* that all must go thither to learn. It suits Itself to the need of all, and thus the crucifix is put as its first book into the hands of the little child, and held up as the last lesson of love and hope before the failing eyes of the dying.

He set Himself two tasks when He came upon earth, "to redeem us from sin and Hell and to show us the way to Heaven." Three hours on a Friday afternoon He gave to His first work, by dying for us on the Cross; and three-and-thirty years, all the years of His Blessed Life, to show us our road to Heaven.

The way in which a campaign turns out depends very much on the opinion the men have of the commander, as we

---

1   St. John 1.

have seen. This is why it is so necessary for us to come to know our Lord. But this is not enough. We must go on to admire, and trust, and love, and imitate Him.

Admiration, confidence, love, imitation. By these four steps all the saints became perfect Christians and followers of Jesus Christ. The first, at least, is easy, for admiration means wonder, and everything about our Lord is so wonderful that this is one of His Names. *"His Name shall be called Wonderful."*[1] In no other life do we read of marvels such as we find in every page of His. Admiration, then, is easy, but we must not stop there.

Lord Wolseley tells us only what we all feel when he says that for a chief to fire his troops with enthusiasm and get from them all they are capable of, it is not enough that he should have the most splendid military qualities. These will win the admiration of his men. But he must have more than this. He must have their confidence, affection, and their devotedness.

Confidence in our Chief comes from the knowledge that He can defeat our enemy and any number of enemies, and that He will stand by us in the fight. That He *can* conquer, needs no proving. "He is King of kings and Lord of lords,"[2] *to Whom is given all power in Heaven and on earth.* At His Name every knee is bent, in Heaven, on earth, and in hell.

He has led on millions to victory; can He not fight *my* battles! Of all the countless hosts of His Saints not one has been disappointed of his hope, and shall I fear! He has never failed one soul that trusted in Him; shall I alone be forsaken by the *Faithful and True?*

Confidence leads straight to love; indeed, it is hard to see which comes first. And when we love, all the rest is easy. Love

---

1   Isaias 9.
2   Apoc. 17.

can do all things, À Kempis tells us. It is "strong, faithful, long-suffering, courageous,"—just the qualities of a loyal soldier. It "feels no burden, values no labours, would willingly do more than it can, complains not of impossibility because it conceives that it may and can do all things."

See what men will do in the service of an earthly sovereign. The gallant Picton[1] who fell at Waterloo had had two ribs broken at Quatre Bras,[2] but in spite of the agony, he had concealed his wound for fear of being invalided by the doctor's orders and missing any fighting. You all know the story of the attack on the Dargai Heights during the Afridi Campaign of 1897,[3] and how Piper Findlater, after being shot through both feet and unable to stand, sat up under a heavy fire and played the regimental march to encourage the charge of the Gordon Highlanders.

So with seamen.

During the war between the United States and Spain in 1898, a young American lieutenant signalized himself by an act of heroic daring, which, it has been justly said, has few if any parallels in the history of the world.

1   Sir Thomas Picton had retired from the army, but at the Duke of Wellington's request, he returned to a High Command post in the allied English and Dutch armies at Waterloo. His troops held the center of the battle line against Napoleon. His baggage did not arrive in time, so he fought in his civilian clothes: a frock coat and a top hat. When the French Lieutenant General d'Erlon advanced against his troops, Picton bravely rode forward, encouraging his men to charge. They succeeded in driving off the French, but Picton fell when a bullet struck him in the head.
2   Quatre Bras was a preliminary battle to Waterloo, as the English and Dutch forces attempted to turn back Napoleon's advance toward Brussels.
3   The Afridi were a tribe from the far north of what is now Pakistan. For sixteen years, they had been paid by the government of British India to guard the important trade route through the Khyber Pass. In 1897 they revolted, capturing the Pass and the surrounding areas. The Gordon Highlanders, a Scottish infantry regiment, successfully stormed the Afridi position at Dargai Heights. Findlater later received the prestigious Victoria Cross medal for his bravery.

Piper George Findlater continued to play while propped up
against a rock at Dargai Heights.

The ships of the Spanish squadron having taken refuge in
the harbour of Santiago, he undertook to sink a huge collier
in the narrowest part of the channel and thus prevent their
escape. His plan was to swing the *Merrimac* crosswise athwart
the channel, drop anchor, open the valves and explode the
torpedoes on the port side. Then, preceded by the crew, leap
overboard and escape, if possible, in the small lifeboat towed
astern. Any who survived the explosion and failed to reach the
boat, were to attempt to save themselves by swimming ashore.
Laden with torpedoes for her own destruction, the *Merrimac*
was to set out at three in the morning and make her way into
mid-channel, under the guns of the Spanish batteries, and over
the submarine mines that guarded the entrance to the harbour.

Having laid this programme before the officers and crew
of the flagship, Lieutenant Hobson asked six men to volunteer

for the desperate work. Would you believe it—every officer and hundreds of men offered themselves! More wonderful still—when the doomed ship came to be searched before starting, stowaways were found hiding and had to be turned out by force.

Are the rulers of this world to have all the loyalty and enthusiasm men have to give? Are there to be no eager spirits on the side of the Heavenly King, *Jesus Christ our Lord,* as the Church is never tired of calling Him! His war is more necessary and more honourable; the terms He offers are more favourable than those of any earthly King. He invites us to join Him for our own sake, and tells us our reward shall be in proportion to our labour. No other King can undertake to do all his soldiers do; to bear whatever they have to bear; to be at the side of each in the fight. No other can promise that all shall live to see the triumph if they will be brave. In the service of an earthly King it is the bravest who run the greatest risk of being killed, and as a rule they have all the hardships and suffering of the campaign without any of the honours and rewards.

Again, the rank and file rarely see the face of the Commander-in-Chief, perhaps scarcely know him by name, and certainly cannot have recourse to him in their needs. But in our Lord's service it is not so. Our Leader is not far from His soldiers. He reaches them not merely through officers and proclamations. He lives in their midst. The last and the least have been called personally by Him, and can come to Him freely at all times. He knows all by name, knows them intimately; cares for each, one by one; appoints his post to each; stands by him in the battle, watches him fight, and rewards him with His own Hand after the victory. Who would not fight for such a King!

You remember how the Welsh chieftains in the reign of Edward I[1] clamoured for a prince of their own race, and promised to obey and serve him. They did not bargain that he should be wise, or just, or kind, but only that he should be *one of themselves.*

The petition of the chiefs comes home to every one of us. We all know how comradeship on the part of a captain pleases his men. "Why are you all so devoted to this officer whilst you have not a good word for that one?" a French soldier was asked. "Ah, monsieur," was the ready answer, "*c'est que celui-ci dit toujours '**Allons!**' mais cet autre '**Allez!**' *"[2]

Our Leader does more than go before us and cheer us on. He takes care that, even in His company, hardships shall not be over hard. There is a legend which tells a beautiful story of His tenderness for His own. It is said that during those three years in which the Apostles were His constant companions they sometimes spent the night with Him on the mountain side, sleeping around Him while He prayed. When the nights were cold—and in Palestine they are often very cold—He would interrupt His prayer to go and look after them, and if He found their feet uncovered, He would wrap them up tenderly. He would not have His Apostles blamed for not fasting whilst He was with them. When they were hungry He let them eat the corn as they passed through the corn-fields. On that awful night in the garden when the agony of death was upon Him, He thought of their comfort even then. "*Sit you here till I go yonder and pray.*"[3] *Sit* you. It was because He made their watching so easy for them that they fell asleep. Well might one of His Saints exclaim, "We have a good Master!"

---

1   Edward I of England (who reigned from 1272-1307) suppressed the first Welsh rebellion without serious consequences, but the second resulted in a full-scale conquest of Wales and its being heavily settled by the English.

2   "It is that this one always says '*let's go*' but the other '*you go*.'"

3   St. Matt. 26.

98

And so it is not only "a great glory to follow the Lord,"[1] it is also sweet and easy. He Who goes before us to lead the way is our Elder Brother. Our fellow-soldiers are apostles, martyrs, confessors, virgins—all the best and noblest that this earth has seen. The labour is short, the reward great.

"Still, it's hard, I think, to imitate our Lord—harder than going to battle."

It *is* going to battle, and therefore it is hard. But He will help us. He does not expect us to conquer all our enemies at once, as we shall see later. And He does not leave His soldiers alone in the fight. Whenever temptation comes, He is at hand with His grace—enough grace to overcome—and plenty more to make it easy to overcome if we choose to ask for it.

But we must try not to be so terribly afraid of what is hard. The true soldier thinks more of honour than of hardship. He takes it as an insult to be kept from the fight. "*What have I done that I may not go and fight against the enemies of my lord the King?*"[2] said David, in an injured tone, when he was serving in the army of Achis. In every army the true soldier makes the same complaint.

At St. Pierre, the most desperate battle of the Peninsular War, the colonel of the 71st, for some unaccountable reason, withdrew his regiment from the fight. It was one with a splendid reputation, full of eagerness and daring. Imagine then the disgust of the officers and the indignation of the men. But discipline prevailed over impatience, and despite black looks on every side the mysterious order was obeyed. The brave fellows, however, were not doomed to disappointment. From a post where he stood surveying the whole army, Hill, the general in command of 14,000, saw what had happened. Hastening down, he met the 71st with the order, "Right about

1   Ecclus. 23.
2   I Kings 29.

Face," and led them himself to the attack. Think of their delight. So eagerly did they follow him and so tremendous was their charge, that the French were instantly driven back and victory was secured.

We have now studied three sets of soldiers who follow the King into the field. The first serve because they are afraid of the consequences to themselves of not serving. These do as little as they can, and do that little grumbling. The second set are, let us hope, numerous in the army. They are not heroes, but they do honestly and well what they have undertaken, and, whilst avoiding hardships which they are not bound to face, take their share of those that come in the ordinary course. Lastly there are those who, by studying the character of their Leader, have conceived such unbounded admiration for Him and such deep, personal love, that they are resolved to follow Him everywhere and closely, out of love. "*The men of Juda stuck to their King.*"[1] So will these soldiers of "The King's Own."

I cannot help hoping that they will be your favourites, and that some of you, at least, will want to belong to this regiment, where are found, not the King's servants only, but His trusty friends. It will be worth our while, therefore, to study it somewhat more fully.

---

1   2 Kings 20.

VII.

The King's Own

In what place soever thou shall be, my Lord King,...
there will Thy servant be. (2 Kings 15, 21.)

How men volunteer when their country is taking up arms!
Before the week was out, in which America declared war with
Spain, in 1898, over 100,000 men had joined the National
Volunteer Reserve in New York alone. All the inhabitants,
of course, could not go out to fight, but the stay-at-homes
thronged round the recruiting tents cheering those within. In
one day a million flags fluttered out over the city. Every building
raised a flag-staff, and unfurled the Stars and Stripes. All the
windows were gay with bunting. Booksellers, grocers, hosiers,
tailors, arranged their stores with wonderful ingenuity so as to
display the national colours only. The roofs of the cable-cars
were decorated with banners. The horses in the drays and vans
tossed the flags proudly above their heads. The dogs and the
cats ran about with red and blue and white ribbons round their
necks. Bicyclists, of course, were not behindhand, and flew
along with flagstaff and tiny banner stuck into the lamp-socket
of their machine. Everywhere the same enthusiasm prevailed.
A millionaire begged to serve with the first expedition to Cuba,
and besides fitting out a battery of artillery at his own expense,

offered his fine steam-yacht as a gift to the Government, and free transportation of troops.

On the other side of the water, enthusiasm took a different shape. Before leaving Cadiz, the Admiral and crew of the torpedo squadron took a vow never to return to Spain unless victorious. The little King was all eagerness in discussing the chances of the war with his military professor, putting endless questions to him respecting the forces of the United States, and suggesting various plans of campaign, which occurred to him as likely to secure victory. Every morning he entreated the Queen to let him go out to the seat of war: "Madame, I have a favour to ask of you. I wish to go to Cuba to fight the Americans." It was no use to tell him he was too young. His Majesty declared himself old enough to fight, and cried with vexation because he could not serve his country.

All this eagerness for a war which might cost the lives of thousands and bring distress and misery to their country and their homes! A war, too, in which many wise heads must have been puzzled to know on which side the right lay. How different is the case with us! All imaginable right is on our Leader's side, and His bitterest enemies know it. Nothing but good can come to us from joining Him and fighting valiantly under His banner. No enthusiasm, therefore; no ardour can be too great in His cause. How much have I shown?

The Saints tell us that those who find the service of God easiest are the generous—those who are liberal with His Divine Majesty, who think more of what they *can* do for Him than of what they *must*. They say that the best way to conquer our enemies and keep ourselves free from sin, venial as well as mortal, is to try to follow our Lord closely—that is, to imitate Him, even when we are not obliged to do this in order to avoid sin. They bid us look at His Life and try to make our lives little copies of His—to try to speak as He would speak, to do as He would do in our place, to be willing to suffer something for His sake and from the desire to be like Him. This is to follow Him through love. Is it asking too much? He Himself tells us the servant ought not to want to be better treated than His Master. And if the servant follows in his Master's footprints, it will not be so hard.

St. Wenceslaus, Duke of Bohemia, had so tender a love for our Lord in the Blessed Sacrament that he often rose in the night and went a long distance in order to visit Him. If the church doors were locked, he knelt down in the porch and there poured out his heart before the Hidden God. He was wont to take a favourite servant with him on these errands of love. The snow lay thick on the ground one night as they trudged along together, and the fast falling flakes were swept full into their faces by the north wind. The Saint walked bravely forward. On in front was the Divine Prisoner in the Tabernacle, and his heart was with his Treasure. But the poor servant behind followed lamely enough. His hands and feet were numb with cold, and he began to complain, first to himself and then aloud—he could not go on, he was perishing with cold, he must turn back. The Saint looked round with a pitying face: "Tread in my footsteps," he said, "and you will not feel the cold." The man obeyed, and at once there shot up into his heart a flame of love so strong that it took away all sense of pain and made him eager to follow in his master's track.

So it is with us. We follow our Master indeed, but crying out that it is hard; we are cold, we are tired, we cannot keep up with Him. And He looks round lovingly at us and says, "Put your feet into My footprints, child, and you will not find it hard. Think of Me and of what I have done and suffered for you, and it will not hurt so much."

Notice that it was a *favourite* servant St. Wenceslaus took with him. It is His favourites that our Lord invites to follow Him closely by bearing now and then a little extra pain in His company. They need not come unless they like—they may stay at home in ease and comfort, and He will go on alone or look for a companion elsewhere. But the invitation is meant as an honour, not as a hardship. Can we see it in this light? What have our hearts got to say to Him? When David wanted to shake off Ethai the Gethite, a follower who had attached himself to him, he said, "Why comest thou with us? And Ethai answered the King saying, *As the Lord liveth, and as my lord the King liveth, in what place soever thou shall be, my lord King, either in death or in life, there will thy servant be.*"[1] When Elias was about to leave his faithful disciple Eliseus, he said to him, "Stay here. And he said: *As the Lord liveth I will not leave thee.*"[2]

What have we to say to Him Who is Master, King, all in all to us? He does not ask us to leave Him, to stay behind. He wants us to go with Him, to keep close to Him, to be with Him here that we may be with Him hereafter. What are we going to say to Him?

In 1871 a French Marshal was brought to trial for not having done his duty during the Franco-Prussian War. He was found guilty and condemned to imprisonment for life in a gloomy fortress. His friends were very sorry for him, no doubt, and there their sympathy ended. But his wife—did her sympathy end with a few tears and vain regrets? It got about that she meant to break up her home in Paris and go to him in the prison. Friends tried to prevent her. She could not set him free. It would only add to his sufferings to see the sacrifice she was making on his account. Why make two lives miserable to no purpose!

1   2 Kings 15.
2   4 Kings 2.

They might as well have spoken to the moon. Her path was clear for her, her mind was made up. He was in trouble, and her place was at his side. If she could not free him, she could cheer him by her love and her sympathy. What he had to bear, she would bear; his punishment should be hers too. She knew he must suffer, but she could not, would not let him suffer alone. What! did they think she was going to live in honour when he was in disgrace! Could she care for comfort when he was in want?

So, leaving behind her the gay capital, her splendid home, and amusements, and friends, she went where her heart drew her. To be faithful to him when others fell away, to share his lot in trial as she had shared it in prosperity, to stand at his side *always*—this was the desire of that true heart.

Another story—not about a marchioness this time. A little child who dined in the nursery at twelve used to go downstairs in the evening to dessert. There her place was always next to her elder brother. He was a big brother, quite grown up, and she was only a baby. But the two were devoted to each other, and as soon as she made her appearance, room was made for her beside him as a matter of course. When she had taken her seat, a curious little ceremony took place under the table. There was a feeling for hands, and then the little finger of a big hand and of a tiny one were locked together and shaken, and there was a whispered, "Going shares." This done, the smallest shareholder sat demurely with her hands in her lap awaiting her portion of the profits. Sometimes, indeed most times, her brother left the choice to her, and then, when he had peeled the apricot and taken out the stone, it was divided and each had half. As long as it was a question of apricot, or sugared strawberries, she sat by his side radiant. But now and then his turn to choose came round, and when something she did not like landed on her plate, Babs' countenance fell. It was only a wee bit of ginger or banana that he passed to her; enough, however, to make the small face pucker. Yet Babs was a brave and a trusty little shareholder. And though she looked up to him pitifully with quivering lip and brimming eyes, she stuck to her compact. His hand came across the little finger feeling for his to renew comradeship, and the bad bits were gulped down in spite of—perhaps, with the help of—tears.

Are we going to let our Elder Brother have all the hard things? Can we not brace ourselves to "go shares"? He will not give us more than we can bear. What if we were to make an effort to overcome ourselves, even when this is not necessary to avoid sin—to smile when we are in a humour to pout; to say a kind word instead of a sharp one; perhaps even to hold our tongue and make no excuse when we come in for a word of blame! And this, as the loving St. Francis Xavier says, "not for the sake of winning Heaven or of escaping Hell," but to show our love to Him Who bore so much for us, and make a little return, even if it be only a little, to that dear Heart of His.

Oh, what shall we do, what shall we do when we meet the children Saints in Heaven! Little St. Basilissa, virgin and martyr, whose feast the Church keeps on September 3rd, was only nine years old when "by the power of God, she overcame stripes, the fire, and beasts,"—just the things to strike terror into a child's heart. St. Agrippina and St. Eulalia were twelve. One of the Japanese Martyrs, a boy of twelve, when he saw the crosses prepared, ran to his and clung to it fast till they came to nail him to it. Another, a baby martyr of four, was waked one morning and told that the big soldier who stood by, had come to take him to the place where he was to have his head cut off. His father had gone on before to be killed. Little Paul got up and dressed. Then putting his hand into the executioner's, he trotted along by his side till he reached the place of execution. The first thing he saw there was the bleeding body of his father, whose head had just fallen beneath the axe. The child knelt down beside it, joined his little hands and began to say his prayers. The headsman took the axe. But the sight of his baby victim unnerved him. His aim was unsteady, and the first blow, though wounding grievously, failed to kill. Little Paul prayed on. Again the man aimed, again the blow missed. Then, losing all control over himself, he struck here and there till the child was literally hacked to pieces.

More wonderful still was the heroism with which mothers took their little children with them to martyrdom. We meet with more than one such example in the records of early Christian ages. But the tradition of high-souled courage did not stop short with them. A day famous for ever in the annals of the Church of Japan, was the Great Day of Martyrdom, September 22nd, 1622. Fifty-two Christians, men, women, and children, were led out to a little hill on the sea-shore in the neighbourhood of Nangasaki, there to die for Christ. Some were to be beheaded, others burnt to death. Among the former was a Portuguese lady whose husband had suffered martyrdom the year before. She had a little boy four years old, whom the saintly Jesuit, Father Charles Spinola, had baptized by the name of Ignatius. The child was a great pet of Father Charles, who always called him his little Ignatius.

Surrounding the place of execution on this September morning were some 30,000 Christians, drawn together from all parts by the desire to do honour to the martyrs, and to be encouraged by their example. Father Spinola, like a good shepherd, was there in the midst of his flock, and from the stake where he was to be burnt to death by a slow fire, he spoke brave and noble words, strengthening and animating with his own courage those who were to die. Near him, kneeling in prayer, was the Portuguese lady, but as far as he could see she was alone.

"Where is my little Ignatius," he cried in alarm. "Have you left him behind?"

"No, Father, how could you think so," she replied, with a smile, "shall I not offer to God the dearest thing I have on earth?" And lifting her mantle she showed the boy kneeling by her side.

"See, child," she said to him, "here is the Father who made you a child of God, ask for his blessing." Folding his hands, the little fellow cried out: "Please, Father, bless me." Then he looked around, for the executioners, having completed their preparations, had begun their dreadful work close by. Three heads rolled near him, but he showed no sign of fear. The fourth was his mother's. Without cry or tear the child of two martyrs bore the fearful sight, and then bowing his head offered his neck for the stroke. Another moment—and mother and child, beyond the reach of cruelty and pain, were rejoicing together before the throne of God.

To suffer for Christ as soon as they were ranked among His followers, was an idea which came so naturally to the Japanese Christians, that they looked upon persecutions and a cruel death as a matter of course. Children went with their parents to the place where martyrs were to suffer, and helped to gather up the precious relics when the crowns were won. They were brought up to think of their own martyrdom quite simply, as of a thing that was sure to come sooner or later. And so when two little brothers were hurried away to the place of execution, they tore off bits of their clothes as they went along, and gave them as relics to the Christians who accompanied them.

Painters are always on the look-out for beautiful subjects; will none of them give us for the schoolroom wall a scene that must have charmed the angels, and the Lord of angels—the boy

THE CHRISTIAN MARTYR.

From the picture by Delaroche.

martyrs distributing their relics to eager hands on their way to martyrdom?

You will say, perhaps, that these heroes and heroines lived long ago. What difference does that make? They had the same fear of pain, the same terror of stripes and lions and bears that you have. Any way it was not long ago that a boy, who had to undergo a painful operation, told his mother he would not have morphia "because our Lord did not have it on the Cross."

And it was not long ago that we heard of little African slaves going straight from Baptism to the most frightful torments for the sake of the new Master Whom they had but just come to know.

Are Japanese children and little negroes to shame us out?

"But we don't live in Africa or Japan."

No, we need not go so far in search of tyrants and tormentors. There is one close at hand. No farther than our own hearts, a fierce persecutor sits enthroned. His name is "Self." Our life's work is to fight him and dethrone him. For he is a usurper who wants to take the place of our rightful King and lead us, not to glory and happiness, but to everlasting pain and misery.

The true Leader does not ask us to run to a cruel death like His eager little Japanese soldiers. But He expects all to be brave in His service, and He does love the eager ones—Peter, who must needs throw himself into the water to get to Him sooner, who ran to the Sepulchre and only came in last because he could not run as fast as John; and the Holy Women, who "*went quickly* from the sepulchre, *running* to tell His disciples."[1] His Blessed Mother went "*with haste*" into the hill country to visit her cousin Elizabeth. And He Himself "rejoiced like a giant *to run the way*."[2] When the time of His Passion was come, He

1   St. Matt. 28.
2   Psalm 18.

took the Twelve up to Jerusalem. "And Jesus went before them, and they were astonished." He went so fast.

He does not like slowness in seeking Him, in works of charity, in going to duties we dislike. Children resemble Him in this; they cannot bear people to be slow. As it is an effort to an express train to "slow down," so it is a trouble to them to slacken their speed. Walking, driving, cycling, they must get on, push ahead, "hurry up." Slow coaches are a trial to them. None so eager to admire, to applaud as they! When the gallant Highlander, Findlater, fresh from Dargai, made his appearance at a military tournament playing the very same march which led the Gordons to victory, he was greeted with ringing cheers by all. But the boys of the Duke of York's military School, who saw in him a comrade-in-arms, wearing the same uniform as themselves, and decorated with the Victoria Cross, which they hoped to get some day—these beat the rest of the audience hollow; their shouts as he passed them were simply deafening. The Commander-in-Chief, who was present, must have been pleased. Such appreciation will easily lead to imitation, he said to himself, and the country may expect great things from these shouters when their time comes to go into the field. It is to call forth this eager enthusiasm for the brave and for the service, that such displays as reviews and military tournaments are held.

Our Lord shows off His heroes with the same intent. He comes to us, holding little Basilissa by the hand, and says to us: "Cannot you do what this little thing has done? I will not ask you to bear as she did the sting of the scourge, the scorching flames, the cruel eyes and teeth of savage beasts. But I do ask you to overcome your too great love of ease and comfort, for love of Me; your fear of pain, by the greater fear of losing Me."

What shall we answer Him? And what shall we say to Basilissa herself when she comes running to meet us as we enter Heaven, and asks with a child's curiosity, "What have you done for our Master?" There is no sinking into the ground there, you know. We shall have to say something, to show something—what are we getting ready to show?

We can imagine the admiration and applause of the Blessed as the baby-martyrs of Japan, little Paul and Ignatius, were ushered into Heaven and made their way to their thrones. We can imagine the great St. Paul and the great St. Ignatius coming down to meet their tiny namesakes and show them reverence.

"Mummy," said a little boy, who had been listening with rapt attention to these stories of the children martyrs of Japan, "shall we have to go to the same Heaven as them?" "*Have* to go"—as if he hardly thought he could face it, or as if it were high time to be getting ready.

But it would be the greatest mistake to suppose that the glories of Heaven and its joyous welcomes are for martyrs and wonder-workers only. "*The small and great are there,*" holy Job tells us. He himself, among the greatest, did not get there by *doing* but by *bearing.* Greatness is not measured in the next world as even good people measure it here. Here we say: What has such a one *done* for God? There they say rather: What has he *suffered* for Him? It is not the life that is outwardly glorious, nor even the brave death before the eyes of the world, at which God and His holy Angels look. But at the hidden martyrdom, the struggle with self, daily, brave, persevering, that all the Saints, and not the martyr-band only, must go through. St. Mary Magdalen of Pazzi says of St. Aloysius that he was a hidden martyr. He did not shed his blood for Christ. His martyrdom therefore must have been that *dying daily* of which St. Paul speaks.

We may all, then, be great if we will. On our will, helped by God's grace, all depends. How surprised we shall be at the Day of Judgment when we see the truly great *and where they come from!* From the cabins of the poor, patient Irish; from the close factory; from the one miserable room where a charwoman and her children lived; from the apple-stall in the street corner where the old woman used to sit telling her beads; from the desk in the office where the young Catholic braved the sneers of his fellow-clerks; from coal-mine, and from hospital, from the workhouse, and the poor school—from the dark and despised corners of this world the great ones will come out and take their places beside the King. They have been true to Him though the campaign was long and hard; they have fought the good fight; they have kept the Faith; the crown of justice is laid up for them.

"But how have all these people been soldiers? When did they fight for the King?"

St. Paul gives us the description of a true soldier when he says that in all he does he tries "*to please him to whom he hath engaged himself.*" [1] Such a one is thoroughly in earnest. He is following his Leader seriously, like our German forefathers of old. You have heard perhaps of the *gesiths* or companions, the later *thegns*, who formed the bodyguard of each King or prince. The life and fortunes of the follower were bound up with those of his chief. He lived for him, fought for him, stood by his side in battle and defended him at the risk of his life, followed him into captivity and even to death. This was a follower indeed.

> They lay thegnlike their lord around,

says an old Anglo-Saxon poem in its description of some of the King's followers who perished with him on the field of battle.

We have bound ourselves to follow our Chief. If we would follow Him closely, we must study His actions and try to imitate Him. Watch and see how He behaved when people were unkind to Him; when He was cold, or thirsty, or in pain.

---

1   2 Timothy 2.

How He treated children and troublesome people who came to Him when He was tired; disagreeable people who contradicted all He said; unjust people who found fault with all He did. How gently He answered when He was blamed; how readily He forgave; how He obeyed when He was told to do hard things, things that hurt.

Only members of the body have a right to be united with the head, but they have a distinct right—where else should they be? We have to prove ourselves members of our Head if we are to be united to Him in glory. We must be like Him if we are to take our place in the court of Heaven. They are all like Him there. Likeness to Him is the ticket that gets them shown to their places. When a soul passes into the next life, Almighty God takes it, as it were, into His Hand and examines it on every side to see what resemblance it bears to His Son. The measure of its resemblance will be the measure of its reward. No resemblance, no reward; great resemblance, great reward. He has determined that the likeness of His Divine Son shall shine out beautiful and glorious in every one of the Blessed. And that likeness has to be brought out in them here on earth. In the dark-room the photographer "develops" the little dark picture which is to be transfigured into the dear face of father, or mother, or friend. In the darkness of this world the change must be worked out that is to transform us into the likeness of Christ our Lord. *Worked out*—it will not come of itself.

When you sit for an examination in model-drawing, you find yourself grouped with other candidates round the object you are to copy. It has been arranged with a view to your copying it and all is provided that you require. The light falls differently for each of you and no two see the model exactly the same. But each is expected to copy what he sees, as well, and as much as he can, in the time allowed. At length the hour strikes, the work is called in and sent up to head-quarters for examination. Those whose copy is excellent get honours. Others whose work is fair just pass; the rest fail. So is it with the imitation of Christ. No two see Him alike. Some are in a better position and have more light, others work under great difficulties. But all must try. The Saints try hard, and bring out splendidly, according to their light, the different aspects of the Divine Model—St. Francis de Sales His meekness, St. Francis Borgia His humility, St. Francis Xavier His zeal, St. Francis of Assisi His poverty and gladness of heart. What are *we* trying to bring out in ourselves? Let us make haste—there is no time to be lost.

We look at our Lord when He was hurt or unkindly treated and we notice how He spoke and acted. Then we look at the copy. When I am hurt or snubbed, how do I act? Something has happened which makes us doubt how we ought to behave. At once we ask ourselves what would Jesus have done in my place? This is copying our Model.

The imitation of Christ means two things—effort and self-denial. Without these nothing can be done. We must rouse ourselves, put our hand to the work, study our Lord and see what He teaches us in the lessons of His life—this supposes effort. And when we have *seen*, we must *go against* ourselves and our bad nature in order to bring ourselves into likeness to Him—this is self-denial. "He that will come after Me *let him deny himself and take up his cross and follow Me.*"[1]

In the English army there is a regiment called "The King's Own." Our Lord, too, has His own—those who follow Him for His own sake, those who love Him for Himself, who give without counting the cost, who are ready for anything and for everything He asks of them, whose only desire is to be with Him and to be like Him. These are the "King's Own." These

---

1 St. Matt 16.

have no "buts" and "ifs" with Him; they are generous. They volunteer to serve here or there, to fight this enemy or that, just as He likes; they only wait the word of command.

"The martyrs, I expect."

The martyrs have a distinguished place in this splendid regiment, but it is not composed of martyrs alone. Any one may belong to it. There is no need to be six feet high and thirty-eight inches round the chest, or to score three bull's-eyes in every four shots. All that is needed is a deep strong love for our Blessed Lord, a determined will to follow Him *seriously*, and to *make ourselves*, by dint of quiet persevering effort, something like Him at last.

Does any one want to be in "the King's Own"?

> In the thick of the fight I marked them,
> The valiant, the "*corps d'elite,*"
> Wherever His banner beckoned them
> They followed with flying feet:
> Red tokens of many a hidden wound
> Did their battered armour bear,
> Yet ever into the thick of the fight
> They pressed—*for the King was there!*
>
> A little, a very little while
> And that band I saw again
> Glittering and white their raiment now,
> And oh, for their loss, what gain!
> Labour with Him, and wounds, and pain
> It had been their joy to share,
> And now, whence the innermost glory streamed
> They stood—*for the King was there!*

VIII.

A Black Banner

They have talked of hiding snares; they have said: Who shall see them?
(Psalm 36, 6.)

DID you ever hear of "the skag," the American hunter's device for getting a good shot at his game? On the great Lakes that separate Canada from the United States, ducks congregate in enormous flocks, a tempting sight to the sportsman. But they are timid birds and suspicious, as they have every reason to be. The only chance of getting near them is by cunning. Unfortunately for them, there is no lack of that. This is what happens. Some fine afternoon whilst they are sporting about, heads in the water, tails cocked, splashing, quacking, enjoying themselves after the manner of their kind, there drifts into their midst a harmless-looking canoe covered with long reeds. It attracts little attention; why should it? All looks quiet and safe, nothing stirring, not even the duck peacefully squatting at the boat-head. Poor things, could they but see beneath those reeds the hunter lying flat, his gun at his side; could they but know that dummy duck is there only to deceive them and prevent any suspicions of man's presence or his designs! Nearer and nearer comes the boat. The right distance now, the right moment. Bang! Bang! The hunter has suddenly risen for a shot, and now he fires away, right and left.

Something after this fashion *our* enemy sets to work. The devil does not care to show himself when he goes a hunting. He prefers to use the "skag."

So far, we have been studying the True Leader in order that admiration of Him may spring up in our hearts, and trust, and love—the love that leads to imitation. It is sweet to look at Him, to learn His ways, to linger lovingly about Him. But there is another leader to study now. There are other ways to learn— crafty, cruel ways, frightening to learn about, yet necessary for us to know, that we may be on our guard against them. Our enemy loves concealment. He keeps a set of masks to hide his ugly face. Let us pull off his disguises and see what he looks like as he is. And let us ask for help to find out his deceitful snares, that we may not be caught in them.

We have no words terrible enough by which to picture the Wicked Chieftain who is the enemy of the True Leader, our Lord Jesus Christ. Holy Scripture speaks of "beasts full of rage, breathing out a fiery vapour, sending forth a stinking smoke, shooting terrible sparks out of their eyes; whereof not only the hurt might be able to destroy, but also the very sight might kill through fear."[1] The devil is worse than these—oh, worse by far. For if one mortal sin makes a soul so frightful that the sight of it would kill us, what must he be like who *sinneth from the beginning,*[2] as St. John tells us. The gentlest of the Apostles, the Apostle of love, has no words too fearful for him. He is *"the angel of the bottomless pit,"*[3] *"a great red dragon," "the old serpent."*

Some foolish men have written about the devil as if he were something grand, a kind of noble rebel, like those brigands whose daring courage attracts us in spite of ourselves. It is the

1   Wisdom 11.
2   I St. John 3.
3   Apoc. 9.

father of lies who gets men to think of him and write of him like this, that he may arouse interest for what he is not, as he cannot get it for what he is.

If we feel drawn to something like admiration for the brigand, it is because we see underneath the cruelty, injustice, and recklessness of his life some noble traits which redeem his character. But in the devil there is not a redeeming point. He is bad through and through and through. It was no lofty independence like Simon de Montfort's[1] or William Tell's[2] that made him raise his standard of revolt and cry, *Non serviam!*[3]—"I will not serve." It was not the noble sacrifice of self in conflict with the tyrant and oppressor. It was the selfish revolt of Absalom, the revolt of the favourite child against the best of Fathers, the most privileged of subjects against the most royal-hearted of Kings. Nay, it was infinitely worse. It was the rising up of the creature against Him Who had drawn it out of nothing into magnificence and glory; the treason of one so gifted that his very name means brightness, so trusted as to have the command of the angelic host. Is there anything to admire in this? How you hate the traitor in your story-books and histories; how you hope he will get found out and be punished as he deserves! How in school life you despise the bragger, the bully, the coward who takes unfair advantage of the little ones, the sneak who promises and never means to give, who wheedles himself into your favour to get something out of you, offers to go shares with you in some underhand

---

1   De Montfort is known for leading a rebellion against Henry III of England in 1264, when the king refused to abide by certain provisions of the Magna Carta. Though the rebellion was put down, De Montfort succeeded in establishing the first parliament of elected officials.

2   William Tell led a rebellion against the Austrian rulers of Switzerland in the 1300s, leading to the formation of the Swiss Confederation.

3   This phrase is attributed to Lucifer, and is often used as a literary reference to his refusal to submit to the authority of God, resulting in his fall.

business, and when he has gained his own end makes off and leaves you in the lurch! Does not your blood boil when you are treated, or see others treated like this? Then do not be led astray by high-sounding words—were they those of the grandest poet that ever lived—into thinking the devil anything but what he is: a traitor to be hated and *despised*. These are days when the youngest of us needs to be warned against believing all we find in print. As children of the Church, we have a safe rule by which to guide ourselves always. Whatever agrees with the teaching of the Catechism is true, and we may believe it; whatever is contrary to that teaching is false. No matter how boldly or how bewitchingly it is put, it is false and we must fling it from us as we would a poisonous reptile.

Our Lord is called "*a Teacher of Justice*."[1] We go to Him to learn. He is the Truth, Who cannot deceive, Who cannot exaggerate, Who cannot be harsh. Now, by what name does He call the devil? By the only one that properly describes him. It is very terrible, that name given him by One Who knows him thoroughly—"*a murderer from the beginning*."[2] If there is a word that makes our flesh creep it is the word "murderer." It brings to our minds all kinds of horrors: the deadly hate, the deep-laid plot, the long tracking of the victim, the luring into dark places, the stealthy step, and at last the fatal blow. All this cruelty and cunning, all this persistent malice we find in the "*murderer from the beginning*." Many, thank God, have escaped him, but so far as lay in him, he has been the murderer of all. Then there is the name by which we all know him, devil (*diabolus*), which means the *slanderer*. He slanders God and God's Providence. He tells us that God commands what is impossible, that He will not keep His word to us, that there is no truth in what He has revealed. He was a slanderer when he told Adam

---

1   Joel 2
2   St. John 8.

and Eve that God had uttered idle threats—that they should not die, but themselves become as gods.

St. John has another name for him—"*the beast.*" And it is one that suits him admirably. For as the wild nature of a beast is roused at the sight of man, so is this monster lashed into fury at the sight of man, woman, and child, each and all of Adam's race as they pass him on their way through the world. One, "beautiful above the sons of men,"[1] passed on His way, doing good to all. It was the Man-God. Not even Him did the beast spare. It hated Him with an insatiable, with a double hatred— because He was Man, and because He was God: because of what He was in Himself, and because of the work He came to do for us. For four thousand years it was on the look-out for Him, lying in wait for Him. And when at last He came, it sprang upon Him, it fastened its fangs in His innocent flesh and never rested till it saw Him lying, full of wounds and still in death, at the foot of the Cross. But the meek Lamb was stronger than the beast. St. John tells us He overcame him "*because He is Lord of lords, and King of kings.*"[2] It was just by that death on the Cross which the wicked one had tried to bring about, that he was conquered and his captives were set free.

And now the King calls round Him those whom He has died to save, that He may lead them against the foe. They are not to be afraid, he is a beaten foe now, and the King will go with them to the fight.

On the field of battle, it is important to be able to distinguish the figures of the leaders. Cruelty and cunning are, as we have seen, two characteristics of the Wicked Chieftain. Another is the tumult and the gloom that follow him always. Just as gladness and peace show our Lord's presence, so darkness and

1   Psalm 44.
2   Apoc. 17.

disturbance mark the devil's. Like a black shadow he darkens every place through which he passes. We may drive him away fast, but still there is a dull mist hanging about for a while, a sign he has been there. He is overjoyed to see us all in a flutter, fretful, upset by trifles, discouraged by our faults. He does all he can to stir us up into a fury, or to sink us deep in gloom.

"I know he likes to get us into a passion, but I can't see what good it can do him to make us gloomy."

Only this: that he counts as gain for himself whatever harms us. Now, these dismal fits harm us so much that he thinks he has done a good day's work if he can get us to give way to them. We shall see why later on. Here it is enough to say that there are no days, perhaps, when our examination of conscience shows so many faults as those which have seen us, I do not say in trouble, but in the dumps.

Would you suppose cowardice could be another trait in the devil's character? Seeing how much stronger he is than we are, it seems strange that it should be. But strength and courage are not always found together.

A gentleman tells us of a curious sight he saw one day in India. Riding out one morning, his little terrier at his side, he came up with an elephant ridden by a native. The dog, occupied with his own concerns, took no notice of the huge beast, but trotted along in front, now on this side of the road, now on that. The elephant, on the contrary, showed signs of much uneasiness, never taking his eyes off the little creature and shuffling out of the way whenever he came near. Perhaps the presence of his master had something to do with the terrier's indifference. Anyway there was an amusing contrast.

The devil is a great coward. He has often tried to frighten the servants of God by appearing to them under hideous forms and making horrible noises. But a few drops of holy water quench his courage, and at the sight of a baby's hand raised to make the sign of the Cross, he takes to flight, like a dog when you stoop down to pick up a stone.

Before a campaign opens, the Commanders-in-Chief carefully think out their plans and determine how it shall be conducted—when and where an attack is to be made, what troops and what engines of war are to be employed, what is to be the order of the fight, and what is to be done in case of victory or defeat.

The Wicked Chieftain has laid his plans carefully, neglecting nothing that will improve his chances and bring about our ruin.

"He can't have many new plans now, that's one comfort, for if he has been fighting against everybody all this time, he must have used them all up."

Unfortunately he does not need new ones. He works on the same old plan that he made in the beginning, and tries it on every man, woman, and child.

"Oh, but that's silly, because you know people will find out how he has caught others and they'll take care not to be caught themselves."

One would think so, but he has such silly people to deal with, that he can afford to act in a way which, as you say, seems extremely foolish.

"Do we know his plans?"

The most important we know. St. Paul could say of the Christians of his day, "we are not ignorant of his devices."[1] And the Saints, who are always finding out his secrets, let us into them.

"Then I think it is our own fault if we let him catch us."

Please, bear that discovery in mind, it will come in usefully

---

1   2 Cor. 2.

later on. Our business now is to study the "devices" of which St. Paul speaks, for surely common prudence requires us to look into the ways of an adversary who is always prying into ours. No watchfulness in the warfare of this world can be compared with his, and we know how diligently an enemy is watched. Lord Wolseley says:

"By reconnaissance and scouting every movement of the enemy should be ascertained, his intentions divined, and reported—if possible by telegram, to the general officer commanding the army...Officers, particularly those on the staff, should study the general habits and customs of the enemy, his hours of *réveille*, his practice in relieving sentries, &c...The glittering of the sun upon the arms of troops in motion indicates the direction of the march. If the rays are perpendicular, he is moving directly towards you; if slanting from left to right downwards, he is moving towards your right, and vice versa. If the rays are intermitted, he is moving away from you."

Sentinels "are to be always on the look-out to report any unusual signs—firing, its direction, amount, distance; dust and smoke, its direction and distance; the flashing of a heliograph, lights, signals, rockets, torches: unusual noises, trampling of horses, rattling of carriages, barking of dogs; lighting or extinguishing of watch-fires. Study attentively the many indications of intended movements which an enemy may unwittingly afford. If large magazines of stores or provisions are collected anywhere, it is clear that no retreat is contemplated; if on the other hand stores and ammunition are being sent to the rear, a retreat is being prepared for. The dust raised by columns is a fair guide in some countries as to the numbers and composition of the force marching. That raised by cavalry forms a high light cloud, by infantry a lower and dense one, by baggage one more dense still. In following a retreating army much can be learnt from its trail; large numbers of graves indicate the existence of disease in the enemy's army. The places where they halted for the night should be carefully examined and all indications carefully noted. Did they bivouac or pitch tents, was their camp laid out with regularity? &c. The most insignificant circumstances afford sometimes whole pages of information to officers who, having studied the manners and customs of an enemy, know how to interpret them aright."

See the vigilance with which every movement of an enemy is noted.

For nearly six thousand years an enemy has been studying our manners and customs. Our inmost thoughts he cannot tell unless by some outward sign we betray them. But he is quick in reading such signs. Our most insignificant actions are worth pages of information to him who knows well how to interpret them. What we like, what we run after, what we are afraid of, is no secret to him. He knows us well. The conclusion to which his careful study has brought him is this—that he has to do with those who are not by any means all bad. Passions indeed they have and corrupt inclinations. But there are the remnants of great things and the makings of greater things in them—still.

The members of a noble family that has fallen into poverty and disgrace, often retain evidences of their birth and rank. In their bearing, in their ways, in their tastes, there is a dignity that tells of what they were in days gone by. So it is with us. There are many things inherited from our Heavenly Father that cling to us yet—the love of beauty, the love of happiness, the love of truth. How we delight in the beautiful things God has made, and love to surround ourselves with them! Happiness we are running after all our lives long. Truth attracts us irresistibly. We stand up for it, with a kind of chivalrous loyalty. We hate a lie and fire up at unfairness and trickery.

The devil knows all this and he considers what is to be done. He has quite made up his mind to get hold of us, but these instincts deep down in our nature create a difficulty for him. We love beauty, and he is ugliness itself. We love truth, and he is a liar. We love happiness, and he has nothing to offer us but misery. We go after only that which we take to be good, and there is not a shred of goodness about him, everything bad as bad can be—a bad chief, a bad end, bad means to the end. He cannot *make* us go over to his standard and fight on his side, we have our free-will and cannot be forced.

Here, then, is a grave difficulty for him. But he sees his way out of it. We are free indeed, but we are foolish too, foolish and incautious. We can be enticed and we can be deceived. His hope is in that.

"Yes," he says to himself, "there is one thing in which no one is a match for me—*cunning*. If I cannot *win*, I can *deceive*. I can promise things I never mean to give, and could not give if I would. I can pretend I have something good to offer them if they will leave the true Leader and come over to me. I can make out that by doing a wrong thing just this once, they will satisfy themselves. And as they amuse a child with a bright toy and then take it away and leave the baby crying, I can distract them with useless things, and then, having gained my own ends, can turn round and laugh at them for being so silly as to believe me."

This is true. He can hold out nice things to us as we bait the hook for the fish. Moreover, by watching us carefully, he has discovered the baits we like, just as the angler knows the kind of worm that will make the fish bite:

Riches and whatever makes life comfortable;

Pleasures of every kind that make it enjoyable;

Honours—notice, admiration, all that makes us consequential.

"Is it wrong, then, to like riches and pleasures?"

I knew you would ask that. It is a sensible question which we will answer by another: What end are riches and pleasures meant to serve?

When a small child just beginning to think sees an object for the first time, it asks, "What is it for?" And if there is an idea in its mind that the thing may possibly hurt, it takes care to get a satisfactory answer before meddling with it. On our side, we take care to tell the child what the thing is for and how it is to be used. "That is a see-saw," we say. "Jump up and have a ride. But take care not to get your fingers trapped in the hinge, or they will be dreadfully crushed. And don't be late for lessons. Come off when you hear the bell. No, we won't put Baby on, she would only fall and hurt herself."

Used in a certain way and with moderation, the see-saw is useful, that is, good for the child—indeed, it was made expressly for the child's use. Only, if it is to remain useful, it must be used as was intended by the maker. Careless and immoderate use would make it harmful.

Now, all the things we see around us are to be used according to the same rule, that is, for the purpose intended by the Maker. All things are His, because out of His three Kingdoms—mineral, vegetable, or animal—all come. If they are His, we are naturally bound to use them as He wills. And as He is our Father, we may be sure of His will being what is best for us. The rule He gives us is the very simple one given to our First Parents in Paradise: "Use whatever you find in the world around you, any of My creatures, *as far as it helps you* to reach the end for which you are created—Eternal Life. No further. You must keep your hands off anything that would harm and hinder you." Wise, loving rule! the one given by every good father to his child!

Everything we see around us is a creature of God—flowers

and fruit, books, animals, friends. Studies too, and games. And all that happens to us. For St. Paul says, "Neither death nor life nor things present, nor things to come, nor height, nor depth, nor any other creature, shall be able to separate us from the love of God which is in Christ Jesus, our Lord."[1] If He can call things such as these creatures, we may surely bring everything under this name—events, circumstances, changes, cold, heat, health, sickness, talents, success and failure, disappointment, kindness and unkindness, joy and sadness—everything except ourselves and God.

All these creatures we are to use according to the same safe rule. "Will it help or harm?" we are to ask ourselves. The answer is to guide our choices and decisions *always*. We are not free, you see, to use things belonging to our Heavenly Father in a reckless way, any more than we may use wastefully and to our hurt what belongs to our father here on earth. Above all, we are to see as St. Paul tells us, that no creature comes in between us and God so as to separate us from Him.

"But it's impossible to think all that before we use a thing."

Instinct works quickly. How long does it take you to decide whether it would be helpful or not to take up in your fingers a bit of hot metal shot out of the grate, or to jump from the top of an omnibus that is passing your door? Instinct and experience guide us promptly and surely in our decisions when the body is concerned. Conscience will be as ready, if we take pains to train it aright. You know well enough when a book does you harm, or whether a certain habit you are taking up is good or bad for you. No process of reasoning is needed here.

"But why did God make things that are bad for us, and a lot of things that can't help us?"

All things can help. Let us see how. Some—a very large number, serve us by our *use* of them, like the meat we take

1   Romans 8.

six days in the week. Others serve us by our abstinence from them, like the meat we do *not* take on Fridays. Therefore these last help us too. Like the apple in Paradise, they give us an opportunity of showing obedience to God—a big step to Heaven surely. The Church knows we profit so much by this kind of help, that she obliges us to get it at least in one shape every Friday. Even our temptations and passions, temper, greediness and laziness can be turned into steps for getting up to Heaven, and thus *all things* work together for the good of those who love God.[1]

But we have not finished yet with the first set of creatures, those which we may *use*. There are two ways of using things. We may remember our rule and use them as far as they help us and no more. Or we may forget all about the rule, and use them just because they are nice. If we do this, they turn from helps into hindrances. Food and amusements are such helps that we cannot do without them. Yet if we use them immoderately, they harm us seriously.

Our enemy knows all this and he sees his chance. If he can get us to give up the right rule and take his instead, he can turn whatever we use into a net to catch us. Here is his rule:

First: Take the things you like—novels, amusements, bicycling, cricket, good things at table, and use them just because you like them. Take as much of them as you like, and use them as long as you like—then you will be happy.

Second: Have nothing to do with disagreeable things— hard work or study, reading that does not amuse you, dry prayers, self-denial, giving up your own way, yielding to others, everything that is uncomfortable. You are not the sort of person who can manage to do those things and be happy at the same time. Saints can, but you would never make anything of it, and it would cost you a great deal to try. Don't try. Enjoy

1   Romans 8.

yourself. You will have plenty of time to deny yourself later, and it will be easier then.

Having whispered this advice into our ear, he takes the three things we are so fond of and dangles them before us like baits. If he can get people to love riches immoderately, all their thoughts, desires, cares, fears, are about money-making. Their one business in life, their one thing necessary comes to be this—if they are poor, to get rich; if they are rich, to get richer.

"But there's no harm in being rich; people can't help being well off if they are, and poor people must try to earn money, mustn't they, for their wives and families?"

Undoubtedly. They may even strive to earn what will enable them to live in moderate comfort, and to make their homes bright and pleasant. Please remember that it is the *immoderate* desire of riches that does the harm.

"What harm?"

Our Lord tells us in some very startling words, so startling indeed, that if any other had said them, we might be inclined to think them overstrong, and try to explain them away: "*Woe to you that are rich, for you have your consolation here.*"[1] Riches bring the good things of this world within our reach, and to go in immoderately for the good things of this world, is to lose those that are to come. And so the Church, in one of her beautiful prayers, bids us pray, "that we may so pass through the good things that are temporal, as not to lose those which are eternal." The immoderate love of riches, by which we mean all the good things that money can buy, makes people think only of having their consolation here, and care nothing for the consolation to come.

"Like Dives.[2] But we needn't love them immoderately. We

---

1   St. Luke 6.

2   In the Vulgate, the story of Lazarus and the Rich Man (Luke 16) refers to the Rich Man as Dives—*dives* being the Latin word for *rich man*.

can just love them as much as we ought, can't we?"

That seems to you easy? How to do it is a problem that has puzzled the wisest heads from the beginning. Old Greek sages and Christian Saints have tried to solve the problem. All who at this moment are serving God in earnest are trying to solve it. We *can* love riches just as much as we ought—our Lord tells us this expressly; but it is difficult, and He warns us to take care. If the bait were not tempting, you know, there would be no danger in it. Riches attract like the sugared paper you see here and there in the summer-time, and on it the poor, feebly-struggling flies. They thought they would get just as much of the sugar as would satisfy them, but they sucked in the poison too.

One need not be a Saint to know that we have to be on our guard against these sugary things. All men who think seriously tell us that riches are dangerous. You are too young to care much for Mr. Gladstone's thoughts. Yet you may like to know what the great statesman spoke into the phonograph in 1894. He knew his country well, and he would leave her a warning word when he should have passed away. His warning word to England was this:—

"Wealth is the mother of temptation, and leads many of its possessors into a new form of slavery, more subtle and not less debasing than the old. From this slavery may all lands of the English tongue hold themselves for ever free!"

We Englishmen and Englishwomen reduced to slavery, and by riches—the very thing we fancied made us free and independent—think of that! You spoke just now of Dives. His miserable life and miserable eternity show us the harm that riches do when they are loved to excess. Think what a selfish life his was; of the wretched pleasures that were all he cared about—nice things to eat and drink, soft, rich clothing, the best of everything and plenty of it. These, our Lord tells us, were the "good things" for which he lived. He cared for nothing better or higher. Poor Lazarus might lie on his doorstep and beg in vain for the crumbs that fell from his table. That face pinched with hunger, that body shivering with cold and wasted by disease, woke no pity in his soul. Selfishness had dried up all tenderness in it, all thought except for self.

"How can we keep ourselves from loving riches more than we ought? Did our Lord tell us?"

Yes, and we will hear another day what He said, but your questions have kept us sadly too long at the devil's first bait, we must go on now to the second.

Plenty of money is the way to plenty of pleasure. This is the bait our enemy dangles before us when we are young. "See here," he says. "When you leave school or college you will be able to do just as you like; mind you have a *good time*. Get all the enjoyment you can out of balls, theatres, races, picnics on the river, garden and tennis parties, betting, card-playing, novel-reading. Don't listen to those who say you ought to employ your time usefully, to have some regular occupation and all that sort of thing. You have had that at school. Your business when you get home is to enjoy yourself."

"But mayn't we enjoy ourselves when we go home and go to balls and picnics and garden parties? And if we go we can't help enjoying ourselves, you know."

Of course you cannot. No one pretends that pleasure is not pleasant. And certainly no one wants you to live without pleasure. But you have missed out a very important word in the enemy's bit of advice. He does not merely tell you to enjoy yourself when you get home, but to *make it your business* to enjoy yourself.

There is no harm in enjoyment any more than there is in riches. It is only when there is immoderate love of it that

harm comes in. If you want to know what harm, just watch
the life of a girl who, on leaving school, has made enjoyment
a *business*. You will find it alarmingly like that of Dives—the
same round of selfish pleasures, and neglect of duties towards
God and man. Notice this too—such a life is not wrong only,
it is miserable. Yes, in spite of all the pleasure squeezed into
it, it is miserable. This is because earthly things are not made
to satisfy us. Our hearts are too big for them to fill. Pleasure
is like egg-flip,[1] which looks so frothy and tempting. Take as
much of it as you like, it will not satisfy your hunger. Neither
will the good things of this world. Enjoyment and excitement
have a pleasant taste, but we shall find them disappointing if
we try to live upon them. All the world knows this. Those
who lead fretful, dissatisfied lives are those who are always on
the hunt for amusement, who make stunning enjoyment *the
business of life.*

If the devil can bring us to this selfish love of pleasure for
its own sake, so that self is our aim in all we do or plan, we are
not far from independence of God, the precipice to which he
is edging us on.

He does not try all his baits on every one. He knows our
tastes, and chooses his worm accordingly. Some are caught
by the love of pleasure and some by the love of honour. The
slaves of honour must be first always and everywhere, must
be noticed, praised, made a fuss about, followed with incense
wherever they go. Like the Pharisee, they cannot bear to be
"as the rest of men." They must have their first seats, and their
salutations in the market-place, and their trumpets blown
before them. Every one must give way to them, bow down
in their presence, attend respectfully to all they say. We know
what our Lord thinks of such as these.

---

1   A drink similar to egg nog.

"Mustn't we want to be first then?"

Want it by all means; want it very much; St. Paul tells us to do so. He who "laboured more than all the Apostles," and would have us "press towards the mark," is not likely to hold us back. We see the eager, zealous character of the great Apostle in his repeated use of the word *run*. He cannot do with slowness. All his converts, all to whom he writes, Romans, Corinthians, Galatians, Philippians, Thessalonians, Hebrews, must *run*. To every one of them he speaks of *running*. "*Let us run to the fight proposed to us*."[1] "*All run indeed but one receiveth the prize. So run that you may obtain*."[2] He speaks to the Romans of him "*that runneth*."[3] "*You did run well*," he says to the Galatians, scolding them for having stopped. Of himself he says "*I run*,"[4] and he tells the Philippians he has not "*run in vain*."[5] So St. Paul will not quarrel with you for wanting to get on, or to be first.

"But you don't see what I mean. I mean wanting to come out first at exams and things like that."

Even in such things there is no harm in wanting to be first. God has given us certain powers of mind and body which we cannot help using. If they are in a healthy state we feel the need of using them vigorously. There is real pleasure in hard study, in football, cricket, rowing, racing. And it adds zest to this exercise and pleasure to see others at our side, aiming at the same end and eager as we are. We may try to distance others in examinations as we try to outstrip them in the games.

"There is nothing wrong in a Catholic striving to win what are called 'the prizes of life,' high position, wealth, influence, professional success. If these things were evil things, Catholic

1 Hebrews 12.
2 I Cor. 9.
3 Romans 9.
4 I Cor. 9.
5 Philipp. 2.

134

educators would sin in seeking to set young Catholics in the way of obtaining them. But they are not what Holy Writ calls 'all man.' They are not the highest interest of man, they are things that every man who gains them must resign some day."[1]

We must be careful, too, that our emulation is without envy. These two things are apt to run into one another; we have to be on our guard.

"I think it's hard not to envy. Because if somebody else gets first and we wanted to, we can't be quite glad, can we?"

When this happens, it is a good plan to think more of the somebody else's pleasure than of our own disappointment. This is not always easy, and if we have let the desire to be first grow immoderately, it becomes very difficult indeed. Here, once again, we see how these three things, riches, pleasures, and honours, though harmless in themselves, may be very hurtful if we let them become our masters.

The immoderate love of honour leads straight to independence and pride. Here the devil has attained the end of all his scheming. He has brought God's reasonable creatures to such a pitch of folly that they behave as if they were independent of the God Who made them. "Professing themselves to be wise they became fools,"[2] turned by self-conceit into such ridiculous objects as to be a laughing-stock to devils and to men.

You know how ridiculous people look in clothes that were not made for them and do not fit them. "Pride was not made for man," the Holy Ghost tells us,[3] and the devils laugh when they see us strutting about in it. Pride, if allowed to grow, makes people act as if they had lost their senses. They cannot stand anything which brings home to them that they are what they are—creatures—therefore, subjects. They will not submit

1 Father Joseph Rickaby, S.J.
2 Romans 1.
3 Ecclus. 10.

to the authority that comes from God—not to parents, nor masters, nor to magistrates—no, nor to God Himself.

We see to whose likeness we have come now. We are frightened at the resemblance to him who bears on his black banner, "*Non serviam!*" And well we may be. For in the next world all who are alike will be together. Just as we are fit for our Lord's society and that of the holy Angels when He has brought us by humility to His own likeness, so are those ready for companionship with the rebel angels whom their chief has brought by pride to likeness with himself.

We have now seen something of the hunter who glides into our midst, hidden under harmless things. Must we not be on our guard lest we come within reach of his shot?

You are tired, I expect, of hearing about his wiles and ways. I am, and heartily wish we had finished with them. But unhappily there are more to come, of which we must know something if we want to keep out of his way.

It would be bad enough if he came alone on his wretched "skag" hunting. But he has his accomplices to help him when he cannot get on by himself.

One of these, sad to say, is a traitor. His name is "Self." He is an awkward person to deal with, because he cannot be got rid of altogether. He is useful to us on the whole, and sometimes we think we have got him safely on our side. Then, just when we begin to trust him, off he runs to the enemy's camp and betrays us to him. His treacherous ways we shall have to see to by-and-by; we have another accomplice to look at now.

All creatures feel safe when they are with those of their own kind. Wolves hunt in packs, elephants and buffaloes keep together in herds, birds travel in flocks. When cavalry have to transport horses across a river, they get one horse over, then the others will swim to him. Our Lord knew how much easier it would be to get us to Heaven if we had one like ourselves to follow. This is why He took our nature and went before us leading the way. Encouraged by His example, millions have gone after Him and reached their journey's end in safety.

The devil looked on in dismay. What was he to do? He would like to have become incarnate too, that we might follow him into the pit of Hell. This was beyond his power. Yet something must be done. Ha!—a capital plan, and not beyond his power—*the skag*. After all it would never have done for him to show himself. We should have been frightened to death at the sight of him and run away. No, he must keep out of sight. Hidden under harmless things—that would be his way of getting at us. And as the hunter had a decoy duck at the boat-head to attract the ducks, so would he find human beings to decoy one another and bring his prey within shot.

Alas! that his stratagem should have succeeded as it has— that men, women, even children, should be found on his side, ready to let him do *through them* the evil work he cannot do by himself. Were he to appear himself, we should be terrified and fly from him, but we are not terrified when people like ourselves lead us to do wrong. He has his agents everywhere— in the school, in the play-ground, in the streets, in the shops, even in the churches—every-where devils working together with men, women, and children, to lead to eternal misery the souls for which Christ died. It seems too dreadful to be true. Had it happened only once or twice, it would be frightful. But to think it is the commonest thing in the world for people to try and lead others into sin and push them into eternal fire!

We all know how eager the leaders in a game are to secure the best players for their side; how much a cricket team makes of a good bowler, or batsman, or wicket-keeper. The leaders of whom we are speaking are most anxious to have us all on their side. They go about inviting, urging each and all of us into their ranks. But whom do they want most? Over whom do they dispute most persistently? Would you suppose it to be the children? Yet, so it is. These are the helpers that both leaders are trying with an earnestness of which we can form no conception, to win for their side.

"Why?"

Not only because of the value of those innocent souls for which a God has given His life, but because each child will become, later on, a recruiting officer, gaining over others for its leader.

The Children's Crusade in the Middle Ages was a failure. Humanly speaking, it could not have been anything else. That army of poor, helpless little ones must needs have been cut to pieces! But had the children really been chosen, as they fondly hoped they were, for the grand work of saving the world in that time of peril, they would have succeeded beyond a doubt.

"I wish they had been. It would have been nice for them to have conquered the Turks."

They were to have their chance later. God meant to call them to a Crusade in modern times, with the promise that if they would join in the Holy War and be true to their colours, there should be no defeat for them.

"Oh, did He? And when will the time come? And will all be able to join, big and little, girls as well as boys?"

All may join, for He wants all under His Standard. He cannot spare one. And, children—the time is *now*. *Now* He wants the help of your fresh strength and your brave wills for His holy cause; *now* He wants you to fight His battles. The children of other days were not wrong in believing that God's victory in the world and over the world was to be won by them. And the time is *now*.

Yes, our Lord wants you on His side. But, alas! there is another who wants you, too—that chief who, like his own false prophet, is always making war on Christian lands and against the King's Crusaders. The Wicked Chief is most anxious to have you, for he wants his to be the winning side.

In the Turkish army of olden days there was a celebrated body of soldiers called the Janizaries, or "new troops." It was composed entirely of the children of Christians who had been forced, generally whilst they were quite little, to adopt the religion of Mahomet.

They were torn from their parents, made to renounce the faith in which they were baptized, and to profess the creed of Mahomet. They were then carefully trained for a soldier's life, in a way that was at once trying and flattering to human nature. They were taught to render an instantaneous and unquestioning obedience to all orders given them, and to bear without complaining hunger, fatigue, and pain. But, on the other hand, they had high pay and many privileges and honours. What wonder, then, that this terrible body of infantry became the scourge of Christendom!

Three things in its history are useful for us to note, because they bring out clearly the character of the Wicked Chieftain and the wiles of which we have been speaking:

It is baptized souls that he covets most. For three hundred years the corps of the Janizaries was recruited by an annual enrolment of one thousand Christian children, so that no fewer than 300,000 of the baptized were used by him for fighting against Christ and against His Church.

The means by which he won over these Christian children were those we have been speaking of—love of riches, love of pleasures, love of honours. By means of these three baits he brought them to such a degree of independence and pride, that they would submit to no one, and becoming at length a terror to their own sovereigns, they were destroyed to the number of 20,000 by Sultan Mahmood in 1825.

Here we see the end to which the devil's service leads. Tempting people on by promises of riches, pleasures, honours, he brings them at last to the precipice—pride, and independence of God, and so to everlasting ruin.

It is a terrible thought, this multitude of baptized souls having been used by the devil as his tools. Three hundred thousand is a frightful number. Yet, would to God, he were able to boast these only. But alas! They are only a small portion of his gains. Not for three centuries only, but in every century of the world's history, every year, every day, he is using baptized children as instruments for doing his deadly work. They do it by bad example—teaching others harm they did not know before; by laughing at those who are better than themselves; by getting those who are trying to serve God to give up prayer and the sacraments and devotion to Mary. They do it by lending books they have no business to read or to lend; they do it by getting those who cared once for God and holy things to care for nothing but the vanities and pleasures of this world.

Oh, children, it is a fearful thought that Satan, seeing how we follow the lead of those who are like ourselves, and unable himself to come down among us for our ruin, as our Lord has come for our salvation, should secure the services of children—Christian children—to do his work for him, and drag down to Hell the souls which, but for their help, he could not reach.

The Janizaries did not know they were fighting against their Saviour and doing the devil's work. But children who range themselves under his standard in these days know quite well the harm they are doing. They know that, by the vows of their Baptism, they have promised to renounce Satan and all his works and all his pomps. And here they are, in league with him, bringing to his service just the soldier he likes best—a baptized soul, torn from the ranks of the true Leader to fight against Him.

140

What wonder that among the countless multitudes the Church has to tend, the children should be her chief care! That she should speak as if on them depended the salvation of the world! That her heart should break when the little ones are torn from her, or scandalized, or neglected—the faith she has given them, the helps she has ready for them, the Precious Blood with which she has washed them, the Divine Food with which she has fed them—thrown away! Every now and then a wail goes over Christian lands, sadder far than the wail of Rama long ago—the Church of Christ "*bewailing her children and will not be comforted because they are not.*"[1]

O True Leader, my Lord and my God, keep me always safe on Your side! Do not let the Wicked Chieftain entice me over to him. Let me see the snares he lays for me, and help me to guard against them. Never let our holy Mother the Church have to weep over *me*. And never let me be so wicked as to hurt by bad example any of the little ones she keeps for You, dear Lord.

---

1   St. Matt. 2.

IX.

THE STANDARD OF THE KING

*And it shall come to pass in that day that the Lord shall
set up a Standard unto the nations.*
(Isaias II, 12.)

How glad we are to get back to the King! Because the enemy
comes spying about in the camp to make use of all he can pick
up, it is only prudent for us to be on the alert too, and find out
what he is devising against us. And so we have been over to
his quarters studying his plan of campaign, his wiles and his
snares. It was necessary and had to be done. But oh, how glad
we are to get away from it all, and be back in our own camp!
How refreshing it is to turn from darkness to light; from our
deadly enemy to our best Friend; from Lucifer to Jesus!

We leave behind us the Black Banner and the Wicked
Chieftain, with his miserable followers who hate him even while
they do his bidding; and hasten to where our King, surrounded by
His servants and friends, is waiting for us. He looks more beautiful
than ever after the ugliness we have seen. His gentle majesty,
His graciousness, the sweetness of His smile, the tones of His
voice, are all the more charming for the hateful things we have
left behind. Dear Lord and Master! We kneel before Him and
feast our eyes upon Him, and fling our hearts brimful of love
and praise at His Feet. We have asked Him for light to know

142

the most Wicked One. May He give us more light to know and
follow Himself.

These two Chiefs are at war for mankind, *for me*. Each of
them is saying, "Follow Me!" The tricks by which the Wicked
Chieftain allures and deceives his followers we have seen. We
turn now to the True Leader to learn His ways. His *"ways are
beautiful ways and all* His *paths are peaceable."*[1]

Let us look for a moment at His Standard. You know
what a flag is to an army, and why so much is made of it. To a
soldier, the standard of his regiment represents his sovereign
and his sovereign's cause, the cause of right and justice. It
represents his country, the glory of her arms in the past, and
the prosperity that awaits them in the future. It represents his
home with all near and dear to him there. All these are bound
up with the future of the flag, to whose service he has given
his life, and for which he must, at any moment, be ready to
face death. If he lives to see it triumph, he will share its glory;
should disgrace threaten it, he must shed the last drop of his
blood in its defence.

This visible symbol of the cause for which they were
fighting, has in all ages fired the enthusiasm of men and inspired
heroic deeds. Whether the standard were the Roman eagle, the
Labarum[2], the *Oriflamme* of France[3], the Lions of England—
in all days, as in our own, it has been guarded with the most
courageous vigilance and the most absolute devotedness.

At the Battle of Albuera, the bloodiest of the Peninsular
War, the standard-bearer of the Buffs,[4] seeing the enemy closing
round him, threw the colours on the ground and flung himself

1   Proverbs 3.
2   A military standard topped by a *chi-rho* symbol, used by Constantine.
3   A sacred banner used as a battle standard by the early French kings.
4   The third oldest regiment in the British Army. Caught in a heavy
rainstorm at Albuhera, their muskets were rendered useless, and only 2 out
of the 63 men in the regiment survived.

upon them. He was slain by a dozen lance thrusts, protecting his charge to the last. The ensign who carried the other colours of the regiment, tore the flag from its staff and thrust it into his breast. There, when the fight was over, it was found, stiff with his blood.

America was immensely proud of her first war trophy, a Castilian flag captured from the heights of the Cavité forts after the bombardment and surrender of Manila in May, 1898.[1] On September 2nd of the same year, the Crescent flag of Egypt, torn down at Khartoum in 1885, was unfurled beside the Union Jack at Omdurman.[2] The black standard of the Mahdi, taken on the battlefield, was borne in triumph before the Anglo-Egyptian troops as they entered the town, and was afterwards sent to England. The 42nd Highlanders, known as the "Black Watch," enjoy the proud distinction of having captured more standards than any other regiment in existence.

Even animals seem to understand the value of the flag. Among the distinguished names that have come down to us from the beginning of this century is that of the French poodle Moustache, which—surely we should say *who*—shared the brilliant fortunes of the army during most of the wars of the Consulate and of the Empire.[3] He was specially honoured at Marengo, and was decorated on the field of Austerlitz for his gallantry in rescuing the colours of his regiment. An Austrian was seizing them from the grasp of the standard-bearer as

1 The Battle of Manila was a short conflict during the Spanish-American War.
2 In 1885, Sudanese forces led by the Mahdi Muhammad Ahmad laid siege to Khartoum, then held by the Egyptians and the British. Before a relief expedition could arrive from Britain, the Mahdi's forces slaughtered both armies and took the city. A harsh Islamic dictatorship was then set up throughout the Sudan. Horatio Kitchener (the Sirdar referred to earlier) was sent to avenge the slaughter of Khartoum and reconquer Sudan. He succeeded at Omdurman in 1898.
3 These are now usually referred to simply as the Napoleonic wars.

he fell mortally wounded, when Moustache sprang upon the assailant, drove him off, and then seizing the tattered colours in his teeth, dragged them along in triumph till he reached his own company.

"The plucky fellow! What became of him?"

That I never heard. But this incident in his history we shall do well to remember. In zeal for *our* colours it will never do for us to be shamed by a dog.

A King bears emblazoned on his standard a figure or ensign emblematic of himself, something which recalls him to mind as soon as seen. It stands for him, signifies him, so that the two are inseparable in thought.

What should stand for Jesus but the dear Cross by which He saved us! What should be *the Sign of the Son of Man,*[1] but that Sacred Tree on which He was lifted up to draw all things to Himself! The Cross, then, is the Standard of Jesus. And as *there is no other name*, so there is no other sign *under heaven given to man whereby we must be saved.*[2]

When the young Emperor Constantine, son of her who was to glorify the Cross, was entering into the battle on which hung the fate of the Roman Empire and the Christianity of the world, the God of armies revealed Himself to him, not in Person, but by His Standard—*the Sign of the Son of Man*. It was a revelation to appeal straight to a soldier's heart. The mid-day heavens were flung open—and there, outshining all sunshine and glory of this world, appeared a heavenly Standard surrounded with the words in letters of light: *In hoc Signo vinces!*

In the strength of that Sign Constantine went forth and conquered. Henceforth the Cross became the Standard beneath which Christian armies fought. The Emperor had a banner made according to the heavenly pattern shown him. Forty picked men

1   St. Matt. 24.
2   Acts 4.

were appointed to guard it, and so well did the *Labarum* guard its guards, that none of those forty, we are told, were ever wounded in any battle.

Our King draws us to His side. He points to His Standard—the Cross—and says to us: "By this Sign *thou* shalt conquer." He explains gently that if we want to follow Him we must suffer, we must deny ourselves. There is no help for it. It is the only way to Heaven now. He has gone along this way bearing His Cross, and His servants have followed Him— men, women, children, popes, kings, beggars—cross-laden every one of them. Weary and bruised, they bent beneath its weight, but it was the Standard of the King, the Sign by which they were to conquer, and they bore it bravely to the end. To the gates of death they bore it. There what a surprise awaited them! There, for the first time, they saw its other side. For the Cross faces two ways. On earth we see its dark side only. In Heaven we behold it radiant with glory as befits the Standard of the King. Yet we shall see it glorified even here.

A day is coming when the whole earth shall be lit up with its glory. "The sun shall be darkened and the moon shall not give her light, and the stars shall fall from heaven, and the powers of heaven shall be moved…

"And then shall appear *the sign of the Son of Man* in heaven: and then shall all tribes of the earth mourn: and they shall see the Son of Man coming in the clouds of heaven with much power and majesty. And He shall send His Angels with a trumpet and a great voice: and they shall gather together His elect from the four winds, from the farthest parts of the heavens to the utmost bounds of them…And all nations shall be gathered together before Him: And He shall separate them one from another, as the shepherd separateth the sheep from the goats."[1]

---

1   St. Matt. 24, 25.

St. John, who saw in vision this tremendous Day when "earth shall pass away," says:

"I saw another Angel ascending from the rising of the sun, *having the Sign of the Living God;* and he cried with a loud voice to the four Angels to whom it was given to hurt the earth and sea, saying: Hurt not the earth nor the sea, nor the trees, *till we sign the servants of our God* in their foreheads."...Of the locusts that came from the bottomless pit, he says: It was commanded them that they should not "hurt the grass of the earth, nor any green thing, nor any tree: but only the men who have not *the sign of God* on their foreheads."[1]

See what this saving Sign will be on that day to the true soldiers of the King! Because, in their lifetime, they were not ashamed of it, not ashamed to sign it on their foreheads, it will be their safety in the tremendous Judgment. Our King bids His followers to rejoice when "all tribes of the earth shall mourn," when men on every side shall be "withering away for fear." "*Lift up your heads because your redemption is at hand.*"[2] Lift them up for the swiftly passing Angel to sign with the Cross. Lift them up to hear once again the words of your Confirmation, "*Signo te Signo Crucis.*"

Why, then, are we afraid to take up a Cross that leads to a Kingdom, that will lead us to victory here on earth, and to the gates of Heaven, when earth, its work accomplished, shall be crumbling away beneath our feet!

"Will you let My Cross lead you where it has led all the Elect, to the fight now and to glory presently?" the King asks us once again.

We look up into His Face. It is grave, yet very beautiful and very persuasive. The tones of His Voice sink into our souls and stir them to their depths. He is not inviting only, He is

1   Apoc. 9.
2   St. Luke 21.

drawing. We know now what His Standard means, we know where it must lead us before bringing us to His Kingdom—and yet we are attracted. The truth is safe, the truth is satisfying. He is the Truth, we can trust ourselves to Him. So when He holds out His Hand, we put ours into it, and ask like the Crusaders of old for the Cross.

We notice here, by the way, that the Wicked Chieftain is at no pains to draw attention to his standard with its absurd inscription: *Non serviam!* Why should he be? Does it represent anything very attractive to his soldiers?—their leader, a rebel; the cause, a shameful one; the end, defeat and the ruin of all who have served under it. "No, keep it out of sight," he says, "especially of new recruits. Wait till they have got drilled in our ways and are blinded by our dust and smoke before you let them set eyes on it." Concealment again, you see; he cannot afford to let anything belonging to him come to the light. How different this to the frank ways of the True Leader!

In the armies of this world the common soldier is not supposed to know the plans of the Commander-in-Chief and the secrets of head-quarters. It would never do to confide to the rank and file matters of importance, which even staff officers must guard carefully and not betray by any imprudence of word or manner. Lord Wolseley warns young officers of the staff not to go about with anxious, mysterious faces, as if they were in the confidence of the Commander-in-Chief and weighed down with their responsibilities.

In the service of our King, there is no such reserve. His youngest recruit is not only free to know His projects, but is invited to study them. Let us see, then, what is the plan of campaign marked out by our Chief, and how He proposes to defeat the designs of the enemy.

To *catch by craft* in one of his traps is the devil's aim. If by the love of comfort, the love of pleasure, the love of honour, we can be brought to independence and pride, he may consider our ruin as secured. And so his followers are told to go about to every place and to every person, and try to bring all to the immoderate love of these things. "Get them," he says, "to put all their happiness in the enjoyments of this life, in pleasure, and in praise. This will bring them to pride. And there you may leave them." Yes, for he knows well that in that trap they will sink down, down, down, till they come to him who, for his pride, fell from the height of Heaven to the lowest Hell.

Now what is our Leader's programme for defeating this horrible scheme? One we should never have dreamed of, never have thought possible had He not brought it about. Go to Bethlehem, to Egypt, and to Nazareth, to the desert of the Temptation, to Calvary, and you will see Him fighting on those strange battlefields the enemy He came to conquer. We have to fight our battles on His plan, so we must go to these places to study Him. But you are looking disappointed.

"Because we don't see any fighting. There wasn't any at Bethlehem or Nazareth."

No? If we try to put in practice what we are taught there, I am afraid we shall find plenty. Look at the palace where the King of kings was born; see its furniture, its conveniences. Is He not fighting there the love of riches and comforts? Is He not showing us what we are to think of them? Can we, without a struggle, imitate in the very faintest degree what we see Him doing at Bethlehem? You asked the other day if our Lord has taught us how to avoid loving riches more than we ought. See how He teaches this from the stable-floor where He is lying.

By His own example, He shows us one means of escaping the danger, one that He was afterwards to give to His Apostles and to the rich young man. It is to use the remedy, "Hands off." Have nothing to do with riches: "Go, sell what thou hast and give to the poor, and come follow Me." This remedy is a strong and sure one, but it is not for all. Most of us have to handle these dangerous things, the point therefore is to know how we can do so with safety. A very good way is to hold them with a loose hand, so that we can part with them readily, either when through some misfortune we come to lose them, or by the blessed habit of almsgiving. Those who give easily and willingly and as far as their means allow, when the service of God or the good of their neighbour requires it, are not likely to be too much attached to their riches. And therefore it is well to accustom ourselves, whilst we are quite young, to give out of our little store, thus to acquire the habit of giving which, as our Lord has told us in so many places, will be a strict duty when we grow up.

The Wicked Chieftain says: Get rich and you will be happy. The True Leader says: Keep down that craving for the things of this world. Be able to see things that are comfortable, convenient, fashionable, pretty, without forthwith wanting to have them. Remember you are on a journey, and must not look here for the comforts of home. Would you be like Dives and have your good things here? Remember, too, you are steward, not owner, of the money you call your own. It is Mine. I have put it into your hands, saying: "Trade till I come." When I come I shall expect to "receive My own with usury."

To give to the poor is trading. To feed the hungry, to clothe the naked, to find homes for those who have none, to take little delicacies to the sick, to give away good books, to teach a catechism class, to amuse the children at school treats—all this is trading. But it cannot be done without sacrifice. We must deny ourselves if we are to win that reward, at the Judgment, of having helped and honoured the King in His "least brethren." But the joy we shall have even now will far exceed the cost. None are so happy as those who have the poor for their friends, none so free and light-hearted as those who, by almsgiving, escape the dangers that riches bring. At all costs we must contrive not to have our good things here. Almsgivings will secure this for us.

Certainly the King fought at Bethlehem—fought *the love of riches*. And then He passed to another battlefield.

Throughout His whole life *Christ pleased not Himself*, St. Paul tells us. In a heathen land He would please Himself least. Egypt, therefore, was to be His place of exile when the cruelty of Herod drove Him from His home. In Egypt He would fight that immoderate love of pleasure which carries away so many of us. We have thought many a time of the suffering of that midnight flight into the strange land, and of the hardships there. But perhaps we have never considered one circumstance that must have made it so additionally, and, as we should have said, so unnecessarily painful to the Holy Family, one that from first to last was part of their trial—uncertainty. Of all trying things, uncertainty of what the morrow may bring is among the greatest. Now think what this was in their case. When the Angel, rousing them from sleep in the middle of the night, bade them leave the little home St. Joseph had made in Bethlehem and take the road to Egypt, not a word was said as to the length of their stay there, whether it was to be weeks, or months, or years. Had there been no other trial than this, what a trouble this must have been! They did not know what to take with them and what to leave behind. Should the few household things be put together, or would their needs be provided for?

"Our Lord knew all about it and what they had better take."

Yes, and as usual His knowledge served to increase His pain. What a relief, what a pleasure it would have been that night and during the weary years in Egypt, on the road to Jerusalem when He was twelve years old, and many and many a time beside, to have said the word that would have lightened their anxiety and brought joy to their hearts. But *He pleased not Himself,* and He was silent.

The little place St. Joseph took in Egypt was very poor, yet to pay for that, and for the coarse food on which they lived, was hard enough. He was glad to get orders for such rough carpentering as he could do. But he never knew whether he would be able to complete them. At any hour of the day or night the Angel might come with the command to return to the land of Israel. Be there "till I shall tell thee." That was all he knew who had to provide for the household and make ends meet. Little money there could have been to hand over to Mary for the house-keeping; food, even bread, was scarce, and as to having enough of other necessaries, they did not know what this meant. There was not much *pleasure,* in our sense of the word, in Egypt.

And there was not much *honour* in the carpenter's shop at Nazareth, when they got home again. All who belonged to that rough village were looked down upon by their neighbours, and, from what we hear of them, were not civil-spoken among themselves. The carpenter's Boy, Who lived in that little bit of a place at the bottom of the street and ran errands and took orders, would come in for a full share of their rude words and ways. Why not? No one outside His home had the faintest idea Who He was. Later on, when He did such wonderful things, they were quite taken by surprise: "Why," they said, "He is only the carpenter whom we have known and ordered about for years, who made and mended our benches and our carts— yes, and was glad enough to be paid for doing it."

And thus at Nazareth, the King fought the immoderate love of *honour.* He did not complain. It was for this He had come. He had a lesson to teach me. All this was *for me.*

For three years our Lord passed up and down through the

152

towns and villages of Judea, Samaria, and Galilee, teaching in the Temple, in the synagogues, on the Lake, in the cornfields, on the mountain side; warning in earnest words all who would listen to Him against the deceitfulness of riches, the broad way of pleasure, the first chairs, and the highest places, and the salutations that men covet so eagerly. "Woe to you rich," He said, "for you have your consolation. Woe to you that now laugh, for you shall mourn and weep. Woe to you when men shall bless you. But blessed are ye poor. Blessed are ye that weep now. Blessed shall you be when men shall reproach you."[1]

It was a new teaching, this, and the crowds listened and wondered. It was a teaching hard to take in, therefore the Teacher followed it up by His own example. They saw Him poor and despised; they saw Him in tears. And meek and humble of heart always. Whether hailed as the Messiah and followed by Hosannas, or reviled as a malefactor and hunted to His death—meek and humble of heart. Humility was the chief lesson He came from Heaven to teach. By pride men had wandered away from God, by humility they were to be brought back to Him. *Pride was not made for man*, the Holy Ghost tells us.[2] But humility is. It becomes the creature as a beautiful robe becomes him for whom it is made. But because, being blinded, we did not see the beauty of this robe, our King clothed Himself in it, that we might at least love it as His and for His sake. Humiliation is less hard to bear since He has borne it and left it as His livery to His followers—a royal livery and therefore a title to glory.

See Him in the white garment, hooted through the streets of Jerusalem as a fool. See Him seated on a bench, bearing the spitting, and the mocking, and the striking of His Sacred Head, whilst the Blood trickles slowly from beneath His Crown of

1 St. Luke 6.
2 Ecclus. 10.

Thorns. Surely He has taught us from first to last what account we ought to make of the comforts, pleasures and honours of this world, of which He made so little.

But it was on Calvary, when He was lifted up, that the King drew all to Himself. Then the three-fold lesson of that Divine Life was taught as it had never been taught before, and with a persuasiveness that has softened, and is softening daily, the hardest hearts on earth. So bereft of all things, that "they parted His garments amongst them, and upon His vesture they cast lots;"[1] so suffering, that "from the sole of the Foot to the top of the Head there was no soundness in Him;"[2] so disgraced as to be "despised and the most abject of men"[3]—He left this world of Whom the Angel had said to Mary: "He shall be great and shall be called the Son of the Most High, and the Lord shall give unto Him the throne of David His father, and He shall reign in the house of Jacob for ever, and of His kingdom there shall be no end."[4]

Was ever defeat more complete? For such it seemed to men. But during the three hours' darkness on Calvary a battle was being fought that men could not see—the fiercest battle that has ever been or shall be. The Wicked Chieftain had found out at last Who He was that had overcome him in the desert. He had discovered the Divine plan by which his power was to be overthrown. He saw how the standard which the King was consecrating by His Blood would be carried into a thousand battlefields all the world over, and that *by this Sign we should conquer*. At once all his schemes were reversed. He must prevent that Death which was to give us life. He must overcome the Standard which was to lead us to victory. A cry

1   Psalm 21.
2   Isaias 50.
3   Isaias 53.
4   St. Luke 1.

154

of despair rang through the vaults of Hell: "*God is come into the camp, woe to us!*"[1] He assembled his hosts and bade them put forth all their strength. He called upon men, his allies, enlisted under his banner to help him. And a cry went up from the earth, a mocking cry to the Crucified: "*Come down from the Cross!*"[2] They knew not what they did, nor at whose bidding they spoke, as so many times that day they had spoken. John, who stood so still by Mary's side, did he know anything of the conflict raging around the Cross? anything of that alliance between men and the Evil One, of which he was to tell us later: "*These have one design: and their strength and their power they shall deliver to the beast. These shall fight with the Lamb, and the Lamb shall overcome them, because He is Lord of lords and King of kings.*"[3]

He did not come down from the Cross. He loved us even unto death. "*All is finished,*" He said, "*and bowing His Head He gave up the Ghost.*"[4]

The darkness cleared away from the earth, and the dark spirits that had been fighting for the souls of men slunk away, defeated utterly. For the meek Lamb had conquered; Life had fought with Death and had overcome; Christ the Innocent One had reconciled sinners with the Father; the world was redeemed.

From the disappointment on your faces just now, it was plain that the King's way of fighting was not the way you were expecting. But is not this just what we might have looked for in so great a King? He could not go to work in our common ways. He had His own. Do we expect our masters to teach us only what we were quite prepared to learn? Which of us says

1   I Kings 4.
2   St. Matt. 27.
3   Apoc. 17.
4   St. John 19.

after hearing a proposition in Euclid, "Ah, yes, exactly so—just what I expected." Most of us hear, day after day, and every hour of the day, what we were so far from expecting, that it takes a great deal of attention to the master and careful study to grasp what we hear.

We should have expected the King of kings to teach in a palace, and to have had the telegraph, and the phonograph, all the "graphs" at work to flash abroad and multiply and perpetuate His words. Or that we should see Him like Samuel, hewing to pieces the enemies of God; or like David, slaying His thousands in battle. Would that have helped us much? He knew what would help, and He mapped out His Life accordingly. There was the world to redeem. There was His Church to be founded and His Apostles taught. There was the example to be set *for me* of the quiet hidden virtues—humility, patience, self-denial—that should sanctify my home life. He divided His Life as these needs required—*three hours* of one afternoon to the redemption of the world; *three years* to the training of His Apostles, the foundation of His Church, and His work of public teaching; *thirty years* of lowly hidden work to *me*.

How different His way to ours! Which way was best? If we had had to go to a gilded palace or to a battlefield for the example we need in the toil and trouble of daily life, should we have learnt our lesson better than when the Master teaches from the stable floor, or in the silence round His Cross on Calvary?

And see how magnificently His way has succeeded. Look at His Saints pressing close on His footsteps, following Him in self-denial, in patience, in love of suffering. Think of the brave servants of His, of whom we were talking some time ago, and see if you can imagine any better way of teaching, helping, and encouraging them than their Lord followed when He planned out for their example His Hidden, Suffering, Glorious Life. Oh, how grateful we ought to be that Our Lord is what He is—that on His first appearance, He showed Himself to us not as "*a powerful King and greatly to be feared*,"[1] but as the sweet Babe of Bethlehem!

I have been watching your faces all this time, and now I am going to tell you what you have been thinking. You have been saying to yourselves:

"All this is true of course. And I see quite well I ought to be glad to be our Lord's soldier. He has done all He can to make it easy for me. And yet I can't help thinking it's rather hard all the same. It's easy enough to belong to armies that only pretend to fight, such, for example, as the 'Kind-Hearted Brigade.'[2] It's quite easy to sign yourself K.H.B. But our Lord's service is something quite different. Something has to be done there, and though I don't know the exact thing, I am afraid it will be something hard. It's mean, I know, but I can't help it."

Now this feeling is, in great part, my fault. I ought to have reminded you that the King's Proclamation has two parts. It does not end with the invitation to share the fighting with Him. Coming directly after, is the invitation to share His triumph. He wants us to go with Him into the fight, that we may have part with Him in the victory as we had in the toils. And as it was the thought of His triumph, the triumph we were to share

---

1   Ecclus. 1.

2   In the 1880s and 1890s, the British newspaper *Weekly Telegraph* ran a "Children's Corner" where "Captain Trim" encouraged them to join the "Kind-Hearted Brigade." The rules which all members promised to keep:

    1. Every member is kind to birds and animals;

    2. Every member is kind and gentle to everybody;

    3. Every member is truthful and honest, and will not use bad language;

    4. Every member is respectful and obedient to parents, teachers and others in authority;

    5. Every member is clean in mind and person;

    6. Every member is helpful and happy in the home and everywhere.

with Him, that made our King go gladly through His sorrows, so it is the joy we are to have with Him when the fight is over that is to keep up our hearts while it lasts. "If we suffer we shall also reign with Him," St. Paul said to Timothy. And he told the Christians of Rome that "the sufferings of this time are not worthy to be compared with the glory to come."[1] Notice, he does not say they are not nearly so great as that glory, but "*not worthy to be compared*" with it.

And it is coming so quickly. "Humility goeth before glory,"[2] and only a little way before. Only a stone's throw from the spot where our Lord lay on His cruel death-bed that Friday afternoon, is the Garden of the Resurrection where, very early on Easter Day, He rose again. What did He think of the pains that were past, when in all His glorious beauty He came forth from the tomb! What, when He stood before His Mother; when He sped here and there—to Magdalen and the other Maries, to Cleophas and his companion, to Peter, and to the Eleven—the Joy-giver of all that Easter day! What did the great Conqueror think of the fight, when leading *Captivity captive* He passed with His rejoicing Saints into His Kingdom on Ascension Day! Rising with all His train above Jerusalem, the scenes of His Passion lay beneath Him—the two Gardens and the Via Dolorosa between; the courtyard of the Scourging; the hall of the Crowning; the place where they cried, "Crucify Him!" the spot where He fell on the way to Calvary; the corner of the street where His Mother met Him. What was it all but the road to His Kingdom, the Kingdom that would be all the more glorious for the valour with which it had been won!

So will it be with us. We, too, shall have our little way of the cross, but He will take care it shall not be too rough. We have a good Master, and it would be the greatest mistake to

---

1   Romans 8.
2   Prov. 15.

suppose that His service is a sad one. Our King is the great joy-giver even now. He is always in the field, and His very presence is gladness and strength. Be the fight ever so hard, there is joy in the hearts of His Soldiers—a joy beyond the reach of pain or loss, a joy worth a thousand times more than anything the Wicked Chieftain has to offer. After all, what *can* he offer, what *does* he offer?

We have come to know something of the two Chiefs. We shall know them truly when we see how they deal with their own in the matter of rewarding when their hands are free, when there is nothing to keep them from showing what is in their hearts. We know that when our Lord gets us into His Kingdom, He has in store for us what eye hath not seen, nor ear heard, nor our hearts dreamt of in the way of reward, and that meantime, when He has to be careful what He gives, all He *can* give in the way of prosperity and gladness will be ours.

And the other Chief?

If we want to see how he treats his subjects in this world, we have only to think of those countries where idolatry reigns—that is—where he is king, though with limited power. Of the car, carrying the hideous image of the god Juggernaut, crushing under its huge wheels the miserable people who have flung themselves in its way. Of the poor little children whose fingers are chopped off to propitiate the gods when the king is going to war.

"But he does not treat everybody like that. Sometimes he gives wicked people plenty of nice things and they are very happy."

Not so happy as you think. We have seen the kind of reward he gives them, and we know from the lips of those who have had most of these "nice things," that they cannot make them happy. Happiness is something more than pleasure, and even pleasure, like good things to eat and drink, disgusts us when we get too much of it. The honours of this world, for instance, that he gets people to run after—what are they? Here is a sample:

INDIA OFFICE, May 21, 1898.
SALUTE.

The Queen has been graciously pleased to approve the grant to his Highness Sir Hira Singh Mahlwandar Bahadur, Raja of Nabha, G.C.S.I., as a personal distinction, of an increase of two guns to his salute of thirteen guns.

Did this increase of honour add much to his Highness' happiness, do you suppose? Salutes, medals, garters, letters after one's name, are not very substantial goods, are they? We all knew Her late Majesty's[1] unfailing sympathy and solicitude for the soldiers who were struck down by wounds or illness in active service for their country. She went to visit the men who had returned invalided from the West Coast of Africa, the northwestern frontier of India, and the Soudan. The Sirdar was at the hospital to assist her in the distribution of medals to the hundred and eighty patients entitled to them for the Atbara and Omdurman Campaign. No doubt the poor fellows were pleased to have their Sovereign and their General pinning medals on their breasts. Yet, are not the honours of this world a very poor affair after all, a miserable compensation for the gallant acts of service done!

It is no one's fault, of course. The brave General could not help coming out of the fray unscathed, and showing himself in ease and in glory to his men lying there in pain. Only it is so utterly unlike the terms on which our King and His soldiers fight, that this decoration of the wounded almost looks like a mockery.

And now we have surely pondered enough and are ready to make our choice. We would not make it hastily or without

---

1   Queen Victoria.

knowing what it entails. After hearing the King's Proclamation, we considered carefully the different classes of soldiers to be found in the army, the characters of the two Chiefs, their plan of campaign, and lastly, the rewards each has to offer.

Now we must make up our mind—not, once again, *whether* we are going to fight under the King's Standard, but *how*. Watch those who have heard the Proclamation with us, as they make their choice.

Some come up to the Standard—frown at it, and go off grumbling into the ranks.

Others look at it steadily—and show their determination to fight under it as good soldiers.

And others, after gazing long and earnestly *at the King*— fall down before it and grasp it with both hands. These are "the King's Own."

Our turn is coming; what are we going to do? He stands there. He smiles upon us. He holds out His Hand ready to help. Do we want to show our loyalty and our love? Do we want to be among His *Chivalry*?

O Sovereign and True Leader, I fall on my knees before You. I put my hands within Yours like a vassal in the old feudal times. I want to give You all I have, all I am; to give You my best service; to be Yours out and out. If I cannot leave all things to follow You, give me grace to leave some; to do without some little luxuries for the sake of resembling You in Your poverty and giving to You in Your poor. Let me deny myself sometimes in my pleasures even when I am not obliged, that so I may be like Him Who *pleased not Himself*. And when I am unnoticed, or blamed, or laughed at, help me to bear it patiently, silently even—oh, that it could be gladly—that so I may follow You, my King!

X.

OUR KIT

We Thy servants all well appointed will march on to the war.
(Numbers 32, 27.)

"WE'VE come to the fighting now, haven't we?"

To the immediate preparation, at any rate. When an English army is to take the field, the men do not rush off harum-scarum, anyhow. There are the stores, the outfit, and the armour to be provided. To this we come now.

Whilst the Crimean War was raging, thousands of our bravest soldiers, left to shift for themselves, lay dying from wounds and disease in the so-called hospitals provided for them. Medicines were either wanting altogether, or were insufficient in quality; washing was utterly neglected; the food was unsuited to the poor sufferers, and their wounds were sometimes undressed for a week at a time. Fever and cholera filled the sheds with long, sad rows of dying and neglected men. The Battle of Inkerman was fought on the very day that Florence Nightingale, with her band of nurses, landed at Scutari. On the preceding day, terrible cargoes of men stricken down in the awful contest at Balaclava, had been landed there. One huge barrack hospital, and another big building near, were filled with close upon four thousand of the wounded and dying. Up and down a path two miles in length, hemmed in on either side with human agony, the nurses went.

Thank God, the shameful neglect which preceded the coming of these heroic women is unheard of now. It is true, Lord Wolseley tells us, that in hot and very mountainous countries, such as India, a towel and a piece of soap carried in the great coat is the only kit required by the English soldier, whilst the coat alone is all the Sepoy[1] needs. He is speaking, however, of what the men are to carry, for the commissariat supplies—provisions, clothing, tents, arms, ammunition, are close at hand, carried by mules. As to provisions, the bread is to be sweet, made of good wheat, well made and properly baked—How much crust and how much crumb is determined by regulations. Meat is to be good and wholesome, and varied in kind. Straw used for bedding is to be frequently renewed. The Index in his *Soldiers' Pocket-Book*, gives us an idea of the wants for which Government now thinks it necessary to provide when an army takes the field:

Ammunition	Onions
Blankets for sick horses	Pack Saddles
Bolsters at sea	Pepper
Centipede, bite of	Photographs
Collar-bone, broken	Plum-pudding, how to make
Cheese	Ponies
Cooking pots	Rations
Dead meat	Scalds
Donkey, rations for	Shoes
Graveyards	Snake-bites
Grease, allowance	Soap-soft, how to make
Guns	Sore feet
Horses, sore backs	Soup
Kicks	Table-linen
Luxuries	Tails, not too short
Music	Tea, advantages of
Mutton	Wasp-bites
Night-caps	Yeast powder
Nose-bags	

---

1   A *Sepoy* was an Indian soldier that served in a European army.

The Commanding Officer should see that his officers and men have something to eat and drink before they begin their work, no matter how early, *e.g.*, a cup of hot coffee and a biscuit before the regular breakfast. The men's rations should be varied as much as possible, and he would do well to take with him on campaigns in wild, uncivilized countries, plenty of mustard and cress seed.

The Commander-in-Chief condescends to such detail as the ingredients of soft soap for cleaning the belts, how to make plum-puddings and lemonade, and enumerates the number of mustard-pots, pickle-jars, pudding-bags, washing-tubs, scrubbing-brushes, dust-pans, saucepans, kettles, dough-scrapers and blankets one of our British troopships requires.

Lord Kitchener will be remembered by posterity as the hero of Omdurman, a new "Africanus," a man who has brought a new epoch of civilization and Christianity to the vast territory over which the English and Khedival flags are now waving. But for nothing will he deserve greater honour and more grateful remembrance, than for the care with which, on the march to Khartoum, every need of his 18,000 men, white, black, and yellow, was provided for. He knew what depended on them, and his knowledge of tropical climates enabled him to get the right sort of rations. As to the arrangements for the sick and wounded, they were simply marvellous, when we consider the numbers to be provided for, the distance to which everything had to be carried, and the difficulties of transport from Cairo, where the base hospital was situated.

How to give prompt and efficient aid to the wounded is one of the great questions of war, and it will not be going out of our way to see how it is done.

The work is divided among three lines, each of which has its clearly defined duties. The first line is composed of the regimental aid and the bearer companies. The second line comprises the field hospitals and the stationary hospitals. The third line is composed of the general hospitals at the base of operations.

"What is that?"

A secure tract of country in which the stores and reserves of men are situated. It is called the base of operations, because from it the operations of war may proceed. Being protected by fortifications, it is a place of comparative safety, and retreat may be made thither in case of necessity. It is like the space in Prisoners' Base or Rounders, beyond which any player is liable to be struck by a hand or ball from the enemy's side.

Every corps or regiment has a medical officer attached to it during the campaign. A certain number of men per squadron are trained as bearers. They know how to render "first aid" to the injured, and they bear the wounded from the field. As men fall, they are attended by the medical officer as far as may be, and carried to a spot under cover. If there is no such place near, the first post of assistance must be set up under fire in the open field. Surgical treatment here is necessarily somewhat rough and ready, as the regiment must be followed. The wounded are removed as soon as possible to the dressing station. There the surgical work, like that of the "regimental aid," has to be of the simplest kind. As the patients are dressed, they are placed in the ambulance waggons, which, when filled, are despatched to the field hospitals in charge of a corporal and a waggon orderly.

The arrangements made by the Sirdar for the comfort of his sick and wounded are probably the most extensive and perfect that have ever been made for any army in the field. We imagine, perhaps, that amid the war and excitement of battle, anything like systematic attention to the wounded is impossible. A glance at the preparations for the fight of Omdurman, as described by one who was with the army, will show us our mistake. There is something terrible in the calmness with which the ghastly needs of the battlefield are foreseen and met.

"With reserves of each regiment there are thirty-two armed stretcher-bearers, who, directly men begin to fall, will run forward and pick up the wounded. They will hurry their charges to any available cover, bush, or sand knoll. Presently camels bearing *cacolets* (chairs), or litters, will come up and carry the wounded to the field hospitals—the tents of which have already been erected as near as possible to the river. There all will be in readiness for the incoming patients—the operating tables fixed, the Röntgen ray apparatus[1] ready for all urgent cases to be immediately operated on, kettles boiling, beef tea prepared—all medical comforts at hand."

"Oh, do they call these comforts!"

In war, remedies, however severe, are considered such. The poor wounded man cries out to be taken to the doctor, though he knows it may mean the cutting off of an arm or a leg.

"As soon as possible, the wounded men will be conveyed to the river banks, where one of the light hospital boats will be signalled for the patients to be taken on board. These boats are simply the sandals or two-decked barges which have transported the troops to the front, rigged up with two hundred beds. Each boat will have a surgeon-major and nursing staff. When each sandal has its full number of wounded, it will be lashed to a stern-wheeler and run down with the current to Port Atbara, where the first hospital is reached *en route* to Cairo. Here the patients will rest till the ambulance train is made up to carry them, *viâ* Berber, across the Nubian desert to Wady Halfa, where those too seriously ill to proceed will remain for a time, while the others are taken on by boat to Shellah. Here there will be a halt to give the patients time to prepare themselves for the final and most trying stage of their

1   Now commonly known as X-ray machines.

journey by rail, *viâ* Luxor, through the dusty delta to Cairo. Once in the ambulance train at Luxor, the worst is over. For the arrangement of the cars allows the stretchers to be so placed as to lessen the pain caused by the jolting of the carriages. To each car there is a kitchen, and an ice-box, in which drinks are cooled for the thirsty and the feverish. On their arrival at the base hospital in the citadel of Cairo, after their long, dreary journey of nearly 1,350 miles, by river, rail, and desert, the wounded will be taken charge of by the surgeon-general till so far recovered as to be able to be sent home to the mother country."

And now what about the soldiers of the Cross in their desert warfare? About their supplies, equipment, refreshment, the care of the wounded, the means of transport Home? Will the provision for their needs be less generous than that which we have been considering? Not if God has to provide. He *must* provide of course. We know that beforehand. As usual, we have nothing and can do nothing without Him. To Him we look to have everything ready for us: "*As the eyes of the servants are on the hands of their masters, so are our eyes on the Lord our God.*"[1] "*He hath done all things well,*"[2] the people cried out in admiration, as they watched our Lord providing for every need. Whatever God does He does well. Whenever He provides, He does it generously. He redeems with a "*plentiful redemption*"[3] He has compassion with "*a multitude of tender mercies*"[4] He opens His hand "*and fills with blessing every living creature.*"[5] We may be sure, then, that when there is question of equipment for a war on which His glory and the eternal happiness of His

---

1   Psalm 122.
2   St. Mark 7.
3   Psalm 129.
4   Psalm 50
5   Psalm 144.

soldiers depends, His aid will be abundant. He will be lavish of His gifts, that "*all, well appointed, may march on to the war.*"

To provide our appointments, He does nothing less than institute a Sacrament in which the Third Divine Person comes Himself to supply our every need. What wonder, then, that the Church urges her children to prepare as they should for such a Guest!

"This Sacrament is called Confirmation," says the Holy Council of Trent, "because the soul, already a child of God by Baptism, receives a new force so that it begins to grow strong and to be a perfect soldier of Christ, putting away childishness and growing up to full manhood."

Think of God finding more to do for us after our First Communion, having yet another Sacrament in which to give Himself to us! Yet so it is. His love for us never seems satisfied, never thinks it has done enough. The gift of Himself in Holy Communion would have contented, we should have thought, even Infinite Love. But the Ever Blessed Trinity had not yet exhausted Its treasures. The Father in creation, the Son in Redemption and in His abiding Presence with us, had given proofs of their desire to make us happy here and to bring us to eternal happiness. What was left for the Holy Spirit to do? All that the Father and the Son had done, He had done with them, for there is only one God. In every Sacrament, in every grace we receive, He is at work. But He would have His own special share in the nursing and fondling of our souls—a Sacrament of His own in which He might come to us in Person and pour out upon us His Gifts and His Fruits. This Sacrament is Confirmation.

"But He came to us in Baptism, why does He come again?"

Confirmation perfects the grace of Baptism. "For those who are made children of God by Baptism, like little infants, have a softness about them, but by the Sacrament of Chrism they are made strong against the most violent assaults of the flesh, the world, and the devil, and their souls are confirmed to confess and glorify the name of our Lord Jesus Christ."[1] In Baptism, as a holy Pope says, we are lifted into the camp; in Confirmation we are armed for the battle. Confirmation is promotion. It advances the child of the Christian family to the active service of the Christian army. Those who at Baptism enlisted as recruits are now called to the front.

The new life of grace and innocence which God gave you at Baptism was seen with bitter envy by the devil, and he began at once to lay his plan for destroying it. As you sat on the nursery floor among your toys, trotted about the house, or played with your brothers and sisters, he watched you with cruel eyes, studying carefully the ways and then the words that let him into the secrets of your little heart. He redoubled his watchfulness as reason gradually unfolded. He noticed the use you were beginning to make of your free-will, that dread power of choice for which you then began to be responsible to God.

The battle of your life had begun. You were all but a baby still, but the battle had begun. Nay, earlier even than this it had begun—as soon as you were able to know right from wrong. A great preacher of our own day says it begins on our mother's knee, and that she is bound to watch and train us gently and carefully from the very first.

"The catechism says we don't come to the use of reason till we are seven."

The catechism says it is about that time that we come to the use of reason, so as to be capable of mortal sin. But there has been a great deal going on to help or hinder the salvation of our soul before then. It is when our inclinations and passions first show themselves that it is so important to check what is bad, and guide and strengthen what is good. This is the work of all

1   Catechism of Council of Trent.

who have to do with us when we are quite little, in the nursery, in the school-room, in church, at our games, up and down the house wherever the small feet go. They will have a strict account to give of their charge of us in these early years. Is it fair, then, when we come to know their duty and ours, that we should be so cross, so stubborn, so upset when they try to lead us right? They are doing only what they are bound to do and what will draw upon them terrible punishment if they do not do.

The struggle, then, with our bad inclinations is going on long before we are seven. But after that, the devil begins to lay his plans more carefully and to be bolder in his attacks; studying to see how we are forming our character; what passion is raising its head above the rest; whether it has really come home to us that we are on a battlefield and have to fight for our lives, or whether we suppose that our only business is to please and amuse ourselves and quarrel with everybody who dares to cross us. Hither and thither he follows us, making his notes. Just as our loving Guardian Angel never leaves our side and helps with all his strength by his whispers and his warnings, so does the Evil Spirit track our steps, seeing how he can harm us; how— poor silly things that we are—he can get us *to harm ourselves.*

Years go on, and the fight is getting fiercer. The enemies of our soul are closing round us, trying to win us over to their camp and make us renounce our allegiance to Jesus Christ our King. *Enemies*, mind—not the devil only, but the world and our own evil inclinations. On which enemy, do you think, the devil counts most? Not on himself, strong and cunning as he is. Nor on any example that may lead us astray. No, but on the traitor passions we have within us. Small yet, he knows they will grow with our growth. Temper and greediness, idleness, selfishness, stubbornness—these, if encouraged while we are young, will be his most valuable allies later. So he must lead us to indulge them till they become almost too strong for us to master.

Yes, the battle of life has begun in earnest; soon we shall be in the thick of the fight. For the most perilous part is not when we are quite grown up, but this growing time when we are taking shape fast. It is when our character is forming that the devil watches and meddles, and tries his best that it shall form badly. You know how careful your father and mother are when you are growing, that you shall grow straight; how they try to get you to sit up, not to loll about, not to stand on one leg; how they provide gymnastic exercises of all kinds to strengthen the muscles, that they may all develop as they ought. Think how indignant we should be if any one were, of set purpose, to injure a child at this important time, to try to make it grow up deformed that so its life might be a suffering one. This is what the devil does. He tries in every way to spoil the forming character, that it may be deformed and ugly and bring us, in the end, to that place where all that is deformed and ugly will be for ever.

"But we can't help our character, you know. It's not our fault if we are dull and selfish and cross and lazy. We didn't make ourselves. The catechism says a 'character is a mark *put upon us.*' "

Ah! that's another sort of character. I am talking of our tastes and habits. Do you say we can't help our character! Of course we can help it. To help it is just the work we have to do when we are young. We are to help it as the mother helps the little tottering feet that are taking their first steps. But you have cunningly mixed together two things that are quite distinct, and which we will please keep distinct. You say it is not our fault if we are dull. This may be true, if by "dull" you mean that we have not any very striking talents. But notice that, even in this case, we must do what we can to improve what has been given to us. The slothful servant who hid his talent instead of making the most of it, got a terrible punishment. And notice further, that we are often far too ready to excuse our laziness by taking for granted that we have few talents. Many and many a man and woman who, as children, were set down as dull, stupid even, by those who did not look beneath the surface, have by diligence and perseverance brought to light talents of the highest order, and done for God and for their fellow-men wonderful and glorious things. We never know what we can do till we try; it is by putting out our strength, as the little child does, that we gain strength, and find to our surprise how much we can do.

But granting even that, as "we did not make ourselves," we cannot help being dull, this has nothing to do with our present purpose. Character has less to do with intellect than with will. And our will is free. Character is the result of the choices we are always making; of the way in which we have accustomed ourselves to use our will. It is the sum total of all the habits we have formed. And these habits come from the repetition of single acts. Take for example, our habit of getting up in the morning—we have all got one by this time. Either we spring up like a jack-in-the-box, or we pay no attention, beyond a grumble, to the summons. We stay where we are as long as we can, and then, at last, when we are obliged to make the effort, we drag ourselves out of bed bit by bit, as if we were afraid of coming to pieces. It is a habit now, our way of getting up—a most blessed habit, one that brings a blessing on the whole day, if it is the first way; a most miserable and mischievous one, if it is the other. But both habits have been formed gradually, by single acts.

It is the same with habits of obedience or disobedience, of reverence or irreverence at prayer, of kind or unkind judgments of others. Put all these together and you have character. Who will say now that our character is not of our own making—home manufacture! It is no use for us to label it "made in

Germany." It is nothing of the kind. In my own workshop, with my own tools, by my own labour, my character has been made, and—oh, thanks be to God that I am still young—*is being made!* I can mould it as I like, it is soft in my own hands like the clay I shape into beautiful forms when I am modelling.

"It's easy to make birds'-nests and shells and things, because the clay goes the way you want it; *but we don't.*"

Then you must use a little pressure, just as you do when your clay is getting stiffish. And you must make haste to press it into the right shape before it gets any stiffer. It will never do to let it harden. Then you may break it before you can mould it. Be quite sure that, with God's help, you *can* correct now what is getting out of shape in your character. But do not put off. It will become more difficult every day, for the bad ways will be growing worse.

So you see that, if character meant originally "a mark put upon us," as you say truly, it is we who helped to put it there. The sheep has nothing to do with the great red letter on its fleece that makes it known to its master and perhaps to its fellow-sheep. But we have everything to do with the character that marks us out, and makes us different from every one else in the eyes of God and His Angels, and of those among whom we live.

We cannot, then, afford to get into bad habits, the way to which is doing bad things once, twice, three times.

"It's much easier, I think, to get bad habits than good."

It may be. Yet we have this thought to encourage us— that by every good act we do, whether it is prompt rising in the morning, or forgiveness, or overcoming human respect, or checking impatience, we are helping to form a good habit. The effort will be less each time, and what was hard in the beginning will come to be not easy only, but pleasant. So Holy Scripture tells us if we train ourselves well whilst we are young, we shall keep in the right way when we get older, just as a well-trained horse goes, through habit, along the right road without need of spur or bridle.

"But in the beginning it's hard, isn't it?"

I wonder how many times you bring in that pet phrase of yours, "*It's hard!*" Have we not made up our minds to do what is hard! Do we not see we *must* do it—we have no choice. If we mean to save our souls, we must go in for all that the saving costs. Yet, after all, we *may* say it's *hard*. We may say it to Him Who knows how weak we are and Who pities His poor little children. Instead, then, of saying it to ourselves in a grumpy way, let us lift up our faces to Him in Heaven and say, "*Father, it's hard. Help me. Make haste to help me!*"

It is just to help us at the time in our life when we most need help, that He comes with another Sacrament. He Who made you His children in Holy Baptism has not forgotten you. He knows that, weak and inexperienced, you have to cope with foes that are cunning and strong. And so He comes to the rescue. He comes with a strong Sacrament to arm you for warfare, to give you strength "to extinguish all the fiery darts of the most wicked one."[1]

"At Confirmation," says the Council of Trent, "the soul is prepared for the *encounter*. The sign of the Cross with which it is marked shows that it is entering into the combat of the Christian Camp. The child of God, covered and protected by the Sacrament of Confirmation, as with the strongest armour, enters into the spiritual fight, the reward whereof is eternal salvation."

Like the young knight in the days of chivalry, you are to kneel before the Bishop and be girded with armour that shall be proof against every assault. "*Signo te signo Crucis*," he will say, and Christ our Lord standing by will add: "*In hoc*

---

1   Ephes. 6.

signo vinces. Yes, conquer foes however strong, however wily, however obstinate; conquer them abroad—overcoming the devil and the world; conquer them at home—overcoming self. The time for active service is come, and all that you will need in your warfare is provided. The habits of faith, hope, and charity poured into your soul at Baptism are strengthened in you. Heavenly weapons are put into your hands to enable you to *'fight the good fight of faith'*[1] and bear away the prize of everlasting glory. In the presence of My Glorious Mother and of all the Heavenly Court you stand under My banner splendidly equipped, and your name is registered in the roll-call of My Army."

"I wish we could see and hear all that—it would make us feel very different, you know."

No doubt. But these spiritual realities cannot be perceived by our senses, any more than they can see or hear the grass growing. And supposing they could, what would become of our Lord's promise, "Blessed are they who have not seen and have believed"? This life is a life of faith. Sight will come by-and-by. Your friends will not see you equipped in gleaming armour like the new knight; they will not hear the clank of the new sword, nor the ring of the gilded spurs. But your holy patrons, your faithful Guardian Angel, the Court of Heaven and its Queen—these will see and rejoice. They will behold you clad in *"the armour of God,…having on the breast-plate of justice,…the shield of faith,…the helmet of salvation and the sword of the spirit."*[2] They will see on your brow a sacred character, *"the Sign of the Son of Man"* And oh, how they will pray that you may never be ashamed of that saving sign, but so honour it by your life as to deserve to be owned by Christ as one of His in the tremendous Day of Judgment! "I saw another

---

1   I Timothy 6.
2   Ephes. 6.

CONFIRMATION

from the painting by Giuseppe Maria Crespi

Angel ascending from the rising of the sun, having the Sign of the living God, and he cried with a loud voice to the four Angels to whom it was given to hurt the earth and sea, saying: Hurt not the earth, nor the sea, nor the trees, till we sign the servants of our God on their foreheads."[1] It may be far off yet, but that day will surely come. What it will be to us depends on ourselves now; on the kind of soldiers we prove ourselves in the service of our King.

The devils, too, see that sign—see it and tremble. They know that through the Cross they have been conquered, first by the King and then by the great army—men, women, children, "of all nations and tribes and peoples and tongues"[2] that have followed Him to victory. Pope Leo XIII says expressly it was by their Confirmation that those who were naturally weak became strong: "The same Spirit gives Himself more abundantly in Confirmation, strengthening and confirming Christian life, from which proceeded the victory of the martyrs and the triumph of the virgins over temptations and corruptions."[3]

Your enemies know He is ready to do for you what He has done for these, to make you brave to fight and strong to conquer even as these. But they do not despair. You are not off the field yet—nay, you are only just coming on to it. It depends on your will to use or not the wonderful gifts now bestowed upon you, to put out the power that is in you, or leave it unexerted.

And your will is weak. Oh, pray God's Holy Spirit to strengthen it that you may follow your King seriously, "*not in word and in tongue but in deed and in truth*,"[4] overcoming yourself, denying yourself as all must do who will come after Him. We are in the position of a general who is expected to send to his base of operations when he is in need of provisions,

1   Apoc. 7.
2   Apoc. 7.
3   Encyclical Letter of Leo XIII, Pentecost, 1897.
4   St. John 3.

reserves, ammunition, arms. All these are to be had for the asking and to be had in abundance. But he *must* ask. The Holy Spirit is ready enough to come to you. Yet He likes to be invited and even pressed. If we want His gifts in abundance, we must desire them and ask for them. God speaks to us as if we were little babes. "Open thy mouth wide," He says, "and I will fill it."[1]

Therefore, says the Council of Trent, "very great care ought to be taken lest in a matter so full of holiness and through which the divine gifts are so liberally bestowed on us, any negligence should be committed. For that which God has offered to all for their sanctification is to be desired by all with the sincerest affection."

Yet, the Church goes on to say sadly:

"Very few endeavour to receive the fruit of grace thereby which they ought." She requires children to be taught "that the Sacrament of Confirmation is to be received with the greatest devotion, lest by their fault and to their great hurt this divine benefit may seem to be bestowed on them in vain."

To meet all the needs of our soul at this important time of our life, two great graces are necessary—light for our minds, and strength for our will. And therefore the Sacrament in which the Holy Ghost gives Himself to us is called the Sacrament of *Confirmation*. He comes to strengthen within us the light by which we are to see our road, and the courage with which we are to walk in it.

How the Three Divine Persons love us! The Father and the Holy Ghost no less than the Son, Who loved us unto death. As children of the Father, as brothers and sisters of the Son, as living temples of the Holy Spirit—how They love us!

---

1 Psalm 80.

XI.

The Armoury

*Prepare ye the shield and buckler, and go forth to battle, . . .
stand forth with helmets, furbish the spears, put on coats of mail.*
(Jerem. 46.)

If we were asked to tell the spots in the Holy Land where the love of our Blessed Saviour was shown most strikingly, we should probably name the Stable of Bethlehem, where He was born, the Supper Room on Mount Sion where He bequeathed us the Gift of Love, the Garden of Gethsemani where He faced for us the Agony of death, and the Hill of Calvary where He gave us Mary, His last sigh, and His open Heart.

We think of that Gift in the Supper Room as the tenderest of His gifts, kept for the parting, and we understand why St. John when he begins to speak of It, tells us that "Jesus having loved His own who were in the world loved them to the end." The *end*, as if there were nothing left for Him to give.

And yet, to use His own words spoken of another time, the end was not yet. That Gift of Himself was not the only gift that made the Supper Room what it is to us. There was another, and another as great, another "*unspeakable Gift*" of which perhaps we think too little. What was it?

Look at the Eleven gathered round the Master there. They have made their First Communion and are united with Him as they have never been before. Their love of Him is more tender, more vehement than it has ever been. But that very love is causing them the bitterest anguish. For He has told them that He is going to leave them. They know now what they could not or would not understand before, when He spoke in plain words of a mocking, a scourging, a cruel death that was to come. "They understood not the word and they were afraid to ask Him."[1] But now He is plainly going away, and going to leave them behind. For three years they have followed Him everywhere, but they may not follow Him now. "Whither I go, you cannot come."[2]

Just think what these words meant to them. They had left all things for His sake. They had been taken out of the common thoughts and ways of a fisherman's calling, and lifted into a most wonderful sphere, where miracles from morning till night were the order of the day; where a Divine Life was lived before their eyes; where a Divine Teacher spoke and prayed with them; where they were the chosen companions and friends of Him Whom they knew to be the Christ, the Son of the Living God.

He had come to be everything to them, more than father and mother, more than home and country, all they had ever had or cared to have. They loved Him with a passionate devotion, for every look and word and act of His was ever drawing them to Him more and more. What we sometimes say of others to express a foolish extravagance of earthly love, was literally true of them—*they worshipped Him.*

And they trusted Him with all the strength of their simple natures, with an abandonment that took no thought for self. What did it matter that they had forgotten to take bread with them into the desert? He was there and would provide. And

1   St. Mark 9.
2   St. John 12.

if the waves beat into the ship so that it was filled, what did it matter? He was with them; they had only to wake Him. When the cunning Pharisees came with their clever questions to puzzle them who were so ignorant, what matter? Their Master was listening and would answer for them. Over and over again, His angry enemies had surrounded them, hating them because they belonged to Him—and not a hair of their heads had been touched, because He was by. In His company they feared nothing, neither threats nor persecution, neither governors nor kings, nor the very devils. "Lord, the devils also are subject to us in Thy Name."[1] In His company, poverty was sweet and labour light, and the hatred of the world not worth a thought.

And He was going away! The three blessed years with Him looked like a dream now. They were going to be left alone. The thought bewildered them, and in their helpless terror they cried out to Him not to leave them, not to go, or if go He must, to take them with Him. "Why cannot I follow Thee now?" said poor Peter; "I am ready to lay down my life for Thee." We cannot form any idea of the blank dismay that filled their hearts when they heard He was really going. Oh, how dull life would be without Him! And what was to become of them when He was gone? Who would teach them, comfort, protect them? Had He not spoken again and again of a great work they were to do for Him? Had He not just spoken of twelve thrones on which they were to sit around Him! What did it all mean? Helplessly they looked at Him with hearts too troubled and too full for words.

Poor Apostles! If we feel for them, how much more did He Who saw into their hearts. What amends could He make to His forlorn little flock for the loss He was bringing upon them?

"He couldn't make any because He hadn't anything as

1   St. Luke 10.

good as Himself to give, and He had given them that already in the Blessed Sacrament."

And yet He did find something. It has been said that our Lord never withdraws a gift from us except to give another and a better. However that may be, He found a Gift that night as great and precious as the Real Presence He was leaving with us on the altar.

"Then it must have been God."

It *was* God. He was withdrawing His visible Presence from the world. But He would send His Holy Spirit to take His place, to be to His dear Apostles all that He had been—Teacher, Comforter, Protector, Light and Strength, and Joy that the world could neither trouble nor take away. Let us listen to His tender words:

"Little children,...let not your hearts be troubled. *I will ask the Father and He shall give you another Paraclete,*" that is, Comforter, "*that He may abide with you for ever, the Spirit of Truth...I will not leave you orphans...The Paraclete, the Holy Ghost Whom the Father will send in My Name, He will teach you all things...I go to Him that sent Me, and none of you asketh Me, whither goest Thou?* But because I have spoken these things to you sorrow hath filled your heart. But I tell you the truth: *it is expedient for you that I go, for if I go not the Paraclete will not come to you; but if I go I will send Him to you.*"[1]

You see our Lord speaks of His going away as necessary, as a gain to the Apostles, because the Holy Ghost would not be sent till He had gone.

"All the same I think it must have been a dreadful loss for them to lose our Lord. How could it be a gain for Jesus to go away?"

Only if He came again in another and a better way. He Who was coming to take His place was His own Holy Spirit.

---

1   St. John 14, 16.

The Holy Ghost is "*the Spirit of Jesus*,"[1] the Spirit of the Father and the Son, proceeding from Both, Himself true God, equal to Them in all things.

"I always think it is very hard to understand Who the Holy Ghost is."

No one can understand God but God Himself. He is infinite, and only that which is infinite can comprehend, or take hold of the Infinite. A little child of seven said, in her simplicity, that she quite understood the Blessed Trinity. We shall never, never understand It, because It is a mystery too deep for Angels, or Saints, or the Blessed Mother of God herself to penetrate. The child on the sea-shore, or rather the Angel in the form of a child, who told St. Augustine it was trying to put the whole sea into the hole it had scooped in the sand with its little hands, was a figure of those who expect to hold the Infinite in their finite minds, and to comprehend the Incomprehensible.

But though we cannot understand *Himself* we can understand very much of the gracious work He comes to do for us—*for us*, mind, as well as for the Apostles to whom He was promised. At our Lord's prayer the Holy Spirit was to be sent, and He Himself said at His Last Supper that His prayer was for all His followers to the end of the world. "*Not for them*"—the Apostles, "*only do I pray, but for those also who through their word shall believe in Me.*"[2]

To us, then, this Holy Spirit is promised, and we, like the Apostles, have to prepare ourselves for His Coming.

When our Lord left them on Ascension Day, He sent them at once into retreat to prepare for their Confirmation. The six weeks that had passed since the farewell discourse in the Supper Room where the Paraclete had been promised, had shown them

---

1   Philipp. 1.
2   St. John 17.

how much they needed Confirmation—that is, strength. One of their number had fallen away for ever and left them trembling for themselves. Their head had denied, and they had all forsaken, the Master they thought they could have followed to prison and to death. Even after the Resurrection, they met together with barred doors for fear of the Jews. Surely they needed strengthening if they were to go forth and catch men as their Master had promised.

Strength they needed, and light no less. Their minds were dense and slow, hard to lift up to Heavenly and eternal things. To be first, to be great men in this world, was what they wanted. Of the work they were to do for the Master, what He meant by "catching men," and how they were to set about it, they knew little. They needed, indeed, the Spirit of Wisdom and Understanding and Counsel and Fortitude, the Holy Spirit with His seven-fold gifts that had been promised them.

"Did the Apostles know anything about the Holy Ghost until our Lord told them?"

The Mystery of the Ever Blessed Trinity seems to have been but dimly known to the Jews, if indeed it was known at all. It was reserved for the Law of Love to reveal to us fully the God of love—not only our Father Who is in Heaven, not only the Son of His love, Jesus Christ our Lord, but that Holy Spirit Who is the Love of the Father and the Son. When St. Paul asked some Jews he found at Ephesus, who from being the disciples of John the Baptist had become the disciples of our Lord, if they had received the Holy Ghost, they answered: "We have not so much as heard whether there be a Holy Ghost."[1]

This was the Gift our Lord came to make known to the world, to give to the world. This was His Gift to His own on the last night of His life, that night of gifts. If we make room in our hearts for the Holy Spirit, we shall want for nothing, for

1   Acts 19.

He is the Giver of all good gifts, "*Dator munerum*," the Church calls Him. All good things will come to us together with Him. "*Thanks be to God for His unspeakable Gift!*"[1]

Let us see now what this Holy Spirit, "the Spirit of Jesus," did for the Apostles when they were confirmed on Whit Sunday. They had learned from our Lord many things during their three years of instruction in His school, and they understood, to a certain degree, His doctrines and teaching. But this was not enough for the work to which they were called. Before they could go out as teachers of the Faith, they needed themselves a much more perfect faith and fuller understanding of the truths they were to pass on to others. The Holy Spirit then came *to enlighten them*. But they were to do more than teach. They were to bear witness, by their lives, and by their fortitude in suffering, to the truths they taught. The Holy Spirit came *to strengthen* them for this.

We have only to notice the difference between the Apostles before and the Apostles after Confirmation to see what this Sacrament can do. On the very night of their First Communion one denied, and the rest abandoned their Master. All Good Friday and Holy Saturday they were hiding away, afraid to show themselves lest they should come in for a share of His disgrace and punishment. After the Resurrection, in spite of the good news that He was alive to care for them as before, they remained all frightened together, shut up in the Cenacle "for fear of the Jews."[2]

But after their Confirmation on Whit Sunday—what a change! No more closed doors, no more hiding. Out they came, confessed their faith boldly before their bitterest enemies, and when they were cruelly scourged for the name of Jesus, went away rejoicing. All through the rest of their lives there is not

1   2 Cor. 9.
2   St. John 20.

a trace of fear. "In prisons, in stripes, in shipwreck, in perils of robbers, in hunger and thirst, in cold and nakedness,"[1] they were *filled with comfort abounding with joy in all tribulation*."[2]

With the same fortitude the martyrs professed their faith and died for it, strengthened by the Sacrament of Confirmation. It was this Sacrament which sustained the courage of our own dear English Martyrs. And when persecution went on increasing in severity reign after reign, and priests were hunted down, and no Bishop remained in the land, so that for forty years the Sacrament was not administered, the poor, sorely tried Catholics petitioned the Pope in touching words to remember their need and send them a Bishop, that they might not, by wanting Confirmation, be tried beyond their strength.

A priest giving a retreat recently in an English Convent was told that the little fellow who served his Mass was quite a confessor for the faith. Not more than nine years old, and the child of bigoted parents, he had made his way into the Catholic Church, and in consequence been turned out of doors by his father. An elder brother took compassion on him and gave him a home on condition that he would not be confirmed. The boy, however, having found out that Confirmation was going to be administered in his parish, got instructed, received the Sacrament, and was turned out of his home a second time.

The graces of this Sacrament were never, perhaps, needed more than in these days. We have to profess our Faith at times when it is unfashionable or inconvenient to do so, when we may get ridiculed for it, when family arrangements and other difficulties may stand in the way. The trials, slights, and affronts our faith draws upon us are signified by the little blow on the cheek which we receive at

1   2 Cor. 11.
2   2 Cor. 7.

Confirmation. But before that little blow comes, an outpouring of sacramental grace, enabling us to be true to our Standard— the Cross of Christ—and rather to die than desert from the service, or go over to the enemy by sin.

By the Sacrament of Confirmation we receive a title to the actual graces we shall need in this warfare. These graces, as we have seen, are to give us light and strength. The Gifts that enlighten our minds are: *Wisdom, Understanding, Counsel, Knowledge.* Those that strengthen the will are *Fortitude, Piety,* and the *Fear of the Lord.*

The Gift of Wisdom is a taste or relish for all that has to do with God and holy things. The Latin word for wisdom means *taste, relish.* Things known in this way by experience, have a much stronger effect upon us than those we know by hearsay only. The knowledge of strawberry-jam that I get by taste is very different from what I can get by any description.

"Very."

The same is true of spiritual things. Prayer, Holy Mass, and Benediction, all that belongs to the service of God, is *relished* by those who have the taste for the things of God.

The Gift of Wisdom also makes us see things as God sees them, value them as He values them and no more. A little child is with its father at a review. The father sees over the heads of the crowd, and his face shows now pleasure, now disappointment, now surprise. The poor little child can see nothing. But it watches its father's face, and holds out its arms to him to be taken up into his. What a change! How different everything looks from this height! Its face kindles with interest and pleasure. Now it claps its hands and smiles with delight, now it is frightened. And when it can make nothing of the manœuvres of the soldiers, it turns to its father's face to know what to think of it all. This the Saints do, and those who try to look at things as God looks at them. They see everything from a height. The pleasures, riches, and honours of this world which people in general care so much about, seem of very little account to them—little, that is to say, by the side of the things that lead to God and help us to save our souls. "What is this to eternity?" St. Aloysius used to say of pleasure or pain. And thus he came to set a true value on these passing things.

The Gift of Understanding helps us to see the meaning and the beauty of those truths which we know by Faith. In this way it strengthens Faith. The sight of the little Babe of Bethlehem on the straw makes no impression on the minds of some people. Others, like St. Francis of Assisi, it moves even to tears, making them wish to suffer with Him and for His sake, and so return Him love for love. The first have very little, the others very much of the Gift of Understanding.

The Gift of Counsel teaches us to seek guidance from God before acting in any important matter; to ask, not "What should *I like?*" but "What does *God want* of me here?"

The Gift of Knowledge is the Gift that makes all the creatures, of which we have spoken so often, a ladder by which we get up to God. It makes the sun, the birds, the flowers, things we like, things we do not like, all serve to remind us of God and to praise Him. "It's a hard winter, the Lord be praised," you will hear the poor Irish say. Some of the Saints were very remarkable for this Gift. Everything in their daily life, all that was going on in the world outside, helped them to think of God and to love and praise Him.

The Gift of Fortitude is necessary to every one of us if we would save our souls. Sooner or later trials must come—unkindness, ridicule, failure, the breaking up of home, the loss of those we love. Difficulties will stand in our way from human respect, bad example, and our own bad passions. We shall need the Gift of Fortitude to make us bear up courageously in suffering, deny ourselves bravely, and keep faithful to God in temptation.

We have seen plenty of instances of this manly virtue in the martyrs. But it is not only at the block or the stake that fortitude is wanted. There is room for it in the humblest little home, the least eventful life, the most humdrum duties. At work, at prayer—wherever trouble or difficulty can find us, fortitude must uphold us, or we shall be faithless to our King. It helps us to bear bravely the little frets and worries that fall to our lot day by day, and gives us the firmness we need when great trials come.

The heroic Duchess D'Alençon, who perished in the fire at the Charity Bazaar, May 4, 1897, had asked her confessor for some practice by which to prepare for the Feast of St. Catherine, May 5—some way of following our Lord more closely, she said. All through her novena, she was preparing by little acts of self-sacrifice for a great one, for the heroic act of love, greater than which no man can give. Thus, when the moment came, she was ready. Together with many ladies of the first families in France, she had organized a Bazaar in aid of the Charities of Paris, and had spared neither time nor labour to make it a success.

It was a little after four on the afternoon of May 4, 1897, when the terrible fire broke out. The flames, spreading with frightful rapidity through the building, which was of wood, leaped up and caught the roof and brought it down a mass of fire upon the shrieking crowd below. There was no time to reflect, to make provision. The conflagration, the panic, the rush to the door, were the work of a few seconds. Many were trampled to death by the densely-packed, struggling mass. But one at least was calm. The Duchess, standing by her stall, resisted every entreaty of those who besought her to escape whilst there was yet time. It seemed to her that to remain quietly at her post would give others a chance of escape, that it was her duty therefore to remain. "We must let the visitors go first," she said. "The President must wait till the last. Duty before all. I shall remain." And so, faithful to her habit of self-sacrifice, to her purpose of following her Lord more closely, she remained, and gave her life for others.

Habit, we say, is second nature. In sudden emergencies, when there is no time to take thought beforehand, we behave as we behave habitually, either according to the instinct of nature, as the crowd did here, or by the force of a virtuous habit like this heroic princess. Her fortitude was the work of grace and of a noble, daily correspondence with grace. She was not one whom Paris would have thought equal to so grand a deed. Those who knew her as a girl say she was naturally shy and shrinking, so much so, that on her appearance in the society of the gay capital she was known as "the timid Duchess." Oh, how God loves to show His power in those whom the world counts weak! This force of habit comes out so well in another story that I think we must have it, although, mind, we have no business to get two stories together.

In certain parts of their course, some rivers are rendered dangerous for navigation by rapids. Rocks in many cases obstruct the flow of the water and occasion strong, swift currents that upset any boat coming in their way.

Some years ago a missionary was crossing a river in Africa with one of his black catechumens. At his feet in the canoe lay his single earthly treasure, the box containing his altar furniture. It had been used for his Mass that morning and was to be used again on the morrow, when in the midst of his dear neophytes he was to offer the Holy Sacrifice. They were awaiting him on the opposite bank, and having already caught sight of the canoe, were testifying their joy after the manner of their race by shouting, leaping, and all kinds of antics. Suddenly there was a cry of dismay.

The boat, swerving violently out of its course, had upset, and, keel upwards, was being carried down with the current. For an instant the two men appeared to view—an instant only, before they sank. But in that instant the priest was seen supporting with a supreme effort the black, woolly head, whilst he poured upon it the baptismal water—his only thought in that last moment—to secure for the soul entrusted to his care a footing in the Church Militant, from which it might pass by a swift flight to its place in the Church Triumphant.

God does not require of us acts like these, which are great even in the eyes of the world. He wants us to show our fortitude by resisting light temptations, and strengthening ourselves in good habits, utilising the many little occasions that crop up every day. This will secure for us His special help when great temptations or difficulties come. And should these never fall to our lot, our daily life provides abundant opportunity of bearing with others, bearing *with ourselves*, keeping our peace in worries and unforeseen accidents, or going steadily through tiresome or uninteresting duties; we need not trouble our heads by imagining extraordinary occasions of displaying a fortitude which, in all probability, is not ours to display.

Little teasing troubles may look small beside bigger ones, but they are not small when they fret and worry every day and every hour of the day. Here is the experience of an old Crimean veteran:

"I wur in the trenches afore Sebastopol till I took ill, then I wur sent down to Scutari, which wurn't so bad if you could move your arms or walk about; but to lie, as I seed some poor chaps, wi'out the strength so much as to lift a finger to knock away the flies hangin' round their eyes, an' nose, an' lips—ah! That wur crool, worse nor any fightin'!"

Yes, fortitude is necessary to every one of us, for we have all to fight against the world and the devil. We have all self to fight. Servants need it to refuse situations they could have at the expense of their faith; to bear daily annoyances among fellow-servants who are Protestants; to secure the time necessary for their religious duties in non-Catholic families. Catholic children brought up by non-Catholic parents and guardians need it to keep them firm in the midst of temptations trying to their faith. Workhouse children need it to put up with the taunts of their companions who bid them with a sneer, "Go off to their priest." You, dear children, will need it, every one of you—need its grace over and over again, no matter how quiet your lives may be. To keep to your appointed days for Confession and Communion, needs fortitude; to refuse a sandwich after a dance when Thursday night has melted into Friday morning, needs fortitude; to say "No" to some tempting trinket because a poor dressmaker is not yet paid, needs fortitude. These, you may say, are *duties*, not occasions of heroic sacrifice which you are free to accept or refuse. True, but it is fidelity to duty that makes heroes. Brave perseverance in duty amid difficulties known only to Him "Who seeth in secret"—this is Christian heroism.

The Gift of Piety fills our hearts with a tender, childlike love for our Father Who is in Heaven, makes us cry out to Him in every need, "Abba Father!" and "*as most dear children*"[1] show Him praise, reverence, and obedience. It is the Gift which enables us to love God with all our heart and soul and mind and strength. It makes us eager to serve Him loyally ourselves and to see Him served loyally by others. "He is my Father; all that I can, I will do for Him"—this is its cry. The sight of sin, the hearing of an offence against their Father, sends a thrill of pain through the hearts of His true children, just as we feel sad when we see our mother slighted, or hear our father abused. No punishment will fall on us, but that is not the point. It is no

1   Ephes. 5.

thought of self, but the injury to Him Whom we love that stirs us to sorrow.

The Fear of the Lord. Oh, how little there is of it now-a-days! Why? Is the need less? Did our Lord, Who bade His dear Apostles fear even when He was with them, say there would be no need of fear in our days? Are dangers fewer now than in the past? Or are we stronger and better guarded than those who have gone before us? No, certainly. Why, then, is there so little of the holy, saving Fear of God among us now? We are told that it is a sign of a strong faith. Is faith, then, growing weak? The very thought makes us tremble, for when faith goes, all goes.

When a storm is brewing, the mercury that stood high in the sunshine drops low. So when the storm of temptation sweeps over our soul, the bright love of God seems to sink almost out of sight. This is the time to call holy Fear to our aid. God gives it to us for times such as these. The thought of the punishment of sin will be our safety then. And so St. Ignatius cried: "If ever through my fault I should forget the love of God, at least let the fear of punishment help me not to fall into sin."

If God has given you a great fear of His dreadful punishments, thank Him for it with all your heart; it is a grace to be prized. And a grace to be prayed for. If you have not got it, ask for it, and ask earnestly. You cannot do without it; you are not safe without it; without it you cannot keep clear of mortal sin. Ask, too, for that loving fear of offending Him even in little things, which all His children should have. This fear will keep you from thoughtlessness by making you afraid of *all* sin—of anything that could leave a stain upon your soul and displease the Eye of your Heavenly Father. It will make you dread unfaithfulness to grace—to the whisper of conscience telling you that what you are going to do is wrong, or that God wants something of you which will cost a bit.

"But why must we fear God? I thought He didn't like us to be afraid of Him."

He does not like us to serve Him simply through fear of punishment—this is the fear of slaves. But He wants very much to see in us that childlike fear which makes us dread everything which displeases Him, and behave always with reverence in His Presence when we come before Him in church, or speak to Him in prayer. This reverence is something very beautiful, very attractive. It shows itself in our way of genuflecting before the Tabernacle, in our posture at prayer, in our behaviour to priests, parents—all who in any way represent God and hold His place.

"But doesn't it make people very dull and miserable to be always afraid of God?"

If it does, their fear is not the right kind, it is not the *loving* reverence God wants of them. He is the tenderest of fathers, and to see us frightened, fidgety children, always afraid that He is angry with us, is the last thing He wants. The Angels and Saints in Heaven fear God much more than we do. Are they very dull and miserable?

Perhaps you know two houses. In one, the children great and small treat their father with the affectionate reverence that the commandment, "*Honour* thy father," requires. They love him dearly, trust him perfectly, run to him for whatever they want, are quite at their ease with him. But they never forget themselves. In their behaviour to him, in the way they speak to him, consult his wishes, leave arrangements to him, dread beyond everything what would cause him pain, there is a joyous reverence for him as their father which is perfectly charming. In this house, there is always the peace and brightness of order, of every one keeping in his right place.

In the other house, things are very different. The children treat their father with a kind of condescension that is simply odious. They seem to think that anything like respect in their dealings with him is beneath them. Anyway, there are no signs of the "Honour" which is commanded. That he should look pained, that his feelings should be hurt, does not seem to distress them at all. There is something so unjust, so cruelly wrong in all this, that when we come across it, it is hard to refrain from showing our indignation and disgust.

But to come to the point: Which of these sets of children is the dull and miserable one? You know quite well. Irreverence never yet brought anything but gloom and discontent. If we want to be always joyous, we must do as St. Paul tells us: "*Let us serve, pleasing God, with fear and reverence.*"[1] "*And the rest of His life was joy, and with great increase of the fear of God he departed in peace.*"[2] This was said of the elder Tobias. And of his son: "*And after he had lived ninety-nine years in the fear of the Lord, with joy they buried him.*"[3] See how fear and joy go hand in hand in the service of God!

Has not our King shown Himself liberal in providing our spiritual armour? "Wisdom against folly, Understanding against dullness, Knowledge against ignorance, Counsel against rashness"—these gifts to strengthen us for firm *belief*. And to make us brave and generous in *profession and action*— "Fortitude against fear, Piety against indevotion, the Fear of the Lord against pride."[4]

Speaking of the Gifts and Fruits of the Holy Spirit which are given to us in Confirmation, Leo XIII says: "The Gifts help us to obey more easily and promptly those secret warnings and invitations which from time to time are excited in our minds and hearts by the Holy Spirit, and without which there is no

---

1   Hebrews 12.

2   Tobias 14.

3   Tobias 14.

4   St. Gregory.

beginning of a good life, no progress, no arriving at eternal salvation. These Gifts are so strong that they can lead us to the highest degree of holiness, and are so excellent that they continue to exist even in Heaven, though in a more perfect way...Lastly, there are those blessed Fruits, . . . Fruits filled with all sweetness and joy, inasmuch as they proceed from the Spirit Who is in the Trinity the sweetness of both Father and Son."

He is called by St. Bernard, *the Kiss* of the Father and the Son, because He is the sign of their mutual love. He is called "the Spirit of Jesus Christ."[1] He is called in a very special way *the Sanctifier*. Not that the Father and the Son do not sanctify us, but because the sanctification of our souls is, by a peculiar appropriateness, attributed to Him Who is the Holy Spirit. In His discourse at the Last Supper our Lord "made it clear that the Holy Ghost would complete the work which He Himself had begun in His mortal life...He Who is the Divine Goodness and the mutual love of the Father and the Son, completes and perfects by His strong yet gentle power the secret work of man's salvation."[2] He is called the *Unction* or anointing of the Lord, because as oil is used to consecrate, to soothe and to heal; to cleanse what is tarnished, and to restore to it its first fairness—so does the Holy Spirit work all these effects within our souls.

The grateful love we should have to the Holy Spirit for the benefits with which He has overwhelmed us, should move us especially to fly from sin: *"Grieve not the Holy Spirit of God whereby you are sealed,"*[3] says St. Paul to his converts at Ephesus. Churches consecrated by prayer and holy anointing are set apart for the special service of God, and are to be treated with great reverence as

---

1   Philipp. 1.
2   Encyclical Letter of Leo XIII. Pentecost, 1897.
3   Ephes. 4.

196

His temples. Our souls and bodies are likewise consecrated by the presence of the Holy Spirit. "The Lord is in His holy temple."[1] *"Know you not that you are the temple of God, and that the Spirit of God dwelleth in you? But if a man violate the temple of God, him shall God destroy. For the temple of God is holy which you are."*[2] With what solemn words the Apostle reminds his converts at Corinth that by their Confirmation they have become the temples of God, and that this temple, body and soul, is to be kept with the reverence due to the dwelling-place of God.

The holy chrism is oil mixed with balsam, a precious plant of Eastern lands. Its fragrant resinous juice, which soothes, heals, and saves from corruption, testifies the preservation from sin and the sweet odour of sanctity imparted by the Holy Spirit to the soul.

The imposition of the Bishop's hands signifies the communication to your soul of the sacramental grace as well as your reception among the ranks of the soldiers of Christ.

You know what the little blow signifies—that very gentle substitute for the "accolade" under which the new knight used to reel. It denotes not so much blows *to be dealt* in the coming fight, as those which the soldier of Christ, in imitation of his King, is called upon *to receive* with meekness and patience.

We are told that, in countries where the new soldiers of Christ are converted savages, the Bishop frequently enforces this lesson of patience by making the blow something more worthy of the name, so that with the vigorous stroke there may be got into those thick heads an experimental knowledge of what as Christians will be expected of them. It would be sad if the Church had to extend the same practice to us!

True soldiers pride themselves on their powers of endurance

1   Psalm 10.
2   1 Cor. 3.

—their strength in bearing blows as well as in dealing them. They do not disguise their contempt for those who make much of "a mere scratch." Am I a true soldier or not?

Perhaps there came into our baby hands at one time or another a box labelled "Soldiers." The military were wrapped up in cotton-wool and needed careful handling. They were not over steady on their legs, and were never meant to see fire. To afford amusement to babies was their only end and object. Are *we* content to turn out to be sham cotton-wool soldiers such as these, fit for nothing but to be the devil's playthings, serving for his diversion? Is it for this that our appointments have been so handsomely provided?

In olden times the young and inexperienced knight would single out in the camp some doughty warrior for special admiration and imitation. His patron would be to him the embodiment of all that was noble and chivalrous—his ideal soldier, following in whose footsteps he might learn the practice of arms and approve himself to the King.

By this last gift to us on our knighting—of a special patron and protector in the warfare before us, one who, having passed through it in safety, is now ready to lend us a helping hand—the Holy Spirit has surely completed our equipment. What is now to hinder us from *"marching on all well-appointed to war"*? If only we do our part, God will take care of us and bring us safely through every danger: "He will overshadow thee with His Shoulders and under His wings thou shalt trust."[1] *"A thousand shall fall at thy side, and ten thousand at thy right hand, but it shall not come nigh thee."*[2]

Holy Spirit, come to me with the Seven Gifts and the Twelve Fruits that will make my soul beautiful and pleasing in

1   Psalm 90.
2   Psalm 90.

Your sight. Come and change me as You changed the Apostles. I am poor and weak and wounded. I am cold, stubborn, sin-stained. Come, Holy Spirit, and mend in me all that is amiss.

Come to me, Spirit of Jesus, and make me a true Soldier of Christ, following my Leader, "not in word, nor in tongue, but in deed and in truth."[1] Make me strong against temptation like Him; obedient like Him, and like Him meek and humble of heart, that He may not be ashamed of me when He comes with the holy Angels at the Last Day. Make me receive fervently this holy Sacrament that I can receive only once. Let the character that it will stamp on my soul be a mark of glory to all eternity. Make me a Catholic, strong in my faith to the end of my life, and a Catholic worthy of my faith.

---

1   St. John 3.

XII.

RECONNOITRING

I will pursue after my enemies and overtake them.
(Psalm 17.)

"I AM glad we have come to the enemy at last! I want to see some fighting; battles are so exciting, you know."

They are, and your military ardour is quite inspiriting. Take care it does not evaporate. We shall want it all presently.

Yes, we are really on the field now and are going to fight—But what?

"The enemies of our Lord, of course."

But where? Not now on the plains of Syria. If we were all ordered off there to meet the Turks, I am afraid many of us would turn tail and the Christian Army would show a very poor front indeed. No, we have not to go abroad to find the foe. Ours is a civil war and has to be carried on at home. We shall, it is true, be called upon to fight our Lord's battles in the world—to stand up for our religion, to show we disapprove of what is wrong. But whether we do this with credit to Him and to ourselves, depends on the practice we have had upon the enemy at home.

In the early part of the Middle Ages, when men looked upon war as the business of life, boys began their military training whilst they were mere children; practice in the tilt-yard was the main part of their education.

So it is now with the baptized child. The sooner the little hands learn to handle their spiritual weapons, the better. Some, quite children, like St. Agnes, have been skilful enough to overthrow the enemy, not in their own hearts only, but in the world outside, and make strong men and cruel tyrants own themselves vanquished.

We must begin our apprenticeship, then, in good time. How? That is what we are to see now. If we want to go to a place across the country, we get our Bradshaw[1] and make out the times and changes of our various trains. If we are soldiers in battle, we fight on a plan that has been well thought out. To take the first train that we find at the station and trust to its landing us at our destination, or to shoot at random, attacking no particular part of the enemy's line, would be acts worthy of a lunatic.

Now, it stands to reason that in the all-important journey we are making, in the battle on which our eternity depends, we must show at least as much common sense as we put into the concerns of everyday life. We must have a plan in our mind. We must know *what* we are going to do and *how* we are going to set about it.

Again: To succeed in any business, we must give our mind to it. If the business is difficult, it must be our whole mind, because when the attention is divided, the work suffers. Therefore the general rule is—one thing at a time.

"We have to draw with both hands at once now."

True, and the feat is easy enough when both are working out the same form, the two sides of a free-hand copy, for example. But not easy when the forms are totally different,

1   Bradshaw's Railway Time Tables. First published in 1839, "a Bradshaw" came to refer to any railway timetable, regardless of its publisher.

e.g., a circle and a square. Here the division of attention makes the guidance of the two movements difficult. Not many of us are Landseers,[1] able to draw a dog with one hand and a deer with the other.

Our forces being limited, we are taught to consider concentration of mind—the power of fixing all its attention upon one point—as a very valuable faculty and the main secret of success.

Let us apply this to the work before us. We are going to fight our Lord's battles in our own soul, and we must set about it in an orderly way if we are to do any good.

You remember that the tastes or inclinations which we call passions hurry us on in different directions—towards the things we like, away from those we do not like. Instead of following the safe, common-sense rule—"use what helps as long as it helps; don't use what hinders"—they urge us to follow the rule the enemy gives us: "Do just what you like whether it harms you or not." Plainly, then, these passions of ours are on the enemy's side; they are his allies, always running over to his Camp and betraying us to him. We must keep a sharp eye upon them and a strong hand, or they will be the ruin of us.

Now, among these traitors there is an arch-traitor. He is said to be the predominant one, that is the lord and master of the rest. They follow his lead and serve under him as vassals, always ready at his beck and call.

"I should think the shortest way to conquer them all would be to conquer him."

Exactly. It seems scarcely necessary to prove what your clear common sense sees for itself. Holy Scripture tells us that

---

1   Sir Edwin Henry Landseer (1802-1873) was an English painter who was known for his paintings of animals, and was rumored to have been able to work simultaneously with both hands.

when the King of Assyria went to war with Achab, King of
Israel, his orders to his captains were: "*Fight ye not with small
or great, but with the King of Israel only.*"[1] The King was killed
"*and the fight was ended that day.*" The victories which made
Napoleon the king-maker of Europe were gained by his habit
of concentrating all his forces upon one point. He did not
attack a place at many points; one was enough. He found out
the weakest and brought all his forces to bear upon that. This
was the secret of his success. Where he learned it, is not for us
to inquire. But it is just possible that his wonderful military
genius noticed the tactics of a very old fighter, one who has
been at war ever since the world began—aye, and before.

This is just the devil's plan—to find out weak places and
come down hard upon them. He will not waste his time and his
strength in besieging all round. One place, the weak place—he
makes straight for that. All his batteries are raised against that:
all his guns point to that: all his forces camp before that. Not
every minute, mind, not always openly—that would only be
the signal to the garrison for a more wary watch and a more
determined resistance. But he has this point always in view,
he returns to it always, his hope is there—"If I enter at last," he
says, "it will be there."

Can we not take a lesson from our enemy? "We are not
ignorant of his devices."[2] If it is worth his while to attack our
weak point with all his force, it must be worth our while to put
out all our strength in its defence.

"Then why don't we?"

Why indeed! The first thing to be done is to find out the
passion which is our chief danger. In some cases this is not
hard. But often enough, it takes a good deal of skill to come
up with the enemy, because of his wonderful cleverness in

1   2 Paral. 18.
2   2 Cor. 2.

throwing us off the track. Hear what Lord Wolseley says:

"By tapping the wires, the enemy can often learn the plans that are being made to capture his party. Immediately before or after an action he may deceive to any extent by this means; messages can be sent ordering you to concentrate upon wrong points, or by giving you false information he may induce you to move as he wishes."[1] Again:

"The commander must determine which are the important parts—the keys, as they may well be called, of the position. He should, for the moment, imagine himself in the enemy's place, and arrange in his own mind what he would do if he were the assailant instead of defendant. Reflections of this nature will cause him to realise his weak and his strong points, and enable him to make his arrangements accordingly. He should then set to work to strengthen himself artificially. A few hours' work bestowed on a village or farmhouse may turn the scale in his favour...Posts of this nature add immensely to the strength of a position, but as the enemy must take them at all hazards, one must be prepared for the toughest struggle for their possession."

"I see what all that means."

Very good. *We* cannot afford to remain in ignorance of the enemy's plans, and any amount of time and trouble is well spent that enables us to know exactly how we stand.

One afternoon in 1885, two soldiers of the camp at Korti[2] were sent out as scouts. Cavalry vedettes had come into camp reporting that they had seen small bodies of the enemy a few miles out. Orders were therefore given for an infantry patrol to reconnoitre along the bank of the Nile.

Two miles out of Korti the scouts came across a ragged Arab resting under a date-tree. He started up at their approach

1   *The Soldiers' Pocket-book.*
2   A town in Sudan.

and holding out his hand came forward with

"*Backsheesh, nin*" (alms, sir).

Taking pity on him, one of them gave him a piastre, for which he received a profusion of thanks in Arabic. Next day two officers were strolling through the camp. One said to the other:

"See that Arab coming along there? That man will make a name one day."

It was the Arab beggar of the previous night, a man named Kitchener, at that time an English spy, now the Sirdar of the Egyptian army.

"What on earth was he doing so far from the camp?"

Spying. Getting information as to the enemy's doings and plans, putting two and two together and thus coming to a conclusion on which to frame his own plans. The splendid victories of Atbara and Omdurman which, in 1898, overthrew the power of the Mahdi, had been long and silently prepared. Fourteen years before, you see, he had been on the enemy's track. No device came amiss to him, no danger stopped him. As to trouble, it was not worth a thought. Any work that would make him more useful to the Intelligence Department must be undertaken as a matter of course. The African sun had burnt him to such a dark hue that he had no difficulty in disguising himself as a native. In this way he obtained much valuable information. But, of course, his disguise would be useless without a knowledge of Arabic. So he picked up the native dialects to help the service in Egypt, as he had learned Hindustani when serving in India. He named his two Arab horses "Said" and "Mahommed," to make himself popular with the Sheikhs. He smoked their *narghile*— the Turkish pipe, and was seen in their tents squatting on the divan by their side, whilst he chatted away in Arabic. More than this. A knowledge of the Koran might help him to understand their ways of thinking and acting; he therefore set to work to get up the book of the Prophet, and at the Viceroy's receptions at Cairo, when all around were engaged in light conversation with the ladies, he would be seen studying a well-thumbed Arabic volume which contained selections from the Koran.

"It must have been horribly dry and stupid."

It was a means to the end, and that was all the soldier thought of.

"That man deserved to conquer."

Why should we not take a lesson from him and imitate his thoroughness in everything he undertook, his contempt for difficulty, his determination to understand through and through the enemy he had to tackle.

On the necessity of reconnoitring and scouting, Lord Wolseley says:...But no, we must really be getting on and not stop to quote any more.

"Oh, please, let us hear what he says. It is not waste of time, you know, for we can see the sense of it all."

That is a consideration certainly. And perhaps you are right. Our military education is of vast importance, and we could hardly have a better instructor than a Commander-in-Chief. So we will take his lessons as occasions serve, on the understanding that you *see the sense of them all.*

"No body of troops, from an army down to a company, should march without being covered by an advanced guard. Its object is to ascertain where the enemy is and what he is about, so that he cannot possibly take it unawares. A commander must get information of the enemy's whereabouts and doings, if possible of his intentions. This intelligence he gets by means of patrols. He must examine the hollow ways that cover the approach of an enemy, and consider all the points from which he is most likely to be attacked...By reconnaissances and scouting every movement of the enemy should be ascertained, and his intentions divined and reported to the General Officer commanding the army. One of the most effective means of learning the whereabouts and doings of an enemy is by means of balloons. Ascents by night are most useful for this purpose, as the fires indicate the enemy's position, and his numbers may be roughly estimated by allowing ten men to each fire."

Suppose, then, we turn into patrols and scouts, and sally forth to see what information we can pick up for the Intelligence Department. The enemy is sure to be hiding, remember. We must keep a sharp lookout and be prepared to come upon him in the most unexpected places.

Some of us are brimful of pride and vanity. We value ourselves a great deal for our birth, wealth, dress, appearance, or talents, and worry ourselves with the thought of what other people think of us. Our own concerns engross us completely, and in conversation we are wonderfully fond of the small pronoun "I." We are greedy of notice and want to be first always. We are anxious to excess when our reputation is at stake. We recall again and again the public scenes in which we came off well. On the other hand, a mistake which makes us look awkward or foolish upsets us to such a degree that we forthwith lose our peace of mind and temper, and settle down into the dumps for the rest of the day. We contradict flatly, and refuse to see the truth when it is as plain as a pike-staff. We easily find fault with others, and cannot bear a word of reproof ourselves. If we fall into a fault that there is no denying, we fall into ten more in our vexation with ourselves. We undertake great things eagerly, imagining ourselves strong enough to make head against all difficulties. But when these come, we lose heart and give up all for lost. We are much given to amusements, to enjoyment, to seeking our own convenience, and not given at all to anything in the shape of self-denial.

Is the enemy here?

Some of us are slow even to laziness. Everything like an effort is too much trouble for us. We are too tired to get up when called in the morning; too tired to examine our conscience at the end of the day; too lazy to fix our attention at prayers or at class, or to study with real application. We are content to do nothing but dawdle about and waste our time in idle talk. We are careless about order and cleanliness, letting things go anyhow. Needless to say, we are too inert to attack vigorously any one of our failings, least of all the sloth which, if we may judge by symptoms, is likely to prove our predominant fault.

We do not easily warm to good; are slow in undertaking it and easily give it up; are changeable and faint-hearted and afraid of every difficulty. Among the things we are slow in is obedience—wonderfully slow of hearing, slow in moving, slow in doing what we are told—but alas, quick enough in grumbling, in answering back. We are unwilling to show respect; to do little services; to set aside our own likes and put ourselves to inconvenience for the sake of others. And the little we do in the shape of kindness is spoilt by the bad grace with which we do it.

Any signs here of the enemy?

It is unpleasant to own to it, but it is a fact, that some of us think a great deal more than we should care to publish about good things to eat and drink. Whatever pocket-money we have to spend, goes in this direction, and never by any chance finds its way into the poor-box or the offertory-plate, except on those public occasions when we are "expected to give." "Dainty," "wasteful," "greedy," "discontented," are ugly adjectives, but we know by our own experience what they mean.

Anywhere here?

Then there are the gloomy and the silent, the world's injured ones, always in "the blues," always going about like martyrs; misunderstood by every one, and without a good word for any one; full of harsh thoughts and judgments, full of suspicions; with no interest in anything outside the narrow rut in which they move; little grateful for the kindness and forbearance of those around them whom they try horribly; cross-grained and testy; finding fault with everybody; only able to see the worst side of things; living in the dismals, and resisting every effort to pull them out.

Perhaps the foe is here, hidden in the darkness.

No? Then we may belong to the class of explosives, who blow up at a touch; whom no one dares to knock up against; who are convinced that the only way of looking at things is their way, and therefore the right way, and who are naturally indignant at the stupidity of those who cannot see this at once. If any one rashly attempts to have an argument with them, there is a flare up. They are cock-sure of everything at first sight, and are never troubled with those second thoughts which the proverb says are the best. Parents and masters have a difficult time of it with such as these.

Any hopeful signs here?

Some amongst us can never see any good in others, are annoyed at any little preference or applause their good looks, cleverness, success—good behaviour even—procure them, and consider this as an injury to ourselves. We have a habit of watering down the praise we hear with little unkind insinuations. There is a drop of bitterness in all we say of others who have done well and outshone us. In fact, blame comes readily to our lips at all times and praise, rarely. Clever enough at spying out our neighbour's faults, we are strangely blind to his good points. We make mischief by telling people what others have said of them, and spread stories that injure our companions and superiors. This jealousy and selfishness is one of the first faults to show itself in the nursery. As soon as a baby emerges from the stage in which everything goes into its mouth, and is set down on the floor to play with another baby, it must have all the best balls or dolls, all the red toys for itself. Nay, there are some little dogs-in-the-manger whose pleasure consists not so much in having things themselves, as in keeping them out of the reach of everybody else. Woe to the younger brother or sister who comes to share with them the good things, the fondling, the notice they once enjoyed alone! And woe to themselves too, poor little souls! For unless those about them are wise enough and *kind* enough to check these risings of envy and jealousy, there are plenty of miserable hours waiting for them long after nursery days are over.

Among the faults which we find in our daily examination of conscience, we can generally single out one which seems to be the most frequent, the most dangerous, the chief and root of all the rest. What is it that I found at once in my examen of conscience last night, and the night before, and the night before that? And last month, and last term? What is it that my conscience reproaches me with most, that my father or mother, masters or mistresses take me to task for oftenest, that I take oftenest to confession? What do my companions complain of most? So-and-so, to whom I unfortunately trusted my secrets in a moment of weakness—what did he say when he turned upon me? It upset me frightfully at the time, I have scarcely got over it yet. *But was it true? Am* I spiteful, vain, greedy? If parents, and masters, and the school were allowed one minute to discover my predominant fault, what would be shouted out when the minute was up? What am I afraid it would be? What is that fault, the disappearance of which would make all the difference in my life? About which I say: If I were rid of that I could go on swimmingly. Or: It's no use, I can't overcome it. *It's my nature.* What will be the chief cause of my Purgatory? I must force myself to answer these questions—they are the scouts sent here and there to force the enemy out of cover. I could answer them in behalf of a friend who should ask me to do him this favour. I must befriend myself; I must do myself this service.

Another plan. What is the one thing I will not own to? I may have this fault or the other, *but that one, no, no!* Now, it is more than likely that that one is the very enemy I am in search of.

What is the one thing I am most down upon in others? For, by a strange inconsistency in human nature, this is likely to be my own fault.

One way of coming up with the enemy is lying in ambush for him. We do not go in pursuit, but hide quietly in his whereabouts, wait till he is passing and then dart out upon him. Some morning, I find myself stirred with sudden and unwonted cheerfulness. I go about singing and skipping, and am full of benevolent feelings for every one I meet. I feel this is indeed a sunny world, in which all sensible people are bubbling over with happiness. Very good. Now in the midst of these reflections, I pull myself up to ask where this overflow comes from. I trace it to its source. There were no signs of it at twelve o'clock. What has happened since that has so elated me? A word of praise that tickled my vanity, some notice, or preference, or victory over a rival—is the cause here? To-morrow comes. And lo! Instead of being on the heights as yesterday, radiant, and full of benevolent schemes, I am down in the depths; the world is once more a valley of tears, and we are all wretched children of Eve. Perhaps we are, but why since yesterday particularly? What has changed the face of all things? I have clearly lost my peace somewhere, and I must go back in search of it. I was all right till the afternoon, when So-and-so was elected captain of the football team instead of me. Any clue here?

One swallow does not make a summer, and one instance does not tell much. But if I find that my spirits go up and down with every breath of praise on the one hand or blame on the other, is not the enemy coming clearly to the front and showing himself without disguise?

Surely we have come up with the enemy now? You look pretty bright all of you, so I think our reconnoitring must have been fairly successful. But in case of disappointment there is still one means left—one that rarely fails to bring us face to face with the enemy.

"Without our having to think! That's jolly."

To find out our predominant fault, we must think about it of course, and this is what none of us like. But here our neighbours will help us.

I can go to my master and say, "I want to find out my predominant fault, will you, please, help me?"

"Oh, but he might tell us, you know!"

And save us no end of trouble.

"*I* needn't go, anyway, because he would be sure to say I'm lazy."

"And *I* needn't, because I know I get into tempers."

"And there's a fellow in the school *I* can't stand anyhow. The very look of him is enough for me, to see him coming along with his hands in his pockets and his ridiculous airs. I can't bear to hear him laugh, or to see him enjoy himself, and I am always glad when he gets a good snub, or does badly in his exams, or is bowled for a duck at cricket."

"Could we have *all* the bad things you said? I feel as if I had."

Scarcely. Children's faults, we are told, are as thick as blackberries, but any child so plentifully supplied as to have all we have been talking about would be a prodigy. Besides, it is not easy to be hot and cold, a racehorse and a snail at the same time. Anyhow those faults cannot all be the *predominant* one, and it is with that only we are concerned just now. So if you have not discovered your *chief* failing, you have not come up with the foe. It is one thing to say: "He is somewhere in that direction," and quite another to come to the touch.

But I think you will all own that we have come up with him. Our scouting has not been in vain. We see now where we stand, and this is no slight advantage. When the Duke of Wellington was asked at a dinner-party if he had had a good view of the Battle of Waterloo, he replied drily, "I generally like to see what I am about." So did St. Paul, that clear-sighted, vigorous soldier of Christ. *"I so run, not as at uncertainty, I so fight not as one beating the air."*[1] When a lecture is given on Venice or Rome, and the magic-lantern throws a picture on the screen, the operator should focus it so that the outlines and colours stand out sharp and distinct. The spectators will hiss if it is misty and blurred. Most people resemble the old Duke in that they like to see what they are about. We do. We are focusing now. For a long time, we have been looking at pictures which concern us greatly, pictures of the great realities which we shall soon see clearly in the light of the other life; frightening pictures—the Wicked Chieftain and his black banner; beautiful pictures—the True Leader and His Standard. And now we have come to a picture of ourselves, not over beautiful certainly, but extremely interesting. It has to be focused. You must move the lens this way and that till you see yourself standing out with startling distinctness. Never mind if the portrait is a bit startling at first. You will get used to it, and meanwhile the vividness will do you a world of good, and clear away, as a good picture always does, a number of misty notions and misconceptions. A clear sight of ourselves is the

1   I Cor. 9.

first thing necessary to us in our spiritual warfare.

Our talks have all been tending to the point we have reached now—the knowledge of our chief danger in the work of our salvation, of that weak place which all who love us and all who hate us are watching with such concern. "If I get them," says the devil, "it will be through that weak spot in the defences." "If they are to get to Heaven," our Guardian Angels say, "that weak place will have to be strengthened." We must concentrate our forces there and prepare for a fight. At the same time, we have to guard against a snare carefully prepared for us here—a dreadful pitfall into which numbers of unwary ones slip. Once face to face with the enemy, they get so discouraged that there "is no spirit left in them." Now spirit, *pluck*, the quality for which our soldiers are so remarkable, is absolutely necessary for us. If that goes, all goes. So instead of calling out with the servant of Eliseus when he "saw an army round about and horses and chariots, 'Alas, alas, alas, my Lord; what shall we do?' "[1] we must get well into our heads that seeing our enemy is of immense service to us. The horses and the chariots were there before the servant saw them, but the sight made him cry for help.

Neither must we be so ashamed of what we see in ourselves, as to conclude straightway that God can never make anything of *us*, therefore it is no use our trying. We are only beginners and must expect to have our work before us; we are raw recruits and, of course, have to be drilled. None of us, surely, are so absurdly conceited as to suppose we are perfect to begin with. Failures of every description come out as thickly in our examen of conscience as on the Division Lists after the examination. If we happen to have failed there, any one who knows our number can tell our weak points exactly. But this does not crush us. We try again.

1   4 Kings 6.

214

A glance down the Cambridge "Rowing Notes" shows how freely University crews are criticized and the faults of individuals shown up. Also how much is made of a vigorous beginning.

"Trial Eights have been doing plenty of work this week, and are beginning to learn how to work hard.

A rather serious fault, which can be cured by experience more than anything else, is that men either will not or are afraid to row themselves out. They do not lay themselves out to work over the first half of a course as they ought to. Of course, it is very nice to see a crew take the boat in to the finish with a good spurt; it is, however, a doubtful compliment to say that a crew rowed the last half of a course very well, as it probably means that they sugared over the first half.

"G. is still very much inclined to hang; he is very slow getting his blade covered, and has a clumsy finish.
N. is slow with his work at the beginning.
S. has shown a good deal of improvement.
C. is heavy with his shoulders, which makes him very slow, and inclined to hang at the beginning.
B. lets the boat run away from him, as he is slow in applying his work; he is a sound worker over both ends of a course.
W. is rather too dreamy, and lacks life and smartness both at the beginning and at the recovery; he is quite a sound worker.
M. is still very stiff, and keeps his arms straight too long; for a young oar he promises very well.
S. work is good; he ought to be an extremely useful oar.
G. is a sound worker; he does not use both legs equally and at the same time, so does not swing straight back. He might be quicker getting his blade into the water at the beginning.

However, the crews have come on considerably; they have a better idea of getting hold of the beginning of the stroke, and the rhythm is fairly good, though at times the men get flurried and tumble forward."

How should we like to be shown up in print like this—as "rather rough though improved a good deal;" "having a clumsy finish;" "slow with our work;" "rather too dreamy," and "lacking life and smartness;" "very stiff," &c., &c. Yet the noting of defects is the only way to their removal. Like the Cambridge crews, we must be prepared to find ourselves full of faults. The great thing is to bear the sight of them with a brave heart and not to "get flurried and tumble forward."

Many girls go unflinchingly through an ordeal that must be trying in the extreme. Before the eyes of experts they give their lessons of arithmetic, history, geography, knowing that every detail of matter, manner, and method, every look, word, and act is being scrutinized, every defect noted, that they may be called to task for it later. No fault is passed over by the critics. And the students do not mind, or rather do not appear to mind in the very least. Their thoughts are so fixed on the object they have in view, that they are ready for all the mortification and labour they must go through to attain it. What is more, the criticisms, however severe, are taken *brightly*. Anything like huffiness or wounded feeling is looked upon as something so foolish and ill-bred that the offender is soon shamed into learning self-control.

We may take it for granted, I think, that the enemy is discovered. This is the first step. On the second all depends. Let us hear the Commander-in-Chief's instructions.

XIII.

Sharpshooting

Fight ye not with small or great, but with the King of Israel only...
And an arrow struck the King,...and the fight was ended that day.
(2 Paral. 18.)

"If you content yourself with watching the enemy when you come in his presence, sending your commander word that 'The enemy is in my front,' you will never do any good. Don't rest satisfied until you have pinched him well. The wider the extent of country over which you can establish the pinching process the better...Hold on stoutly like a bulldog to your enemy when you have caught hold of him: If he shakes off your grip along one particular part of his line for the time being, hold on to him all the tighter at other places. You may even have at times to gallop to escape capture; but at once when his pursuit ends, turn round and worry him again and if you cannot seize him in front, try to catch him behind."

When the Americans were scouring the seas in every direction for the Spanish fleet, and the papers repeating week after week: "No news of the fleet," every one knew that when the hide-and-seek came to an end, a tough struggle would follow as a matter of course. It did follow. There was the attack in the harbour of Santiago, and then the announcement everywhere in big letters, "Total destruction of the fleet."[1]

Our attack must follow as a matter of course, and a vigorous one it shall be, like that of the Americans. We must come to close quarters with the enemy and train our guns well. One of the despatches at that time was the following:

> SIBONEY, Monday.
> The bombardment of Santiago was renewed to-day. The orders to the artillery were to select special points in the enemy's lines for attack. There was to be no haphazard volleying. The machine guns were not to be used, and the infantry were only to pick off the enemy's sharpshooters. These orders were implicitly carried out.

How terribly earnest earthly warfare is! Ours may look paltry beside it. And yet ours is more important by far. The result of ours will be lasting on and on in eternity, when the bombardment of Santiago will be as though it had never been.

Sighted, by some of you sharp ones, are the enemies: *Laziness in the morning, Temper,* and *Dislikes.* Here, then, are three special points of attack.

No. 1 is to mark down *Laziness* and to pick it off remorselessly whenever it shows itself. Here is anything but a paltry foe, since it is probably accountable for all the faults and troubles of the day. How, gallant soldier, are you going to take aim? It is no use saying, "I'm not going to be lazy any more. I'm going to turn over a new leaf and be up like a lark." This is haphazard volleying. You must go into details, and make your resolution—not upon the fault itself, but upon the *means* you are going to take to overcome it: such prudent means as you would give to a friend whose amendment in this particular matter you had much at heart.

---

1   The Battle of Santiago de Cuba in 1898 was the largest naval engagement of the Spanish-American War and resulted in the destruction of the Spanish Fleet.

Of course you jump out of bed as soon as you are called in the morning?

"Well, I can't say I do always."

Not always, but as a rule, excepting when you are ill.

"Well, I don't think I do. But I say some prayers over-night to the Holy Souls to get me up in the morning. And when I'm called I begin to give my first thoughts to God, as the Catechism tells us. Sometimes last winter I remembered, when I was up, that I hadn't given them, so I got into bed again to do it."

Very good. Now just make this little change. Jump out of bed the instant you are called, and give your first thoughts to God *on the floor*.

"Oh, but I couldn't do that, I am too sleepy."

What makes you so sleepy—what time do you go to bed?

"I *go* to bed at ten, but I read a good long time before I go to sleep."

Make a resolution not to read in bed. If you do, you will never be ready to get up when you are called. Don't take a book to bed with you. Leave it downstairs, anywhere out of reach.

"I couldn't do that. And I really can't get up when I'm called. I've tried over and over again."

Alas, alas! Where has all the bravery gone to and the desire "to see some fighting"? Here is what you want to see, and may see as soon as you open your eyes every morning. Real fighting it is. Napoleon used to say that most men are brave, but there was one sort of courage, the rarest of all, which he could seldom light upon even in his best men—"two-o'clock-in-the-morning-courage." Shall not our Lord's soldiers be able to show six-or-seven-o'clock-in-the-morning-courage?

"I've tried, and I can't."

Hush! Never use that word; it is most unmilitary, and forbidden in both camps. If the wind should waft it into the enemy's now, you would have reason to repent it. No peace for those whom he finds saying "can't." He has all his own way with them, and twists them round his fingers as you twist a bit of rag. We must have no "can'ts," please. When Napoleon determined to descend on Italy by crossing the Great St. Bernard, and take an army of 30,000 men with their heavy guns over a mountainous track unsafe for all but the sure-footed chamois, every one, except his soldiers, said: "He can't." He himself thought fit to consult his engineer on the subject.

"Is the route practicable?" he asked.

"Barely, sire."

"Forward!" said the First Consul.[1]   And the march was commenced.

"But you told us once that his poor men were blown over the precipices like snow-flakes. It's very fine to talk and then let other people do all the hard things when they come."

Just what *I* thought when you expressed that wish to see some fighting. But please notice that *our* Leader does not ask us to be blown over precipices like snow-flakes. On the contrary, it is to save us from danger that he bids us fight *Laziness* and the other enemies that will overcome us unless we overcome them...No answer? You want, you say, to overcome this fault which you feel to be at the root of all the others—and you will take *no means whatever?*

No. 2 has orders to "pick off" *Temper,* by which we mean the tendency to explode on the very smallest hitch, annoyance, disappointment, or word of blame. He must be quick in taking aim, for his opportunity comes and goes like a flash. The moment you find yourself excited or vexed, No. 2, check the word that rushes to your lips. Check it by such a prayer as, "Jesus, meek and humble of Heart, make my heart like Thine," or any other aspiration or means you like—but *check* it. You

---

1   This was Napoleon's title at the time.

may feel boiling over; that word will choke you unless you say it—*check it.* Say to it firmly: "*Thou shalt not.*" But it will relieve you, stop unfairness, teach So-and-so to keep his place, prevent your being sat upon in future—all the same, *check it:* "*Thou shalt not.*"   Nothing said at boiling-point ever did any good. Not till the geyser within has sunk down again will it be safe for you to open your mouth. It will take an effort—and a great effort—to control yourself, but it is the only way to fight your battle, and the effort will be less each time. When you are cutting through a piece of mill-board, there is hard work at first, but each time the knife passes along the ruler, the groove deepens, the knife runs more easily, till at last—it is through! Your work is done. So it is with the formation of habits.

"But I couldn't stand there like an idiot, saying nothing."

Why not?

"Because people would provoke me more, or think me a saint."

No fear of that just yet.

"But how would *you* like to stand there, making your aspirations, and everybody wondering what had come over you?"

Not any more, child, than you like it. I should have to make that same effort and pray for grace as you must do.

"I couldn't do it, I'm sure I couldn't, I must have my say out when I'm in a rage like that; then I feel better."

For how long? There is the momentary relief, then—oh! how many hours, days, weeks perhaps, of remorse, for "*who hath resisted Him, and hath had peace?*"[1] It is the enemy that persuades you that you will be better, and we know what his advice is worth. No, make the effort bravely. And when you fail and have spoken rudely to father, mother, master, or companions, make a frank, generous apology.

---

1   Job 9.

"I couldn't. I really couldn't. You don't know what they would think. And then when I did break out another time, they would throw it in my face that I had apologized. I can't do any of those things. But I'll tell you what: I'll save up my money and burn some candles before our Lady's statue."

And forget our Lord's words: "Leave there thy offering before the altar, and go first to be reconciled to thy brother, and then coming thou shalt offer thy gift."[1] It is no use giving to God what He does not ask, when we refuse Him what He does. Nothing that we do will get us into Heaven if we leave a necessary thing undone, and it *is* necessary to check our angry feelings, and to make amends when we have said or done anything contrary to the charity we are bound to have for one another.

One summer morning when the roses were waking and turning to the sun, the breeze came by their way.

"Now roses, shake off your caterpillars!" he said.

And passing over them briskly as they were opening their petals, he shook them well, and all the caterpillars fell to the ground. But a rose there—she was the fairest—said:

"I will give up all my caterpillars except the pretty hairy one with the pink eyes. To part with that one would kill me."

So when the breeze passed over her, she folded her petals tight round the pet caterpillar and kept it safe. To her cost. A few days later the other roses were fresh and fair basking in the sunshine. One, that had been the fairest, lay ugly and withered among the dead caterpillars on the ground, slain by the pet she could not bring herself to slay.

Do not say, "I will take every remedy except the right one" when to take the right one may be a matter of life and death. Remember that deliberate venial sin leads on to mortal, and mortal sin means the death of the soul.

1 St. Matt. 5.

No. 3 has a difficult enemy to tackle. But there is help at hand, and proportioned to the need. How is he to set about conquering *Dislike?* Lord Wolseley says we must be prepared to use different tactics in warfare according to circumstances. Here is a case in point. When you sight your pet aversion, No. 3, what you have to do is not so much to bring your guns to bear, as to keep perfectly cool and steady. Check unkind thoughts of him. Resolve firmly not to say unkind things of him. If you must be doing something, say a friendly word to show you bear him no grudge. Pray for him; ask him to do you some little service—a capital way of killing *Dislike.*

"That would cost me a frightful lot. But I could keep out of his way, and not do him any harm."

Nor yourself much good. No, if you really want to gain a brilliant victory here, you must not avoid the fight. Make a firm resolve first of all not to *show* any dislike or unfriendliness. Turn away your eyes from what provokes you in him, and find out what is good. It is there, and only wants finding. When you find it, praise it, never mind if the praise feels and sounds unreal at first.

"I should feel the biggest hypocrite that ever was, and if it got to his ears that I had spoken kindly of him, he'd know it was all bosh."

That is not your affair. But it is more than likely that his thoughts would be something very different. Praise, then, when you can. And if you see anything you cannot praise, let it alone. It will take an effort, it will cost, but the grace is ready for you. If you really *will* it, you can learn to overcome yourself and thus secure true peace of heart. The special fruit of self-denial is peace. You think that strange? Try, and find out for yourself. The Pax and the stroke go together in the making of our Lord's Knights in Confirmation.

Are you going to spare Agag, whom God has ordered you to slay, and cry out, "I'll overcome any one else. I'll fight fiercely in this direction and that. But touch my dear Agag—I couldn't, indeed I couldn't!" Saul lost his crown through that sparing of Agag.[1] God grant we may not lose ours!

Have you forgotten the Proclamation, and how eagerly you offered yourself to follow the King? He turns to you now and says sweetly:

Follow Me.

Where Lord?

In that struggle against dislike to which I call you. If any one will come after Me, let him deny himself.

Is there no other way, dear Lord? I will do anything else for You, You know.

But how can you follow Me unless you go where I go, and do as I do? I am meek and humble of Heart. Come and be like Me. It will hurt a little, but I will be with you and help you.

"*I'm going to do it.* I shall meet him this morning, and I won't keep out of his way as usual. I'll tell him I've heard he has a stunning new cricket bat and I'll ask him to show it me. That's not much, you know, but it will be a beginning. And as he wants to practise before the match, I'll offer to bowl to him. If I get as far as that, I can't very well go back you see."

Well done, brave soldier! There will be a tussle with nature—many perhaps, but a glorious victory at last. And meanwhile, you will enjoy the peace of heart that is for those only who follow our Lord seriously, and give Him all He asks—the peace which He promised when He said: "Take up My yoke upon you, and learn of Me because I am meek and humble of Heart, *and you shall find rest to your souls.*"[2]

---

1   See I Kings 15 for the story of Agag.
2   St. Matt. 11.

Two of you say you *cannot* overcome yourselves. Is this true? See who they are that *can*. Little negroes and negresses out in Africa; the little natives of India and China; little bits of children in our slums at home, with parents, companions, and example all against them. Boys and girls all the world over can face pain, cruelty, hardship—suffering in every shape—in order to fight their way to Heaven and follow Jesus, carrying their cross. Cannot you do what these are doing?

We *must* deny ourselves. We have no choice. In the heart of every one of us there is some evil thing which, unless we are on our guard, will separate us from God.

You, dear children, have your life before you. If you want it to be a happy life and lead you to a happy eternity, begin bravely to overcome the predominant passion which is your greatest enemy. Set your hand to the work at once. *Now* it may be done without any great labour or difficulty. Later on, it will be so hard, that even with the help of the sacraments, it will be almost beyond your power to master. What is more easily put out than a spark? But let a spark fall on the dry grass of the leagues and leagues of prairie out in the western States of America, and a conflagration is lit which drives men and beasts before it. A child could have extinguished it in the beginning; an army would be powerless against it later. It must burn itself out—there is nothing else for it. And how many neglected faults grown into habits of sin are, at this hour, burning themselves out, "where the worm dieth not, and the fire is never quenched"?[1]

We sometimes hear men and women at the close of life, or far on in life, complain bitterly that those who had charge of them when they were young neglected to check habits which have grown with their growth and come, at last, to be their ruin. This is sad indeed. Yet there is something sadder still—

1   St. Mark 9.

to hear the drunkard, the man and woman who have neglected their religion and lost their faith, cry out in despair: "Oh, why did we not believe those who did warn us, and that again and again! Why did we not try to correct faults that were small once, but have grown great and brought us now to this! God would have given us grace more than enough if we had prayed; and if our temptations and difficulties were too strong for us to meet single-handed, there was the confessional close by where counsel and help could have been had for the asking."

Be down at once upon a bad habit. Pluck it up as soon as you notice it, and so save yourself a world of trouble later. Do not imagine because it is a small thing, the consequences will be small, or that the labour in uprooting it later will be small. If you find a habit forming which at times gives you uneasiness, one that you are obliged to own does not help you; if it is one that you would advise a friend to break off before it grew stronger—make your resolution about it *at once* and do not be foolish enough to think, either that putting off will make its destruction easier, or that "a little thing like that" does not matter.

A well known trait of Mr. Gladstone's was his fancy for hewing down trees. Whether it was that the deep thinker felt the need of physical exertion as a means of diverting his mind from the pressure of public cares, or simply that his irrepressible energy found delight in the vigorous exercise of will and muscle—certain it is that there was no recreation which he enjoyed more thoroughly than to hack away at a lofty elm or a smooth-trunked beech. A woodman on the estate of Hawarden tells us that, having chosen his tree, the great man would fling off his coat, and then in shirt-sleeves set to work, whacking away hour after hour "as if he were a-fightin' of an enemy." And he whacked on until the enemy was conquered.

Day after day he returned to the charge, never dreaming of giving up till the giant lay at his feet.

But one day, the old man learned a new lesson. It was no giant beech or elm that was doomed to die. A holly-tree, gnarled, twisted, ugly—an unsightly thing that had grown up unnoticed, bearing no berries, good neither for use nor ornament—was at last discovered to be such an eyesore, that it was marked for destruction.

Down came the old man to it one morning. Off went the coat, up went the axe, meaning to cleave through the trunk with a blow or two. Not a bit of it, as the experienced woodman hard by knew right well. Surprised but undaunted, Mr. Gladstone struck on. And still came the dull thud of the axe, showing it was making no way with the obstinate wood. Why? Because that wood was holly, and old holly. Perhaps you have had no experience in this direction, but you know how hard it is to pull up a handful of old bracken, or to cut through it with a knife. The woodman could have told Mr. Gladstone from the first what would be the end of his fight with a holly-tree. The end was that, with all his vigour and determination, the veteran had to give in and own himself worsted. Give in thus far—that finding he could not master the enemy single-handed, he sought for help. The woodman looking on behind was called in, and between the two the work was done.

Have you a holly-tree? Ugly, useless, hurting yourself and others? Has our Lord said to you again and again: "Cut it down"? Have you made any way, or is it too hard and tough now to manage single-handed? Then take a lesson from our great statesman. Do not give in, but look for help. Get advice; set to work again, and you will conquer.

XIV.

THE BATTLEFIELD

Thou fightest the battle of the Lord.
(I Kings 25, 28.)

"BUT you've been speaking all the time as if we had only one enemy. It isn't so really you know. There are lots, whole lines of them, just as there are in battle."

"So when we've killed the leader the battle isn't over."

"And we can't say 'the fight was ended that day.' "

My assailants are many, at any rate. I shall have to observe my own rule and deal with them one by one. We have, alas, a multitude of enemies, their name is legion. And for that very reason we must fight wisely and warily, economising our forces. This is a lesson we are taught by our foes themselves. The Greek poets, and those who write after their fashion, concentrate all the interest of a battle in the chiefs, whose fate decides the future of the day.

> Aulus with his good broadsword
> A bloody passage cleared,
> To where, amidst the thickest foes,
> He saw the long white beard.

> Flat lighted that good broadsword
> Upon proud Tarquin's head,
> He dropped the lance: he dropped the reins:
> He fell as fall the dead.[1]

---
1   *Lake Regillus*, Macaulay.

With much greater truth may it be said of the spiritual warfare, that well-directed strokes at the leader are the surest road to victory. But the slaying of him is a long process. Our good broadsword will have to light many and many a time upon proud Tarquin's head, before he drops the lance and drops the reins and falls as fall the dead. One or two strokes will not kill him. There is no such luck for us.

"Then what's the use of trying?"

The greatest use. If you can disable a powerful adversary, and *keep him disabled*, so that he cannot harm you, this is useful surely. If, by brave and frequent victories, we have got our predominant passion well under, so that its attacks are easily put down, we may be thankful indeed. Some one has said it will not actually *die* till five minutes before ourselves. Some one else says—five minutes after! A further use will be that the downfall of this foe will be the weakening of all the others.

> And on the thirty armies
> Came wonder and affright,
> And Ardea wavered on the left,
> And Cora on the right.
>
> .   .   .   .   .
>
> Then burst from that great concourse
> A shout that shook the towers,
> And some ran north, and some ran south,
> Crying, "The day is ours!"[1]

The reason is that vigour and watchfulness in one direction strengthens our character and so helps us all round. Vices, like virtues, are closely linked together; get rid of one and the others fall off. But not to leave emptiness behind them. We can only displace what is bad by introducing what is good; cast out pride, selfishness, anger, by bringing in humility, charity, meekness. And not one of these virtues will come alone, each will bring with her a beautiful train.

1   *Lake Regillus.*

We see that a sturdy, persevering war against our predominant passion is the quickest and surest road to peace. It is turning a rebel out of the castle to make room for our King. Ask Him after confession, ask Him always when He visits you in Holy Communion, to strengthen your hands and help you to dislodge His enemy, that He may have your heart all to Himself and reign there like a King on his throne. Tell Him you mean to ask this whenever you say: "Thy Kingdom come."

Yet the importance of picking off the leader by individual marksmanship must not make us forget to practise other methods of attack that will tell all along the enemy's line. Our soldiers at Omdurman might teach us a lesson here.

"If," said Lord Wolseley, "I were to describe the effect of the volley firing, I would say that from the moment the enemy's line, an immense line filled with the most determined soldiers, came within the zone of fire of 2,000 yards, up to the time when they ceased to advance, because they were knocked down and killed by hundreds and thousands—our line virtually and literally pumped lead upon them. The fire was so heavy that no one could live under it."

"We can't pump lead on *our* enemies when they come against us and make us commit sin."

Make us, what do you mean—who can make us?

"Well, they can tempt us, and that is almost the same thing."

Temptation the same thing as sin! You take my breath away. Why, so far from being almost the same, they are utterly different. One depends on the devil's will, the other on our own, and those two wills are not the same, I hope. No, these two things are as different as horse and cart.

"Well the horse and cart come together anyway, and one draws the other on."

They only come together when we put them together; they can be miles apart always if we choose.

"You don't see what I mean. I mean temptation leads us into sin."

Just as the Frontier war in India and the advance on Omdurman led to crushing defeat. Just as going home for the holidays leads to a frightful death. True, our troops *could* have handed over their guns and rifles to the Afridis and the Dervishes and begged to be shot and trampled on. And I can open the carriage door and leap out on to the rails when the train is at full speed.

"Oh, but that's ridiculous, for I need not open the door and jump out unless I like."

Neither need you open the door of your heart and jump into sin unless you like. It is most important that we should see quite clearly that these two things *are* two things, and very different things. Now two things cannot be one and the same thing, can they?

"Temptation and sin almost the same"—Only think of a Catholic child saying that! But it will never do for us to have misty notions about a matter which should be as clear as noonday. We must dispel the mist and see what temptation really is.

Temptation is an incitement to our will to do that which is wrong. This incitement comes, partly from the devil's envy and hatred, partly from the source of temptation which we have within us in our own passions, and partly from the evil example we find around us. "The life of man upon earth is a warfare,"[1] therefore temptation is unavoidable. Life in this world is as much the time and place for fighting as the battlefield when the charge has sounded. There is simply no help for it. We

---

1   Job 7.

are on the field and into the fight we must go. Notice how the Holy Ghost speaking of the fighters says simply *man*—that is our whole race without exception, beginning with the Head, down to the least members. "The Lord said to Satan: Whence comest thou? And he answered and said: I have gone round about the earth and walked through it."[1] No Saint has escaped, however high, however holy. No soul, however young, however sheltered, however innocent. Every one who is to be happy with God in Heaven, must first have passed through trial and come out in safety, come out a conqueror.

"The life of man upon earth is a warfare." *The life*—Job does not say there is a little skirmish now and again—the devil would never let us off so easily. He is filled with great wrath, "knowing he has but a short time."[2] He makes the most of that time, worrying us with his temptations in all places and on all occasions. If we go to our studies, he will try to make us idle, or so over eager for success and first places that there will be room for envy and jealousy later on. If we do a kind act, he tries to spoil it by human respect or thoughts of vanity. When we go to prayer, he goes with us, to try to get us to give way to distractions.

Whilst we were quite little our parents were able, it may be, to keep temptation from us. But as we grow older, we get outside the shelter of our home, and become more and more responsible for ourselves. Temptation comes more in our way. Perhaps at school we have to mix with those who have not had our helps; things are said and done which we know are not right, and then human respect comes in to make us ashamed of being different from others. We begin then to feel how weak we are. We feel, too, our passions—pride, anger, greediness, sloth—getting hard to manage, and are conscious that whilst

1 Job 1.
2 Apoc. 12.

we have to be on our guard against getting harm from bad example, our own example is none of the brightest, and our neighbours may see no particular reason for imitating *us*.

At this important time in our lives, the Holy Ghost comes with the strong grace of Confirmation to keep us firm and steady in the service of Christ, able to battle with temptation, and to prove ourselves valiant soldiers.

"Do temper and greediness come from the devil, or from our own selves?"

From both. The devil is always on the lookout for help in his evil work, and he has no better helpers than those traitors in our own camp—our evil passions. He rouses them by setting before them sometimes things they like, sometimes things they dislike, and so by coaxing or by craft, he draws us into his snares.

"Wouldn't it be much nicer if the devil were an enemy like Saladin, not mean and cunning you know?"

No doubt, but we seldom find our enemies quite to our liking. Good, old-fashioned commanders like Blucher[1] were sadly put out by Napoleon's new-fangled and ridiculous ways of fighting. Why couldn't he fight in the proper way like every one else? Come at the proper time when one was ready for him; come to the proper place where he was expected; take up his quarters properly, and settle down in a dignified way before the enemy's guns as a proper army was taught to do! Instead of this, he was most unpunctual, never turned up when he was due, and never in the right place. He did not attack what he ought to have attacked, but some post no one ever dreamed of defending. "He knows absolutely nothing of the rules of war!" exclaimed an old Hungarian officer, with indignation. "To-day

---

1   Gebhard Leberecht von Blucher was a German Field Marshal who was instrumental in defeating Napoleon at the Battle of Waterloo.

he is in our rear, to-morrow on our flank, next day again in our front; such violations of the principles of the art of war are intolerable."

Of course they were. Then, instead of besieging according to military rules, he had a stupid way of throwing all his force upon one weak part, which gave way and made him master of the place before the guns could be got into position. He was bent on beating the enemy, when the correct thing for him to do was to retreat. You never knew where you had him. When you were marching to the battlefield, he was a hundred miles away gaining some absurd victory before any one knew what he was about. And then he moved at such a rate, there was no coming up with him.

All this was very trying you know, and it is no wonder the poor, bewildered old generals were put out. But what was to be done! Napoleon had to be fought, and insisted on fighting in his own way. They must make the best of it, and learn, from their troublesome foe himself, how to meet him. When his movements were so well planned and so rapid, theirs must not be clumsy and slow. No, they must learn from him to be ready at all times; to watch weak posts; to keep a sharp look-out on his movements, and never to think they had done with him because he was routed again and again.

Ours is a truceless war. There will be peace when all is over, but not till then. The white flag can never pass between us and the enemy, and those who think to come to terms with him will find, to their cost, how he treats those whom he has lulled into a false security. He has no chivalry in him, no honour for brave resistance, no pity for the weary and the weak. He is not ashamed to measure his strength with a child of seven, or to come down with great wrath to the death-bed when the failing powers are all but spent.

234

"What a miserable life he leads us! Why, we never have a minute's peace."

Look at it from another point of view; you know what a difference a change of position makes when we are looking at an object. Instead of saying, "What a miserable life he leads us!" say, "What a lot of opportunities he gives us!" This is a much truer, as well as a much cheerier and pluckier way of looking at things. It is our Heavenly Father's view. "Blessed is the man that endureth temptation, for when he has been proved he shall receive the crown of life, which God hath promised to them that love Him."[1] He does not call our contest a just punishment for our sins. In bright, chivalrous language it is a *trial* in which His trusty soldiers are to put out their strength and display their valour before Him and His Heavenly Court with the certainty of coming off victorious, and being crowned as conquerors.

We are told that, as Wellington sat at supper after Waterloo, his few surviving officers about him, he repeatedly leaned back in his chair, rubbing his hands convulsively, and exclaiming: "Thank God I have met him! Thank God I have met him!"

Temptation, then, is not an evil. We have to get this well into our heads. From whatever source it comes—the world, the devil, or ourselves—it is not in itself an evil. This is saying too little. It is a positive help.

"Still, I wish there was no devil, and that we could get to Heaven without all this temptation and trouble."

There would be one enemy the less, but remember he is only one of three. The world without, and our bad passions within, would still have to be fought. But is it not rather foolish and waste of time to be always wishing our life here were other than it is? Had it been better for us to have no difficulty in saving our souls, God would have

1   St. James 1.

ordered it so. "What I do thou knowest not now, but thou shalt know hereafter."[1] When we get to Heaven we shall see clearly what at times we find it hard to see—the high and holy uses of temptation.

A man threshes out wheat with a flail. God uses the devil as a flail. The Evil One means mischief when he comes down hard upon us. But he forgets in Whose hands he is, if he thinks to do us any harm against our will. His intention is to crush us out and out, wheat and husk together. But God's intention is very different. God wants the wheat for His barn when the harvest comes. But He does not want the chaff. When is this to be separated from the wheat? When are our faults and imperfections to be beaten out of us? After our death? It is too late. *Now* then. And see how wonderful God's ways are. He chooses our worst enemy, with his worst of intentions to do us the greatest possible service, to purify us, to get us ready for Heaven. But you will say, "Oh, but He lets the devil lay on so hard." Well, what of that, providing He is watching? There are some kinds of grain with such tough skins, or skins that stick so close to them, that it takes any amount of threshing to set them free. They must bear the operation as best they can. They are not expected to like it, only to lie quiet and wait till it is over.

Again, temptation is trouble, and trouble is good for us. We fear it, hate it, try to get rid of it. Yet the truth remains that trouble is good for us. It does for us a work that nothing else can do. So does temptation. "Because thou wast acceptable to God it was *necessary* that temptation should prove thee."[2] It purifies us as the great dashing waves wash the rocks. It strengthens us as the blustering wind that bows the young trees, forcing them to take deeper root. It gives to the soul a beauty, a delicacy, a tenderness, a mellowness that is wanting to those whom trial in this shape

1 St. John 13.
2 Tobias 12.

236

has never touched, or touched but lightly. It gives, among other things, a wonderful power of sympathy:

> Sorrow with sorrow loves to dwell;
> Mourners their tale to mourners tell.[1]

A splendid use of temptation is to prove our fidelity, to exercise us in virtue, to increase our reward. To prove His children before rewarding them is God's invariable rule. "Come hither, that I may prove thee, whether thou be My son or no,"[2] He says to Angels and men—to all except the babes who die before coming to the use of reason, who have Heaven by God's free gift, but without the added lustre of their own works done with the help of grace. "Thou didst try them as a father."[3] And as a noble King Who will have none but tried warriors round Him.

Is this a thing to be troubled at? Does the soldier weep and wail when he hears the bugle call to battle? Does he cry out, "Alas, alas, it is all up with me," or, "Here is my chance!" The knights of other days were delighted to cross swords with a powerful foe, whilst the king and his court looked on. So are the knights of the Heavenly Kingdom. "Prove me, O God, and try me," cries out David's eager heart. "He has tried me as gold that passeth through the fire," says Job. The shout of joyful praise that resounds through Heaven, should teach us what they think of temptation there: "O, bless our God and make the voice of His praise to be heard. *For Thou, O God, hast proved us.*"[4] Of course, they did not like the proving process whilst it lasted, any more than a soldier actually enjoys his wounds. It was the reward to which they looked that made them welcome temptation—or *trial*—the two words mean the same. "Afflicted

1 Oakeley.
2 Genesis 27.
3 Wisdom 11.
4 Psalm 65.

in few things, in many they shall be well rewarded, because God hath tried them and found them worthy of Himself."[1] *Worthy of Himself!* Can even God find higher praise than that! Where shall they be in His favour, in nearness to Him, in familiarity with Him, whom God has tried and found worthy of Himself!

Troubles and temptations here will make Heaven the happier for us. Those only rejoice fully, in the rest and security of the haven, who have been in the perils of shipwreck. Those only who have known the breaking up of an earthly home, can understand the joy of reunion that is to have no parting any more. And only those who have feared continually lest they should lose their God, can cry out with the ecstasy of the Cure d'Ars, "My God, I hold You fast. You shall never escape from me now—never, never!" "How you will enjoy Heaven," said a good priest to one on whom the cross weighed heavily. The weariness of the struggle will make all the sweeter to us that eternal rest which the Church is always wishing for her children. "Eternal rest give to them, O Lord, eternal rest." "There remaineth a day of rest for the children of God," says St. Paul. "Let us hasten therefore into that rest,"[2] like a traveller driven before the storm towards his home.

To be received into that Home, we must be recognized as children. The likeness to the Elder Brother must be clearly seen. And this likeness is, in great part, the work of trouble and temptation. An artist does not use bright colours only. Now and again he dips his brush into sombre greys, into black even, to make the shadows that throw the lights into relief. No portrait could be either beautiful or true without its shading. Only Elizabeth of England could give the foolish order, "Paint my face without shadow." It is just the shadow that gives beauty, pathos, strength, sweetness, expression. God is a skilful Artist.

1   Wisdom 3.
2   Hebrews 4.

238

He wants to produce in each one of us, according to the design and in the degree destined for each, the likeness of His Divine Son, on which our eternal happiness depends. It is to bring out this likeness that He lets trouble, struggle, temptation—all that we call the cross—overshadow our souls for a while.

See, then, how useful temptation may be if we manage it aright, and what a mistake you made in speaking of it "as almost the same thing as sin." How very different God means it to be! When the Israelites, gathered round Mount Sinai, were struck with fear "at the voice and the flames and the sound of the trumpet, and the mount smoking, Moses said: Fear not; for God is come to prove you...*that you should not sin.*"[1]

What we have to learn, then, is so to deal with temptation as to make it helpful, not harmful, to us. With a little skill we can turn obstructions into helps, as there is a talk of doing in Egypt and the Soudan.

A steamer has been imprisoned for six weeks in the pestilential marshes of the Nile between Lado and Fashoda. The river here is a channel, bounded on both sides by tall grass and reeds standing 20 ft. or 30 ft. above the water, and still further choked by floating islands of grass so thick that men can walk upon them. Nothing but water, grass, reeds, and sky can be seen unless you climb to the masthead, whence you may descry the river banks, eight or even twelve miles distant on either side.

"How delicious! I should love to be there."

To die of fever or starvation, as four hundred out of five hundred did on their way to Khartoum. These vast masses of vegetation float down the river in the rainy season and form the barriers, which stop navigation altogether, south of Khartoum. Now some bright genius, pondering the future of Egypt and the

---

1   Exodus 20.

Soudan, and considering what might be made of these vast regions if fuel could be procured to work machinery, has suggested that a source of unsuspected fuel wealth may be found in the masses of water-weed which obstruct the upper reaches of the Nile. All that is needed is to dry it and convert it into fuel.

See how clever men are in turning hindrances and even grave dangers into helps! When temptation comes to block our way, we must treat it in the same fashion and turn it to account.

Our life here is a warfare, certainly, but even war has its advantages for those who can make profit by it—for those whose trade it helps. "Give me a sharp war," said a shrewd business man during the Crimean War. "It's all very well talking about peace and prosperity, but, as a matter of fact, peace time is a dull time and war time a brisk time." He was right. A big war stimulates trade to no small extent by its vast preparations, which call for increased activity in many of our staple trades and industries.

Slack times are bad times for all trades, and temptation does us no small service by keeping us on the alert. Of course, no one dreams of denying that, like war, it is a time of peril. But it is blessedly unlike in this—that whereas the best will and the utmost gallantry, so far from securing us against danger in earthly warfare, only increase our chances of death—in the heavenly warfare it is quite otherwise. Only *will* to come out a victor and you will do so. And in proportion to your gallantry will be your everlasting reward.

A large part of our warfare, as we have seen, consists in vigilance. "The most arduous, while at the same time most important duties that devolve upon soldiers in the field," says Lord Wolseley, "are those of sentinels and videttes.[1] They

1 A vidette (or vedette) is a mounted sentry stationed ahead of an army's position.

must feel that the safety of the army and the honour of the country depend upon their untiring vigilance and activity. They should be the eyes of the army, always peering forward to watch and report what the enemy is doing. Every road and by-way should be carefully watched by them that so the main body may be protected, not only from surprise, but from the prying inquisitiveness of the enemy. If strangers by night approach any sentry, they must be forced to halt until the next relief comes round, when they should be disarmed and taken or sent before the officer commanding the examining post. No matter who the intruders may be—deserters, spies, or an officer with a flag of truce—the least possible conversation is to be held with them."

"I think I see most of that. But what would you call the roads and by-ways that have to be watched?"

The Saints tell us that the roads we have to watch are the senses—eyes, ears, mouth, &c., through which danger may easily reach the soul if they are left unguarded. Again, we must keep up a look-out against idleness, waste of time, carelessness about prayer and the sacraments, ill-advised friendships, newspapers, books, and other things which our faithful sentry, conscience, has stopped for examination.

So keenly alive are European governments becoming to the importance of safeguarding an army, that they use balloons to make observation of an enemy's movements, take sketches and photographs, and act generally as military spies. Moreover, they are beginning to employ as patrols, videttes, and sentries, animals whose organs of sense and perception seem superior to our own. The frontier armies of Italy, France, and Germany now use the dog as sentry, messenger, and scout.

You see, if the outpost stations are well guarded, the army is safe. They are at a distance, often at a considerable distance from it, yet the sentries have to guard them well. No one is to pass them without examination—the enemy is not to be suffered near them. Lord Wolseley, describing an army encamped, likens it to a hand with the fingers well opened; the nails being the outlying picket, where the sentries, videttes, and patrols are; the middle joints of the fingers the supports; the knuckles the reserves; and the wrist the troops or camp to be protected from surprise. Lay your hand down on the table, spread the fingers well out and think of another camp. Here it is at the wrist. The soul is our camp. The knuckles are care to keep the Commandments of God and of the Church, which bind under mortal sin. The middle joints are care to keep the Commandments which bind under venial sin; the nails, care in those spiritual duties which protect the approaches to our souls—daily Mass, regular use of the sacraments, daily examination of conscience, meditation or spiritual reading. These things are not of strict obligation, but we have only to drop them for a little while to find out the mischief we have done. Think of an army in the field without its sentries—why, it is as good as lost. The way is open now to the supports, which will give way next, then to the reserves, and those passed, it will be easy to surprise the army. Carelessness in spiritual duties leads to venial sin, venial sin paves the way to mortal sin and—our camp is in the hands of the enemy.

In these days the soldier's sense of danger has to become keener and keener to keep pace with the new methods of destruction that are being constantly devised. Now that smokeless powder has come into use, he will have to learn how to detect it. He will have to train his ears in future, as well as his eyes. He will have to determine by the sound of the enemy's guns from which direction the firing is coming. He can depend no longer on the smoke to fix the enemy's position.

"That's a pity, because Lord Wolseley said we could learn a lot from the enemy's smoke."

Our enemy at any rate cannot invent smokeless powder; by the black thick clouds darkening every place through which he passes, we may always tell his whereabouts and act accordingly.

Preparation for temptation makes conquest easy and sure. Our Lord conquered the devil after His fast of forty days. See, too, what strength to go through His Passion He drew from His prayer in the Garden. He meant this to serve as an example. But some will object that preparation makes life a weary business, owing to the constant labour of watching. Does it? Take two people—one prepares and easily overcomes his temptations, the other takes no pains, unless when attacked, and consequently is troubled afterwards with doubts and scruples, and probably will not escape sin. Which of these leads the happier life?

Again, it is easier to prepare for temptation than to do penance for sin committed. Some people do not try to prevent, but expect to get through all right somehow—like the Irishman who, when told his house was on fire, remarked, "Perhaps it will go out of itself."

XV.

UNDER FIRE

A thousand shall fall at thy side, and ten thousand at thy right hand;
but it shall not come nigh unto thee.
(Psalm 90, 7.)

THIS is the promise of God Himself to His soldiers under fire, provided they do their part as every soldier is bound to do. Meeting temptation is an art. We must learn it and stick to our rules.

Of the war between Spain and the United States in 1898, we are told that the plans of the Spanish Government were matured too late. Firmly believing to the last moment that peace would be preserved, it neglected to lay in sufficient provision of coals, despite the representations made by one or two far-seeing naval officers. The Spaniards fought magnificently when once they began; ship after ship went down firing from her lower guns as she sank with all on board. But their unreadiness for the struggle showed the valour of the Spaniards under the greatest possible disadvantage. Their mines did not go off; their scouts gave no warning of the approach of danger; their ships were wooden and weak; their guns could not reach the enemy. The American Admiral was too quick for them, and slipped past their batteries in the dark almost before they were aware of his coming.

We must do our part, then. And our part in action is to be *prompt, prudent, skilful, prayerful, and trustful.* We will take these requisites one by one.

I must be prompt. When the top of a match that I have struck falls on to my hand, how long do I take to consider whether I shall drop it? Is it not tossed off instantly, instinctively, without thought or hesitation? There must be no hesitation with us where there is question of sin. We often look at a pedlar's wares without any intention of buying. I must beware of looking at the devil's wares; some tinsel toy may tempt me. "Thou shalt not!"—the order must come with curtness and vigour. It is much the easiest way, as well as the only generous and safe way.

We may learn from the Army Act what thorough whole-hearted service an earthly Sovereign expects from her soldiers.

Notes from the Army Act.

For the following offences a soldier is liable, at all times, to the penalty of death, or of any less punishment:

Shamefully abandoning his post.

Shamefully casting away his arms, ammunition, or tools in the presence of the enemy.

Treacherously holding correspondence with, or assisting the enemy.

Harbouring or voluntarily serving with the enemy.

Doing anything to imperil the success of His Majesty's Forces.

Cowardice before the enemy.

Mutiny.

Personal violence to a superior, or disobedience to his lawful commands when in the execution of his office.

♦ ♦ ♦

For the following offences, if committed on Active Service, a soldier is liable to the penalty of death or any less punishment:

Deserting, attempting to desert, or persuading any other person to desert.

♦ ♦ ♦

On Active Service, penal servitude or any less punishment may be awarded, if a soldier is found guilty of:

Being taken prisoner through neglect.

Creating alarm or despondency.

Notice, please, how in His Majesty's service the "shameful abandonment of a post, the shameful casting away of arms in presence of the enemy, deserting, or persuading any other person to desert," makes an English soldier liable *to death*. Notice, too, how "creating alarm or despondency" is severely punished, as also "being taken prisoner through neglect." Notice, above all, how any cowardice on active service is "*shameful*."

I must be prudent. What care we take to guard things of great value. The army has its guards and its life guards, its advanced guard to meet surprises and give notice of danger in front, its rear guard for protection behind. It has its soldiers on guard, its guard-room, its guard-ship. And, to come to something nearer home, look at your bicycle—a small thing, yet furnished at every point with guards. There is the gear-guard, the dress-guard, the mud-guard, and lamp and bell and brake, all for protection of one kind or another. Is our soul to be less carefully guarded when peril threatens? It is our only one; its safety is the one thing necessary. A soldier is liable to heavy punishment for "being taken prisoner through neglect." His life and service belong to his country and are not his own to throw away. Neither are ours. "You are not your own, you are bought with a great price."[1] There is something very inspiriting in the thought that much depends upon every one of us. By the way we behave in action, much may be done or lost for the cause. The way in which a little child meets its every day temptations is more interesting to the devil than was the behaviour of the Wellington squares at Waterloo.

You remember the old Duke liked to see what he was about there. In the presence of the enemy we must know what we are about. We must be on the alert. "Father, guard yourself

---

1   I Cor. 6.

to the right, guard yourself to the left," cried little Prince Philip as he dashed here and there on his pony at Poictiers, ever at the side of King John[1].

I must be prudent, then. Whenever conscience stops some intruder, it is my duty as officer commanding the examining post, to listen to what it has to say. "Put down that newspaper," it says, "don't—"

"I know—Yes, I often hear that sentry, but I don't always listen, you know, because it's such a bother when you want to go on doing the thing."

We must never turn a deaf ear to the voice of conscience. Those who do so say with the Jews: "Let me not hear any more the voice of the Lord, my God."[2] The greatest evil that can befall them is the granting of this prayer, for when conscience ceases to speak, there must be a miracle of grace to save us. Even when it asks what is hard to give, we must listen, for it is the voice of God. We must say, "Speak, Lord, for Thy servant heareth."[3] Think that the safety of your soul depends on hearing, when conscience bids you give up this or that which is doing you harm. "Beware that thou pass not to such a place, for the Syrians are there in ambush...And the King of Israel looked well to himself there."[4]

I have heard some of you say that you would not like to live in India because of the many dangerous creatures which would make you afraid to go outside the house, even into the garden. Which of these creatures would you fear most?

"The tiger, or the leopards and panthers which hide in the jungle."

"*I* say the snakes. Because tigers and leopards keep in the

---

1 Philip was the youngest son of King John II of France. Both were captured at the Battle of Poictiers in 1356, during the Hundred Years War.
2 Deut. 18.
3 I Kings 3.
4 4 Kings 6.

jungle, and you could at least be safe in your own garden. But the snakes get into the garden and even into the house."

The report of the Government of British India on death by wild animals and snakes in 1897 will surprise most English people. 4,277 persons, chiefly natives, were killed by wild animals, wolves, tigers, and bears; and nearly 21,000 by snakes. Among snakes, the most dreaded is the *cobra-di-capello*, or hooded cobra, which, during the rainy season, from June to September, is the cause of five times as many deaths as result from tigers and other wild beasts.

"Why in the rainy season?"

Because of the inundations. The home of the cobra is the hilly districts of India, where it lies in a state of lethargy, hidden in caves, or behind large stones, during the cold months from November to February. The hot weather draws it out of its hiding-places down into the plains. But when these are deluged by the rains—you know what tropical rain is like—the cobra is forced to seek shelter on higher ground. It hides in shrubberies, in out-houses, under heaps of rubbish, even in dwelling-houses.

"It's just like the devil, hiding wherever it goes, and going everywhere, so that no place is safe!"

We are told that there is no remedy against the poison which the cobra injects into the two needle-like punctures made by its fangs. One drop communicated to the blood is enough to cause death. Cutting off or burning will be successful only when the bite has been at the extremity of a limb, and when these severe measures are taken instantly.

In the hilly districts of India, railway stations are often far apart, and it is necessary to provide sheds along the line where coal may be obtained in case of need.

One dark, dreary night, when a tropical downpour was subsiding into a drizzle, a train stopped at one of these sheds. The driver was helping the stoker to shovel some coals into the tender, when with a sharp cry he broke off, wringing his hand in pain. The men looked about, and there, coiled up on the top of the coals, was a huge cobra, head erect, hood expanded, its deadly eyes glistening, its forked tongue darting to and fro. Settled down for the night, it had risen angrily, and bitten the man who had disturbed it. What was to be done? The poor fellow was hundreds of miles from medical help. And there was no time for consideration. A few seconds for the poison to mount, and it would be all over with him. Should he cut off his arm? No instrument was at hand. Should he lie down on the rail and get the stoker to drive the engine over it? He would bleed to death. And if the heavy wheels failed to sever the arm completely, a thin shred of flesh would communicate the poison to the rest of his body. Like lightning these thoughts flashed through his mind. He looked round, and his eyes lighted on the engine. Yes, there was that chance. Springing on to the footplate, he flung open the furnace doors, thrust his arm into the fire, and held it there till it was burned down to the elbow. Then he sank back and fainted away. The stoker took the train on to the next station, whence the poor fellow was sent to Calcutta for medical treatment. He eventually recovered.

"But he lost his arm."

And kept his life, to save which the arm was welcome to go amid all that awful pain. *Now* do we understand how our Lord could say: "If thy hand scandalize thee, cut it off and cast it from thee."[1] If hand and arm must go without hesitation for the sake of the body, what must we be ready to do to preserve the life of the soul! Must we not be ready to give up this or that, to part with a book, a companion, an amusement, anything— cost what it may—when the life of our immortal soul is at stake!

1   St. Mark 9.

I must be prudent then—and *I must be skilful.* What a difference skill makes in everything! Here is the experience of a Crimean veteran who was in the trenches before Sebastopol: "Folks a-twhoam reads all about they battles fair and plain in the newspapers, an' think as all you've got to do is to go straight forrard an' *kill.* It sounds simple enuff, but blesh you 'taint so simple when you come to do't." If this is the case with privates, it is still more true of officers. They have their general instructions, but are expected to use their ingenuity and common sense in adapting these to circumstances.

"Fertility of resource and quickness in devising expedients are essential qualities for an officer," says Lord Wolseley. "An inventive mind and an instinct for war helps to hit upon plans which, by their very novelty, if promptly carried out, give you a great number of odds in your favour…Your formation must conform to the nature of your enemy's arms, to his known ways of fighting, and to the character of the country you are operating in." So must—

"Yes, I understand."

"And so do I."

"And I do; please go on."

Perhaps the best part of skill is coolness. In battle, this is so necessary as to be simply indispensable. "In advancing to the attack, keep as cool as possible, avoid hurry, rushing, noise, and talking. To be cool and to seem ignorant that any danger exists, is of the first consequence,…come what may, have a smiling face."

"The staff officer should be cool to the utmost extent. If by nature he is excitable, a strong curb must be placed over his manner. He should always look jolly and unconcerned. Excitement is painfully catching. A staff officer galloping in a high state of excitement with an order to a column, may play 'Old Harry' with the spirits of the men, and cause them to think there is an unknown danger, or that things in other parts of the field are not going on as they should; it gives rise to a hundred speculations of a gloomy nature; whereas the man who gallops up, no matter how quickly, but with a smiling face, and gives his orders precisely, without any flurry, having a nod for his acquaintances in the ranks, and perhaps a flying remark for them, spreads abroad a feeling of security and success, which soon reaches the smallest bugler, making all feel that they are on the winning side.

"I once saw a staff officer gallop with an order to a column of cavalry and artillery, which had been drawn up behind a village to be sheltered from fire, and as he was near it, a round shot struck the ground just under his horse. The horse made an effort to swerve a little, which was checked by its rider without taking a cigar he was smoking from his mouth, apparently taking no notice whatever of the occurrence. He galloped up to the column, coolly gave his orders, and galloped back again over the open space outside the village, where the round shot were striking pretty thickly, still smoking his cigar, as if he were taking his morning exercise. A few shots had previously plunged into the column, and caused some excitement, as it always does when horses get knocked over; but the jolly indifference of this officer—in fact the manner in which he appeared to ignore altogether the existence of any danger, had a capital effect on the men, most of whom saw it, as every one watched him coming, thinking he was perhaps the bearer of an order to advance. Every one who has been often under fire with troops knows how much the coolness of individual officers influences those around them; but a staff officer, being mounted, and his approach being always a matter of interest, being generally seen by the majority—he has a greater opportunity of displaying this quality than any other officer; he cannot, therefore, be too careful about his manner."

The battle signal of Admiral Dewey of Manila fame is: "Keep cool and obey orders." In the middle of the fight at Cavité, he withdrew his ships to have breakfast served and allow his officers to get their morning coffee; and he reserved his highest praise for his Chinese servants, who went on cooking, and ironing linen during the fight, as if nothing unusual were happening.

Of Wellington at Waterloo we are told: "Every member of his staff, without exception, was killed or wounded. But the roar of the battle, with its swift chances of life and death, left his intellect as cool and his nerve as steady as though he were watching a scene in the theatre. One of the generals said to him, when the fight seemed most desperate, 'If you should be struck, tell us what is your plan?' 'My plan,' said the Duke, 'consists in dying here to the last man.' Long after the battle, he mentioned at a dinner-table that as he stood under a tree in the centre of his line, a Scotch sergeant came up, told him he had observed the tree was a mark for the French guns, and begged him to move from it. Somebody at the table said, 'I hope you did, sir.' 'I really forget,' said the Duke, 'but I know I thought it very good advice at the time.' "

A good general has been described as one "whom no danger can flurry and no sudden shift in the kaleidoscope of battle disconcert...Never tired, never surprised, never flurried, never slow, cool as on parade." "Hard pounding this, gentlemen!" said Wellington, as he rode past his much enduring squares. "Let us see who will pound longest." Those of the widest experience said of the Battle of Omdurman, that they had never seen a field in which everybody was so completely cool and set on business. Coolness is appreciated and enforced almost as if it meant victory. On the other hand, every commander knows that fear is fatal. Nearly 18,000 of Wellington's army at Waterloo were Dutch-Belgians, whose courage was doubtful and whose loyalty was suspected. Wellington had placed some battalions of these as part of the force holding Hougoumont; but when, an hour before the battle actually began, Napoleon rode through his troops, and their tumultuous shouts echoed in a tempest of sound across to the British lines, the effect on the Dutch-Belgians in Hougoumont was so instant and visible that Wellington at once withdrew them. "The mere name of Napoleon," he said, "had beaten them before they had fired a shot."

At St. Pierre[1] the French were beaten, though they opposed 35,000 men to the English 14,000. "The French, it might almost be said, lost the field by the momentary failure in nerve of the officer commanding the column upon which the 92nd was rushing in its last most dramatic charge...The oncoming of the Highlanders proved too great a strain for the nerve of the French general. He wheeled the head of his horse backward, and the fight was lost."

"To reserve your fire as much as possible," says Lord Wolseley, speaking of warfare with savages, "has an awe-striking effect upon the night assailant; he does not know what you are at, and your cool indifference at his approach tends to frighten him, whereas if your camp is all noise and bustle, your evident confusion gives him pluck, and encourages him to attack boldly."

Ours is a night assailant. Under cover of the darkness he comes upon us suddenly, thinking to frighten us. We must show ourselves true soldiers and keep cool. We have made our resolutions; the time has come to keep them, and with the time, the grace.

"In the Duke of Wellington's day the fire of the individual soldier was not a factor of importance in the problem to be worked out; the effect of men fighting in a formed body,

1   A battle that took place toward the end of the Peninsular War.

shoulder to shoulder, was alone considered of value. *Now*, the great object of all military teaching is to develop the power of each breech-loading rifle and the independent action of the soldier who carries it to the fullest possible extent."

In one sense, God needs none of us. And in another, He needs every one of us, and so much that if we do not do the work He has appointed for us, it will go undone. He wants a glory from us which He will take from us only. Each and every one may say, "The glory of the blessed God which hath been committed to my trust."[1] Surely this is a thought to fill us with ardour, to make us anxious to be trained, to have our powers developed to the utmost, that we may have more to give to the Service!

Another point of skill is to disconcert the enemy by suddenly assuming the offensive and turning assailant.

"But how can we do that? we can't turn round and tempt *him*."

Not exactly, but we can make his position so uncomfortable, and his so completely the losing side, that he will heartily wish he had let us alone. "The best German authors say that the side acting on the defensive has the best of it. Success depends greatly upon the offensive being assumed exactly at the right time...In all attacks there is a moment when the defendant must charge or be defeated. Experience in war teaches the general to feel, as it were, from the pulse of his men when that moment has arrived. Happy is the man who knows when to say, 'Up guards, and at them.' There is no salvation for him who cannot do so. The opportunity passes in the twinkling of an eye, and if not seized upon at the right moment, cannot be expected to return."

You have been struggling for a long time with a secret dislike for some one. It was small at the beginning, but you are alarmed to see how it is growing. His company is becoming almost

1   I Timothy 1.

unbearable; his walk, his laugh, his every movement irritates you. You catch yourself rejoicing at his disappointments, and grudging him well-merited praise. You try, more or less, to stifle these feelings; you think you do not consent; but things are not mending—you make no way. Suddenly an opportunity offers for doing him some real service, for defending him in his absence, for helping him to get something he has set his heart upon. *Now* is your chance, a brave effort now will win you a victory that will do more than years of weak defence, and perhaps leave you in full possession of the field. "Up guards, and at them." *Charge!* do not hesitate a moment. Grace enough, and more than enough, is given you, but the opportunity is passing and may never return. Act, make haste. The Leader is watching…Thank God, the struggle is over, and you have come out a conqueror.

This is war. And if we want peace, we must prepare for war. The victory is not without the fight.

But let us suppose that the victory was not a decisive one; the advantage was not all on your side; you did not comport yourself quite as you would like to have done, and you have not come off with flying colours. Never mind, practice makes perfect. Our Leader does not expect raw recruits to be skilled soldiers all at once. But regular drill will make you skilful in the use of your arms, and a real engagement will do more for you than any amount of wishing and hoping. Put your hand to the work, and the oftener the better. "Let all Commanding Officers spare no time or trouble in making their men learn to charge with quickness and precision, in impressing upon them their real strength…Let their charges be practiced on the roughest ground, being invariably accompanied by a ringing cheer. Drill is now more essential than ever in the formation of an army. Let us drill a soldier day after day, and, if necessary, all day in the manœuvres of battle, until he is proficient in them."

Excellent advice! We are the Commanding Officer: let us take ourselves in hand without delay.

The Saints preferred this offensive warfare. They were thoroughly in earnest, and did their work in earnest. "*Agendo contra*,"—acting against—was the motto of the Soldier Saint, Ignatius of Loyola, whose vigour in the warfare with self has been light and strength to many a soldier of Christ. He used to say: "Incline thyself on the other side to that to which Nature inclines thee." If your prayer-time drags wearily, prolong it by a few minutes; if you feel yourself wishing ill to So-and-so, pray hard for him; if you are lazy and inclined to shirk trying or tiresome work, go to it briskly; if such a one's story wearies you, ask a question that will draw out another. It is wonderful how the effort to do a little more than we are bound to do, helps us to do brightly and easily what we are obliged. Try, and you will find it so. It is the cheer that puts spirit into our charge. If you want to be of use to the Service, to attract the Leader's Eye, to gain promotion in order to be near Him, volunteer sometimes, go in for a bit of work that is not necessary. Seek, rather than avoid, engagements that will reflect honour on His arms. Put your heart into your charge—don't forget to cheer.

"Fire has become more than ever the soul of defence, and should be applied towards preventing the enemy from reaching the position, and not reserved for defeating him when he gets there. He must be beaten during his advance, else by his own fire he will already have beaten the defenders before closing with them. The energy of his attack must be broken ere he approaches sufficiently near to enable it to carry him further, or have it revived by a feeling of success."

Oh, we must be brave, we must be brave! We are not fighting alone, but in the company of God's faithful servants on every side of us, and of Him and His Heavenly Court above us.

Bravery is catching, as the deeds on every battlefield prove. There even animals catch the infection, and do their best for the cause. A dog called "Bob" went out with the 66th to the Afghan War in 1879, and marched with the regiment to battle. During the fighting he kept running to the front, howling and barking. At last a bullet struck him on the neck, tearing his skin off to the end of his back. When the 66th were killed off almost to a man in the *nullah*,[1] Bob, though badly wounded, found his way back to Kandahar, a journey which took him six weeks. He was wounded again *en route*.

"What a splendid fellow! Did he get back to England safe?"

"And was he decorated?"

Yes, he returned home with the survivors of his regiment, and when they paraded before the Queen, Bob was decorated with a medal which was tied round his neck by Her Majesty. But, please, don't confine yourself to admiration. Remember Bob when you come into action, and do not be outdone by a dog.

Two dogs which recently returned to England have been repeatedly under fire in the various armed incursions which have taken place in British Central Africa. They were known as the "Fox and the Lion," and were held in great awe by the natives, to whom the species was entirely strange. In all the engagements they marched at the head of the column, and on going into action spared no pains, by furiously barking and showing their teeth, to express their distaste for the enemy.

"How do horses behave in battle? Aren't they frightened?"

Your questions are apt to take us off our track, and this is scarcely to our p—

"Oh, but do tell us. I'm sure we can learn a lot from a horse."

Well, we are told that after a cavalry horse has been in

1   *Nullah* is a Hindi word for a steep, narrow valley, often containing a dry riverbed.

service six months he knows every bugle-call, and, when in action, partakes of the hopes and fears of the conflict just as his master does. When the troopers begin to cheer and the sabres to flash he will often scream out. His eyes blaze and are fixed steadily in front.

If a volley comes and he is unhurt he will lower his head and toss it right and left, and then take a sudden breath for the crash. If charging infantry, he will thunder straight at a man and knock him down; if against a line of horsemen, he will lift his head and front feet as if going over a fence.

The horse that loses his rider and is unwounded himself, will continue to run with the other horses until some movement throws him out. Then he goes galloping here and there, neighing with alarm, but will not leave the field. He will avoid the dead and wounded, or he will leap over them.

A horse which has passed through a battle unwounded is fretful and nervous for the next three or four days. His first battle is also the making or unmaking of him as a war-horse. If the nervous tension has been too great, he will bolt in the face of danger. If the test has not been beyond him, he will go into the next fight with his head held high and flecks of foam blowing from his mouth as he thunders over the earth.

A military riding-master says: "Once a cavalry horse is thoroughly trained, its intelligence is marvellous. It will obey the bugle-call as promptly as a man. In fact, I have known many cases where it has put its rider right when he has mistaken the order given. You may imagine it is an odd sight to see a horse executing an accurate manœuvre in spite of the efforts of its deluded rider to compel it to perform an inaccurate one!

"Again, such a horse in battle is often as brave as a man. It will chafe and stamp impatiently while waiting for the order to charge. When the order comes, it will dash forward full of fire and excitement, and neighing wildly. It will often rear at the moment of contact with the enemy, striking and biting savagely at the opposing horses, and trampling down the infantry.

"If its rider falls, it will retain its place in the ranks and follow every subsequent movement with military precision. Many a trooper looks upon his horse as a friend and comrade, and the intelligent animal well deserves it."

"What do they do, poor things, if they lose their masters?"

Lord George Paget tells us. Writing of the famous charge of the Light Brigade[1] at Balaclava, he says: "One incident struck me forcibly about this time—the bearing of riderless horses in such circumstances. I was, of course, riding by myself, and clear of the line, and for that reason was a marked object for the poor dumb brutes. They consequently made dashes at me, advancing with me for a considerable distance—at one time as many as five on my right and two on my left, cringing in on me and positively squeezing me as the round shot came bounding by them. I remarked their eyes, betokening as keen a sense of the perils around them as we human beings experienced (and that is saying a good deal). The bearing of the horse I was riding, in contrast to these, was remarkable. He had been struck, but showed no signs of fear, thus evincing the confidence of dumb animals in the superior being."

To be prompt, prudent, skilful and cool, yet with the pluck and daring that carries all before it, one thing is plainly necessary: we must keep up our hearts—we must be cheerful. There will be more to be said about this when we come to speak of marching. But it is a point of such importance, that as commanding officers we must insist upon it in ourselves.

How is this cheerfulness to be kept up amid weary fighting? *By Prayer.*

1   As immortalized in the poem by Alfred, Lord Tennyson. Of the roughly 600 men who made the charge, only half returned, and more than half of the horses died or had to be killed due to wounds.

XVI.

CALLING OUT THE RESERVES

Incline unto my aid, O God. O Lord make haste to help me.
(Psalm 69, 3.)

I MUST pray. Yes, above all else I must pray: "Queen Esther, fearing the danger that was at hand, *had recourse to the Lord.*"[1] He is anxious to help us, but He means us to ask Him, and He has made our asking the condition of His giving. We all know of the repeated messages Wellington received during Waterloo from different general officers praying for support. His answer was always the same: "You must do your best and hold the ground," although at that moment he had reserves at hand that he might have used. The use of reserves at too early a period of the day is, we are told, the most dangerous of faults—in earthly warfare—but in ours, they cannot be called out too soon. This is why, all through the pages of Holy Scripture, Almighty God encourages us in such tender words to call upon Him: "Call upon Me in the day of trouble: I will deliver thee."[2] "If thou say in thy heart: These nations are more than I, how shall I be able to destroy them? Fear not. Do manfully, and be of good heart; for the Lord thy God, He Himself is thy Leader and will not

---

1   Esther 14.
2   Psalm 49.

leave thee, nor forsake thee."[1] "Take courage, therefore, and be very valiant"[2] "I will show thee what thou art to do."[3]

Had we stood in the British trenches before Sebastopol, we should have noticed that an electric wire was run down to them from the army Head Quarters. This was the first wire used in the theatre of war, and we were thus the first nation to force the telegraph into service there. A most valuable servant it makes. So much so, that in future we shall have, with every army in the field, an officer styled, "Director of Telegraph Engineers," to make, repair, and work the lines. By means of wires laid down as each column advances, messages can be sent back to the starting-place, and so to the front, along the road upon which the Commander-in-Chief is marching. He can thus be in momentary communication with all his columns. "During the Indian Mutiny," says Lord Wolseley, "the wire uniting us with Calcutta followed close upon our heels, so close that I have seen the workmen when laying it, actually under a fire of canister."

An army must never be cut off from its Base of Operations—the port or ports on the sea-coast where its provisions and ammunitions are stored—and communication with it by means of the telegraph is invaluable. To lay down a line, therefore, and keep it in good working order is one of the main concerns of the Commandant.

The electric telegraph is a new element in the warfare of this world, but in the spiritual war there are lines of communication as old as the human race itself, between the army in the field, and the Leader who controls it. Those lines are Prayer. By Prayer, a constant communication is kept up between us and our Commander-in-Chief. Swifter than the electric current, Prayer carries its message to Him Who is all-powerful to aid

1   Deut. 31.
2   Deut. 28.
3   I Kings 16.

us, and in the same instant there comes back the succour we need—grace and strength, courage, confidence, perseverance.

And here, please, take notice that in an earthly campaign the Commandant at the Base of Operations has instructions to forward to the front all reinforcements of men and horses, and all supplies and stores required there. To say that he does not like the General Officer commanding the army—a good-for-nothing fellow—would be ridiculous. He may be worthless enough, but what difference does that make? It is not the man who asks for help, but the interests of the service that are considered, and succour is sent off at once. Much the same is true of God's dealings with us. We must never be so silly as to say, "It's no good *my* praying. I'm not good enough to get what I want."

Now, is it likely that an enemy will leave the British troops in quiet possession of their helpful lines? Certainly not. In the science of war there are directions for the demolition of bridges, gates, guns, provisions—anything and everything that can serve the purpose of an adversary. But the telegraphs by which his succours come—these, above all, must be seized or rendered useless. That communication with the Base of Operations and with the Commander-in-Chief must be stopped somehow. How is it to be done? Lord Wolseley tells us. "An admirable way for destroying communication is by means of a non-conducting wire having the outward appearance of the ordinary wire in use. Being furnished, before starting, with some of this wire, and the tools used in repairing telegraphs, send a man experienced in such work up a pole, and let him then cut the wire close to it, uniting it again with the non-conducting wire spliced on in the usual manner. This should be done in several places along a line, and always at a pole. The result will be that, although all galvanic communications will have ceased, a man merely marching along the line will not be able to discover where the break exists; one must go from post to post with an instrument to test each intervening portion of wire before the exact spot can be ascertained. It is advisable that a pole here and there should also be destroyed, and the wire cut, so that it should be supposed at first that the interruption simply resulted therefrom. Another plan is to unite the several wires together by a thin platinum wire thread. Done close to the pole, it is imperceptible from the ground and diverts the current, acting as a leak and as a confusing medium. If there is only one wire, the platinum thread should be brought to the ground to cause a leak."

All that trouble and cunning to cause leakage and confusion, to stop the communication with Head Quarters! And now, do you know, I think there is something very like it in our warfare—on our lines! The devil will be at mischief if he can. It is well worth his while to divert the current of prayer and grace, to introduce disorder and confusion. His methods are not very different from those we have just been reading about, and they are in various ways adapted to places, persons, and circumstances. But his main object is always the same: to interrupt our communications with our Heavenly Leader. His agents have instructions to be watchful. Wherever a line is started, a prayer begun, they must try to destroy it, or at least to divert or intercept the message. Whatever other business they are about, whatever else has to be left, time must always be found for this. Quietly and imperceptibly, but unceasingly, their work is going on. You pass up a church where the bowed heads and the clasped hands make a show of union with God. But it is a show only, the communication has been broken. "This people honoureth Me with their lips, but their heart is far from Me." [1] Thoughts of business and amusement, plans, work,

1   St. Mark 6.

study; thoughts of vanity, anger, rash judgment, revenge—how often these come in and cause a break in the current, diverting it down to the earth.

"Can we help the devils distracting us?"

"And if we can't, is it our fault?"

Useful questions both of them. To answer them fully would take us too far out of our way. But this much may be said:

1. We may do a good deal to prevent distractions, but to keep them off altogether is not in our power.

2. What we cannot help is never our fault, and we may be quite sure God will not let it harm us.

"Are common things distractions when they come into our heads; I don't mean play, of course, but lessons, exams, rows, and all that sort of thing?"

The thoughts and cares of daily life—work, studies, troubles—can hardly be thrust out of our minds the moment we go to prayer. And why should they? Why should they be kept out of prayer, which is a conversation with our Heavenly Father? Are not these just the sort of things we talk over with a friend? There can be no harm whatever to talk them over *with* Him. The harm is when He is left out altogether. Work, trouble, anxiety, talked over with Him *is prayer*.

"And the Philistines coming spread themselves in the valley of Raphaim. And David consulted the Lord, saying: Shall I go up to the Philistines, and wilt Thou deliver them into my hand? And the Lord said to David: Go up; for I will surely deliver the Philistines into thy hand. And David came to Baal Pharisim and defeated them there.

"And the Philistines came up again. And David consulted the Lord: Shall I go up against the Philistines? He answered: Go not up against them. And David did as the Lord commanded him."[1]

An artist said she got her best ideas in her visits to the

---

1   2 Kings 5.

Blessed Sacrament. *She went to our Lord for them.* In the quiet afternoon or evening when there was no one in the church, she went in, and after her adoration sat down quietly in front of the Tabernacle, thinking out her subject and consulting our Lord as to how He would like it done, asking for advice and lights, begging her work might be well done so as to bring Him praise and glory. Were these distractions? If so, I fancy our Lord's recommendation to us will be, "Go thou and do likewise."

Despatches and Reports of military operations are to be forwarded regularly to Head Quarters. "The rule is that the senior general present at any action great or small, writes a description of it in the form of a despatch to the Secretary of State for War." These official letters are considered of such importance, that every detail concerning them is regulated—the paper, margin, paragraphs, even the folding. Notice the words "any action *great or small.*" *Our* Chief does not count anything small that concerns His soldiers on the field. But lest we should think He does, He would have us report *all*, that we may have His sympathy and help in all.

One important caution we need. When we find we have lost time in prayer by distractions, whether faulty or not, we must not lose more by seeking for the place where the leakage occurred. Here we have an advantage over those who have to go from post to post with an instrument in order to ascertain where the current has been diverted. As soon as we find out that communication has ceased, we must cast away the non-conducting wire, and supply its place without delay.

One who followed the troops in the great Egyptian campaign of 1898 says: "I sat and meditated on the full significance of the simple military phrase, 'line of communication.' It is the great discovery of the Sirdar that he has recognised that in the Soudan the communications are the essence and heart of the whole problem." Let us recognise it too. When we see the telegraph wires, along which countless invisible and noiseless messages are speeding and crossing—questions and needs followed, often instantaneously, by answers and help—we may think of that more wonderful and constant intercourse between Heaven and earth which we call prayer, and thank God for giving it to us and making it so easy and so sure.

Besides destroying communication between a general and his Base of Operations, an enemy may turn such communications to his own profit. A telegraph operator can, with a small pocket instrument, tap the wires at any place. He may learn the messages that are passing along them, and perhaps the plans that are being made to his detriment. In the war between the Northern and Southern States of America, this practice was frequently resorted to. Tampering with the telegraph is so serious a matter, that men have cast about for some means of establishing communication with Head Quarters which should be beyond the reach of an enemy.

"I know. Carrier pigeons."

Yes; Government services of dogs and pigeons are equipped on a scale unheard of before. The pigeon post is being organized for naval and military purposes over the whole of Western and Southwestern Europe. In 1897 the German military authorities did rather a cool thing. They sent to Dover 2,000 pigeons, which when released, flew back to Dusseldorf and other centres. The object, clearly, was to see whether, in the event of a German descent upon England, information of its progress could be transmitted to Germany, even if the cables were cut or in English hands.

"How mean of them!"

"It's a pity we've no way of preventing the enemy stopping *our* messages before they get to Head Quarters."

We *have* a way. "Lord, think of me."[1] "Lord help me!" "O Lord make haste to help me!" "Jesus mercy!" Could any enemy be sharp enough to stop one of those flights? Direct and swift they have sped on their way and reached the Throne of God, and returned with help before the enemy had the remotest idea there was any message going. We might make a collection of these brief ejaculations or aspirations of which the treasury of Holy Scripture is full. Take those you like best and make favourites of them, so that they will spring to your lips in every need. None are more helpful than acts of love. An act of love in temptation is better than an act contrary to the sin to which you are tempted. "My God, I love You," when a troublesome thought comes. And then we turn to other thoughts. Think out that problem in Euclid which puzzled you. Or say the multiplication-table backwards in one breath—! If the troublesome thought will not go, or comes again and again, keep calm and cool like a good general. "Jesus, dear Jesus! My God, I love You, I love You." There is merit each time, and each time the enemy grows weaker. You are making him an Angelus bell, a call to prayer. He hates this, and after a while will leave you in peace.

"As I shall not be rewarded for the good thoughts of the good Angels," says St. Ignatius, "so I shall not be punished for the bad thoughts of the bad angels." Of course not, for the simple reason that neither are my own. This is mere common sense, but very helpful.

Here are a few aspirations for choice:—

"In my distress I will call upon the Lord and I will cry to my God."[2]

"Help me, who have no other helper but Thee, O Lord... Thou knowest my necessity,...deliver me from my fear."[3]

1 Tobias 3.
2 2 Kings 22.
3 Esther 14.

"Alas, alas, alas, my Lord, what shall we do!"[1] *We* mind, reminding Him that we are His soldiers and that our cause is His.

"Strengthen me, O Lord God, at this hour."[2]

Or you may like a prayer shorter still: Jesus, Mary! Jesus, I am Thine, save me! Stay with us, Lord! Lord save me, I perish! Lead us not into temptation. Deliver us from evil.

"I like the Scripture prayers best."

"I don't. The short ones suit me. I can't get along far before the enemy comes splicing his stupid wire on to my line."

"St. Aloysius determined to go for a whole hour without having a single distraction."

"Fancy! How glad he must have been when he was getting near the end."

We shall do well here to note a direction of the Commander-in-Chief's. "Never trust to one messenger for the safe delivery of important messages; send a duplicate, and sometimes even a triplicate, at two or three hours' interval." The interval in our case need not be one of hours. Of course you will not forget your good Angel; when should he be your guardian, if not in danger!

Lastly, call upon Mary in time of temptation. Run to her, as a child runs to its mother.

One sultry evening after dusk, an Indian girl, twelve years of age, was crossing a room whose open windows overlooked the garden. Indian ladies, even of the highest rank, wear no shoes or slippers within doors, and the child's bare feet moved noiselessly across the floor. Suddenly she stopped, trembling from head to foot, rooted to the spot by some terrible fear, yet unable to utter a sound. At last there broke from her lips a wailing, agonized cry:—

---

1   4 Kings 6.

2   4 Judith 13.

"Mother, mother! I—I've trodden on a snake. My foot is on its head. Oh, mother, come quick, come quick!"

"Keep still, child! Keep still! I am coming! Don't move. I am coming."

There was a stir in the next room, a lamp shone through the curtained doorway, and the mother was on the spot. It was a terrible sight that met her gaze—the child in her piteous terror pressing with all her light weight on the foot that held the head of a cobra. It had wound itself round and round the slender ankle in its struggle to free its head. Plainly the little one's strength could not hold out much longer. The mother came, and standing by the side of her child, put her arm round her waist. She laid her foot over the little foot and pressed with all her weight. There they stood a while—mother and child over the serpent's head.

Presently the struggles ceased; the coils relaxed their hold; then fell away and lay in lifeless rings upon the ground; the serpent's head was crushed.

"That's a beautiful story. But is it true?"

Quite true. It happened lately. And times without number during nineteen centuries has it happened that a child has been rescued by its Mother. It is happening all the world over now. Wherever there is a struggle with the Evil One, and the weak trembling soul calls on Mary, she flies to the rescue. She places herself by the side of her child; she puts her arm round it; and again the promise in Eden is fulfilled—the serpent's head is crushed.

> Maria, Mater gratiæ
>   Dulcis parens clementiæ
> Tu nos ab hoste protege,
>   Et mortis hora suscipe.

When temptation presses hard, we may find help in the holy Fear of God, one of His Seven Gifts to us in Confirmation, and given specially for times of danger. "Blessed is the man that shall think of the all-seeing Eye of God."[1]　There are times when this saving fear is our best protection. There are others when a loving loyalty to our King moves us more. He is watching. Our soul belongs to Him more than to us. We must run no risks with it.

I must trust in God.　Surely, surely this will not be hard—to trust Him in the fight, Who only lets us go into it that we may conquer. "The Wisdom of God kept him safe from his enemies, and gave him *a strong conflict that he might overcome.*"[2]　We are only asked to meet a disarmed enemy. So we must not cry out with fear as we see his big sword, but meet him like David, "in the name of the Lord of Hosts," take his own sword—those very temptations of his— and turn them against him.

"God is faithful Who will not suffer you to be tempted above that which you are able."[3]　We lower the flame of the lamp when we see the glass being tried beyond its strength. Will not our Heavenly Father prevent temptation from being too fierce for the frail lamps that are His constant care?

"But I'm so afraid I might do a mortal sin without thinking or knowing."

Not the cleverest person in the world could do that, and certainly you couldn't. Take the mariner's compass in your hand; stand with your face to the north, to which it is pointing—so. Now turn suddenly round to the south, and see if you have changed the position of the needle. No, it may have swerved a little, but its tendency to the north has prevented it being moved right round to the opposite direction. It would have been out of sorts altogether to have gone that far. The

---

1　Ecclus. 14.
2　Wisdom 10.
3　I Cor. 10.

needle is your will. When its usual state is to be fixed on God with a determination never to offend Him by mortal sin, it is not easy for it to twist right round and give its full consent to a grievous offence against Him. And as to its doing this without knowing it—that is simple nonsense.

There is no gliding unawares into mortal sin. Full knowledge is necessary. Those who love God and are trying at all seriously to serve Him, know at once if their will has turned round suddenly and set itself against Him. In a shower-bath you cannot doubt as to whether you have pulled the string or not. Neither can you doubt as to whether you have fully consented to what you knew perfectly was a grievous offence against God. The shock that follows such consent makes it plain enough. Doubt shows this at least—that consent was not full. And if we have the blessed habit of turning to God at once, we need not even doubt. We may be happy in the conviction that there was no consent at all, and trouble ourselves no more about it.

If only the devil can succeed in making us unhappy, he is delighted. It is a wicked thing to make mischief between friends. But this is just what the devil loves to do. And if he cannot do it, cannot get us to turn against our best of friends, he tries to make us *think* we have done it, and so be miserable. He says to us, "There now, you have done it. Don't call on God any more; don't make any more acts of love. He is angry with you and doesn't want your love." And God says to us, tenderly: "Don't be afraid, child; I am here, close to you. I love you dearly, and you love Me. Your very trouble shows that you love Me. Never mind your thoughts and your feelings. I don't mind them. Your will is all I care about, and that I have quite safe."

Some of us say: "If I only knew I was in the grace of God, I could go on bravely." Can we know this? Not with complete certainty. Yet with that amount of certainty which is enough

St. Michael

to make us go on brightly and hopefully. We can tell when we lose grace. The devil lets us know when we say "Yes" to what we know to be wrong. Then we can surely know when we have not done this. If the driver can tell when his engine has gone off the lines, he can tell when it has not. So with us and our will. For mind, it is a question of *will*. We can sin by the will only—not by the understanding, nor by the memory, nor by the imagination, but only by the will. And my will is my own, not the devil's. I have the ruling of it. Let us keep it on the right lines and all is safe. The devil can never *make* us. All he can do is to try. As long as our will says "No," he tries in vain. Why, then, are we so silly as to give him the satisfaction of seeing us miserable about nothing? Temptation, as we have seen, so far from being a sign that God is angry with us, proves the direct contrary. "Whom He loves and trusts, whose promotion He has at heart, the Leader keeps by Him and puts to the test." Is there anything here to make us miserable?

"But the devil is very strong, isn't he?"

And God, on Whose side we are fighting, is "an invincible King for ever."[1] When the servant of the Prophet Eliseus saw an army round about the city, and horses and chariots, he cried out for fear. But the Prophet answered: "Fear not, for there are more with us than with them. And Eliseus prayed and said: Lord, open his eyes that he may see. And the Lord opened the eyes of the servant and he saw; and behold, the mountain was full of horses and chariots of fire round about Eliseus."[2] Any one of that multitude of heavenly spirits was a match for the devil.

"Then the Angel Raphael took the devil and bound him."[3] "And I saw an angel coming down from Heaven having the key

---

1   Ecclus. 18.
2   4 Kings 6.
3   Tobias 8.

of the bottomless pit, and a great chain in his hand. And he laid hold of the old dragon, the serpent, who is the devil and Satan, and bound him. And cast him into the bottomless pit and shut him up, and set a seal upon him."[1] Notice the perfect ease with which they handle him, and his utter helplessness in their grasp.

"Do you know why I think a serpent is more like the devil than tigers or leopards, and other wild beasts? Not because it is fierce and kills more people, or because it is always hiding. But because it hurts people who don't hurt it, or want to do it any harm, and when they can't be of any good to it for food— just out of spite. That's what I hate him most for."

And because his malice is turned, not against us only who have done him no harm, but against God, Who made him and has done him all manner of good.

"It's a pity they don't hunt the serpent or set traps for it, or that it hasn't an enemy to kill it, like all other creatures."

But it has. The cobra, strong, cunning, cruel, has an enemy—an insignificant one, you would suppose, too small to deserve notice, and certainly too weak to excite fear. But this is not the cobra's experience. The mongoose, a little creature about the size of a rat, is anything but a contemptible foe. Inoffensive in appearance as well as defenceless, its vigilance, wariness, and rapidity of movement make it more than a match for its terrible enemy, which it fearlessly attacks. A combat between the two is a curious sight to watch. In vain does the cobra with an angry hiss erect its body in the air, and with glittering eyes and forked tongue darting incessantly to and fro from its hooded head, seek to fascinate or to frighten its puny foe. In vain does it swing its long curve backwards and forwards, intending to take the mongoose by surprise. The little creature remains motionless and watches. Not a movement of the cobra, not

1   Apoc. 20.

a change in the varying attitudes escapes it. But it keeps quite still, waiting and watching; trusting not to its strength but to its agility for victory. And when the cobra, losing patience, thrusts itself forward with a sudden dart to fasten its deadly fangs on its enemy's head, quick as lightning the mongoose springs to one side, beyond the range of those poisonous fangs, which fall harmlessly on the ground in front. Again and again the cobra repeats its attack, and with the same result, only spending its force upon the air, and tearing its mouth by the fall upon the ground. It seems to be a question of which will tire first.

"Does the mongoose ever attack the cobra?"

Oh dear, yes. It does not lack courage, I can assure you. Whether it will remain on the defensive and tire out its enemy, or boldly come out of a thicket and begin the attack, depends on circumstances. In each case it knows what to do. Its mode of attack is this. Seizing its opportunity when the cobra has fallen forward after a fruitless stroke, the mongoose leaps upon its enemy from behind, buries its sharp teeth in the cobra's head, and with teeth and claws rends it asunder.

"The brave little creature! But *we*—of course every one knows who the mongoose is—*we* can't kill our serpent outright like that; I wish we could, and have done with it."

"Does the mongoose always win the fight?"

Not always. Sometimes it is lazy to begin with, and lets the cobra wind round it and crush it slowly. Sometimes it gets tired of the battle and neglects precautions, and so gets bitten. But even then, observe what happens: instead of giving up all for lost, it runs at once to the jungle, seeks out some herb known only to its instinct, applies it to the wound, and then returns to finish the battle. This, at least, is what the natives say!

"Well, if the mongoose can't do that, *we* can, anyhow."

Not only we *can*, but we *must*. We shall be bitten plenty of times before our final victory, and so there is no habit more necessary than that of seeking out our remedy and applying it at once.

"Before the poison gets into the blood, you know."

The mongoose running off for its medicine reminds us to think for a moment about our falls and our wounds. Is it possible that, knowing our own weaknesses, we expect to get through every battle without tumbles and wounds? Yet to see the surprise of some of us on such occasions one would suppose we thought ourselves invulnerable.

There is a picture somewhere of a famous modern General getting his first wound. The scene is the nursery, where the hero is falling off his rocking-horse, and tumbling screaming on to the floor, into the midst of his tin soldiers and toy guns. He must have picked himself up, you know, or he would not be on horseback to-day. All men, even heroes, have their falls. But there is nothing in this to drive us to despair. We are not Humpty-Dumpties, we can be put together again. We come to grief time after time—so does the worm, and to more serious grief perhaps. But it does not lose heart. When the gardener's spade has accidentally chopped it in half, it becomes two worms. One part grows a new head, the other a new tail, so that it is really a gainer in the end by its mishap.

Higher creatures, too, can make good their losses. Lobsters and crabs grow lost claws, lizards grow new tails. Young flies and spiders grow lost legs. It is to be noticed, as very much to our purpose, that the younger a creature is, the greater is its power of mending itself.

And *we* can mend—mend easily and quickly, if we are young and set about the work in earnest. Lobsters and crabs take from six weeks to six months to grow fresh claws. We need not take so long by any means. If the devil has injured us, we can have our claws ready for him the next minute. A good act of contrition is all that is wanted.

Why should a Queen's soldiers be so brave and our Lord's so cowardly? A bagpiper with both ankles shot through could not, of course, go on marching. But he could sit down and go on playing, and forget himself in the thought of serving the army still. When we sit down it is to cry over ourselves, not to cheer up our neighbours.

"He who never made a mistake never made anything." Failure teaches us how to do better next time and how to profit this time by humbling ourselves. A fall opens our eyes, Holy Scripture tells us. It may do us a world of good *provided we rise quickly*. We should get up as fast as if we had fallen on the line in front of an express train. And this ought not to be hard, for our Lord is so good and generous, so ready to forgive. He shows us again and again in His beautiful parables how He longs to get back His lost sheep, His prodigal child. How He is ready to forgive seventy times seven times—as often as ever we come to Him for forgiveness. His Army Act is not a list of the punishments we are to have for "shamefully deserting," "shamefully abandoning" our post, "cowardice before the enemy," "getting made prisoner." He does not, like the War Office, wait for "three years' exemplary conduct," or "till good work has been done in the field to grant restoration of service." He meets us with, "I absolve thee," whenever we come to Him striking our breasts and saying, "I am sorry." He wants us to use our faults as we use the rungs of a ladder, to mount by them higher than we were before. He even comforts us for our wounds and losses. "Let not this discourage thee, for various is the event of war."[1]

Before we commit sin, the devil tries to prevent our seeing the harm to which he is tempting us, lest we should be struck with horror and draw back. But as soon as we have yielded to his temptation, he puts our sin before us in all its malice—

1   2 Kings 11.

not to move us to contrition—oh no!—but to bring us to discouragement and to give up trying. Now we must do the exact contrary of what he wants us to do. When he tempts us to sin, whether mortal or venial, we must look at its hatefulness and its terrible consequences. But if, in spite of this, we are so unhappy as to fall, we must look, not at our misery only, but at the goodness of God, in order that, helped by His grace, we may rise again *and at once.* It was this that was wanting to Judas. He repented of his awful crime; he confessed it; he restored the money for the sake of which he had sinned. But he did not remember the mercy of God; he did not return to the Feet of his Master and make his act of contrition there. Of all the good resolutions we can make, there is none perhaps better than this: "Whenever I fall into any fault, I will make a good act of contrition and try again as if nothing had happened." "A tree hath hope: if it be cut, it groweth green again, and the boughs thereof sprout. If its root be old in the earth, and its stock be dead in the dust, at the scent of water it shall spring and bring forth leaves, as when it was first planted."[1]

One word about moderation in victory:

"The General Officer commanding must make up his mind quickly as to what he intends doing: there is a general tendency to idle during the first moments of relief to the strained nerves which victory brings with it; the best men even are apt to indulge in idle talk of the events that have just taken place, instead of making arrangements for what still remains to be done. The enemy has retreated, is he to be pursued? if so, by what force and what troops?...In war there are frequently such changes of fortune, that even when victorious you must be prepared to ward off dangers. A battle cannot be won every day, and the general who, having won one, fails to reap all due advantage from it should never be employed again."

1   Job 13.

Some make so bad a use of victory by elation and pride that the enemy gains more than he had lost. And some, on the other hand, make so good a use of defeat, that the enemy wishes heartily he had never meddled with them.

"The safe custody of prisoners the night of an action is often embarrassing. All men should be at once disarmed when taken, except those officers who will promise on their word of honour not to attempt to escape, who may be permitted to retain their swords."

Our enemy has no word of honour, we can never trust him—we must always stand on our guard, even when he is worsted after a defeat.

"Do not be dazed by victory, like the savage who halts to plunder or to rejoice; but let it operate upon you in different fashion. Let it quicken your movements and give increased energy to the blows you follow it up with... Destroy the enemy's railways, the signal-stations, the water-tanks, and all the arrangements for watering the engines. All electric wires to be cut and twisted, and all batteries and their apparatus broken in pieces. Blow up bridges with gunpowder. In destroying woodwork by fire, whatever oil can be obtained from the neighbouring houses should be poured over it to make it burn quickly. Tear up the rails and bend and twist them. Burn the carriages, the piles of coal and fuel, and all shops for the repair of engines, &c. Everything that will burn, set on fire."

Is not this following up victory with a vengeance!

John Sobieski, King of Poland, having routed the Turkish squadrons and raised the siege of Vienna,[1] entered the city in triumph, surrounded by his victorious soldiers, and hailed by

1   Jan III Sobieski led the largest cavalry charge in history to secure victory at the Battle of Vienna in 1683, a battle which formed the turning point in the 300-year struggle against the encroaching Ottoman Empire.

JAN III SOBIESKI OF POLAND AT THE BATTLE OF VIENNA

From a painting by Jerzy Siemiginowski-Eleuter.

280

the cheers of all the inhabitants as the saviour of Europe. He went straight to the Carmelite Church, and ordered a *Te Deum* to be sung in thanksgiving for his victory. But no singer was at hand to intone the chant, and the King, eager to give to God the praise which the world was attributing to him, could brook no delay. So he intoned it himself in a loud voice and continued to sing alternately with the people, ending with the words: "*Not to us, O Lord, not to us but to Thy name alone be the glory.*"[1]

Often and often we have a Turk near at home to fight against. When we get the victory over him, we may sing away like King John. But let us not forget it is to be a *Te Deum*, and to wind up with *not unto us*.

---

1 Psalm 113.

PART THE SECOND

XVII.

OBEDIENCE

*All that Thou hast commanded us we will do, and
whithersoever Thou shall send us we will go.*
(Josue I, 18.)

"IF I see Lord Wolseley when I'm grown up, I shall tell him we
know all about fighting, because he has taught us."

All right. Mind you are able to answer his questions
satisfactorily. He will be sure to ask if you act according to his
instructions, for it is not *knowing* but *doing* that a commander
looks at. He will want to know how you show on parade, and
behave in barracks; how you clean your rifle and polish your
buckles and buttons. A soldier is not always actually fighting.
He has duties besides those on the field, and unless these are
properly discharged, he will cut a sorry figure when he comes
into action. Drilling, camping and marching are as much a
part of a soldier's training as learning to shoot straight. But
one word sums up all his duties, all his equipment of mind and
body, all that goes to make up our idea of a soldier: *obedience*.

What is it that in reviews, military tournaments or battle
calls for our admiration chiefly? Is it not the ready and cheerful
submission to authority; the prompt, instantaneous obedience
to orders at any risk, at any cost?

Sir Henry Havelock, the reliever of Lucknow, had a house a little way out of London. One dull afternoon in November, having business at the War Office, he went into the City, taking with him his son Henry, a boy of ten, whom he left on London Bridge to walk up and down until his return. Difficulties and complications detained him longer than he expected, and instead of getting his work dispatched in an hour, he found himself obliged to devote to it the rest of the day. It was quite dark when, engrossed in the affairs he had been transacting, he took a late train home.

"Where is Henry?" exclaimed the anxious mother as she came to meet her husband.

"Henry! Good Heavens—I've forgotten him! He'll be on the bridge still."

A hurried explanation, and he was off to the station. He caught the next up train and arrived in London at midnight. Would the child have remained through all those hours? By the light of the lamps blinking through the fog on the deserted bridge, he made out a little figure dragging itself wearily along. The boy welcomed his father with a smile, and putting his hand in his, asked simply if they were going home now. No questioning, no repining—he was a soldier's son.

Another story. It is told of Robert Clive that, as a clerk in the service of the East India Company, he was guilty of some insolence towards a superior—one of the directors, I think it was—and in that case, a very great personage who could have had him dismissed at once from the service. His misdemeanour was reported to high quarters, and he was ordered to make reparation. This he did in the following fashion:

"I am ordered, sir, to apologise to you for my conduct of yesterday." The gentleman received him with a friendly smile, begged him to think no more of the occurrence, and as he held out his hand, said:

"And now you will come home and dine with me?"

"No, sir," replied the young man as he drew himself up. "I was ordered to apologise, not to dine." And refusing the proffered hand, he turned away.

Now I want you to notice something rather curious. Tell this story to a youngster who is up in rebellion against authority. Notice the timing, please, for this is all important. Not *was* in rebellion a week ago and all is past and set right, but actually *is* in rebellion at the moment. Tell the story, and say: "Now do you admire that speech of Clive's?" You will probably see the eyes go down, the eyebrows go up, the foot work about on its heel, the lips compress, and a cautious smile spreading over the countenance. The meaning of all this is, "Well, if you want to know the truth, I rather do admire it. I wonder whether you do. I think it's rather manly."

Suppose, instead of letting out what *we* think, we ask what the kind-hearted director of the East India Company thought, who had made the offer to the friendless youth. Did *he* think it particularly manly? Or take an ordinary looker-on, what would he have thought? Take Clive himself that afternoon, when he had returned to the use of reason, and could look back quietly on the interview of the morning. What was uppermost in his mind as he sat at his desk with his head buried in his hands? Was it pride at his manly conduct, or was it shame?

If, in spite of this unanimous opinion, you still feel the glow of admiration, force yourself at least to account for it. Chemists get at the nature of a thing by analysing it. We can tell the worth of an act by taking it to pieces, looking particularly at its cause and its motives, for these determine the nature of an act. Now what is there in that act to admire—its *cause*? It came from wounded self-love and from a conscience ill at ease. The apology, instead of being what it might have been—a frank, generous acknowledgment that he had been in fault, was nothing but a cowardly—not to say hypocritical—speech, made for the sole purpose of keeping his place in the service. Like all cowardly acts, it contented nobody, the doer least of all; hence his vexation broke out afresh, kindled by the very act which ought to have extinguished it. So it is with us. Conscience will be our ruler, as it was meant to be, or it will be our tormentor. If we obey it readily, we keep our souls in gladness and in peace. If we disobey it, there will be neither rest nor contentment for us, and on the least provocation the turmoil within will lead to a fresh outburst.

The *cause,* then, does not call for much admiration. Does the *motive?* He was vexed at having been compelled to appear in his true position as a servant of the Company. He knew he was dependent, but chafing under the yoke, he had wished to look independent. He would show his spite by an assumption of superiority which he hoped would hurt his superior? Is there anything very noble in this?

What we have to note—I expect you have noted it already—is this: that independence, or rather our desire to be independent, is foolish as well as wrong, and only looks manly *when we are out of sorts.* Shall we see why this is?

At first the little child runs here and there, does as it is told, and asks no questions. It feels that it knows very little and is very weak and helpless. Therefore it submits readily, without expecting reasons. But as time goes on, the powers of its soul which were folded up like a bud, begin to unfold; its likes and dislikes become more marked; its will grows stronger. It begins to *think* when it hears the order, "You must go to bed." "You must not touch that." And at last the question comes—first to the mind, then to the lips: "*Why?*" The probability is there were plenty of "Whys?" in our nursery when we were small. Nurse told us there is no such word as "Why" in the dictionary, and that good children do as they are told, asking no questions. But this did not satisfy us. We wanted to know *why* we have to do what we are told. And we had a right to know. Not, mind, why we have to obey this or that order in particular, but why we have to obey at all. God has given us our reason to guide us in what we do. Enlightened by faith, it will have to guide us all along our road to Heaven. So those who have charge of us cannot make clear to us too soon why we must obey those who are set over us—in other words, *the duty of obedience.*

Little children readily take in what is said to them. Fresh from the Hand of God, lit up with the glory of baptismal grace, and guided by heavenly instincts which have not, as yet, been dulled by self-will, their souls are beautiful with the beauty of *truth.* There is no pretence, no hiding of ignorance and weakness, no affectation of independence. Submission and obedience come naturally to them, for the mind is docile and the guileless heart unspoilt by passion. Mind and heart are as soft wax on which the least impression remains, it may be for ever—remains for weal or woe.[1] How grave a duty lies on all who have charge of them in those early days, to see that the impression made is such as will teach the opening mind, and guide the trusting heart aright. The first lessons will never, never be forgotten.

But God was guiding the little heart even before the first lesson came from without, guiding it by a wonderful power called instinct, which taught it to look up to its parents and reverence and obey them. This instinct, as its mind unfolds, must be lifted up and strengthened. It must be taught *why* it has to obey. Therefore nurse would have been wiser to try to answer our childish "Why?" The right answering of that question may shape a life. Once we have grasped the idea that

1 *for weal or woe:* that is, for better or for worse.

because God made us, we belong to Him and must do as He tells us, we fall naturally into our true position as servants. We see that we must serve God by obedience if we want to be happy, and we see how naturally the disobedience of Adam and Eve, "brought death into the world and all our woes with loss of Eden."

"Oh, of course. But *God* told them not to eat of the fruit. It is not so bad when God tells us things, but when people make stupid little rules—why must we obey them?"

That is what we are coming to. You wanted some time ago to know exactly what the King's orders are. It was a very natural and sensible wish, and the time has now come to satisfy it. Only you must not require Him to come down from His throne to give His orders. You will hardly expect Him to speak to you as to Moses, face to face. This would be presumption, surely. Suppose we were to insist on the examiners of the University of Oxford travelling all over the world to put the "Regulations" into the hands of candidates, because we could not do with delegates and preferred to get our orders at first hand—would this be reasonable? Or suppose King Edward had to sally forth from Windsor and go all over the country to drill the men—would that be reasonable? Yet this is what would have to be done unless His Majesty could pass on his authority to others with power to command in his name. This he does. His officers can exact obedience, but it is the King always who is obeyed, whether the Commander-in-Chief, or the colonel, or the corporal gives the orders. Volunteers often make themselves very ridiculous in the eyes of a true soldier by their absurd difficulty in obeying those whom they consider beneath them. The Militia man says, "Why should I take orders from Brown, who keeps the baker's shop next door; I'm as good as he any day?" The true military spirit is wanting here.

If it is so natural and necessary that the King should have

his substitutes, how much more the King of kings! And if He sends His orders through these ambassadors of His, must we not obey Him—*Him,* mind? It is He still, He always Whom we obey. An army would stand aghast if the Commander-in-Chief were seen scouring all over the field in the midst of an action to give directions. From the height where he stands he surveys all, and staff-officers are sent here and there with orders as occasions require. So is it with our Lord's commands. He gives them really and truly, but through His lieutenants, those who hold His place. Our father and mother, the Pope, our bishops and priests, our sovereign, our magistrates, masters, mistresses—all these are His staff-officers sent with His orders, and by obeying them, we truly obey Him.

"It would be much nicer if He gave the orders Himself."

Unquestionably, but what has niceness to do with it? We are real soldiers. We cannot enlist, and then say as soon as we begin to know something of army ways: "Oh, I didn't think it was going to be like this, I thought—" What we thought cannot be helped. Here we are now in barracks or on the field, and we must take things as we find them. Soldiers do not expect to find Lord Roberts[1] waiting for them in the drill-yard, and when the sergeant thunders out: "Attention!" "Stand at ease!" "As you were!" no one dreams of stepping out of the ranks to ask: "And pray, who are you?"

Some of us, however, are inconsistent. The very thing that we admire in the army, we despise and cry down everywhere else. Well no—not quite everywhere.

"Five or six years ago," writes a Londoner, "when crossing Trafalgar Square, I stayed for a moment on a refuge at the Square end of Northumberland Avenue. The policeman on

---

1   Field Marshal Frederick Roberts was Commander-in-Chief of the Forces at the time this book was printed, having succeeded Garnet Wolseley in 1900.

point-duty was regulating the traffic, his back being turned towards the Avenue. Suddenly, up went his arm. The first carriage to stop was the Prince of Wales', containing the Prince, the Duke of York, and two other gentlemen. They seemed much amused at the incident, as were also the onlookers. I gave a slight whistle to draw the policeman's attention, and nodded to him to look behind. He then saw that he had been ordering Royalty. Instantly, of course, he allowed the carriage to proceed, saluting the Prince in proper fashion.

I chaffed him on his authority, and jocularly prophesied his getting into trouble. He had his answer ready, however: 'No fear of that—he's all right—No row from him.' "

This is only what one would expect. The policeman represented the Queen, and the Prince of course must obey. It is all right and proper for His Royal Highness and such-like people to knock under—but *me!* We admire the obedience of the Light Brigade, not to the Queen far away in London, but to the officer who gave a blundering order. We admire Outram submitting cheerfully to fight under Havelock,[1] whose superior officer he was. But there we stop. The army may keep all its glorious submission and discipline to itself. *We* want none of it. Dependence for the soldier, independence for me. This is our rule. Is it a rational one? We must examine this question.

Insubordination is the spirit of the day. It has found its way into well-nigh every nook and corner of the land—no place escapes, not even the nursery. In all probability we got infected there, and we must take care that the poisonous germs do not develop and bring on grave disease later. There are men

1   During the Indian Rebellion of 1857, Sir James Outram temporarily waived his rank as Commander of the Bengal Army to Major General Henry Havelock—who had been fighting bravely for months to relieve the siege of Lucknow—thus allowing Havelock to command the relief force, in which Outram then served as a volunteer.

and women who want to be free of every kind of obligation; to do away with all laws and government, that they may be able to think and speak and do just as they like, without any one to check or punish them.

"Why, that's like the French Revolution. And do they think they would be happy so?"

"And good?"

"And what would they do with thieves and murderers if there was no one to send them to prison?"

"Good people would be miserable, because they would be robbed and killed. So every one couldn't have what they wanted, but only the bad and the strongest, as it was in the Reign of Terror."

There would be a Reign of Terror all the world over if these haters of authority had their way. They try by plot after plot to sweep away rulers, not for being cruel or bad, but simply for being rulers. "*There was no king, but every one did that which seemed right to himself.*"[1] This is the state of things they want to bring about.

God never meant a state such as this to be. He knows that order and law are necessary for our happiness, and therefore He places us under them. They have not been invented to fret us and spoil all our fun. On the contrary, there is no real enjoyment without the feeling of peace and security. What made the Reign of Terror? The want of law. What made Napoleon the benefactor of his country when his wonderful career began? The strong grip with which he seized the reins of government that had fallen to the ground, mastered France, and restored order and law. What made him one of the greatest tyrants the world has ever seen? The disorder and distress into which he cast his rescued country with many others, by giving himself up to his lawless passions.

---

1   Judges 17.

"I read yesterday about a dog that has been decorated for stopping runaway horses, by jumping up and seizing the reins in his teeth."

Instinct taught that dog that harm would come unless those runaway horses were stopped. How is it that reasonable men will not see the harm that comes of the unbridled spirit of independence? We must be ruled by some force—if not by the law of God and by submission to those He has placed in authority, then by our own bad passions, which will hurry us to destruction.

Among the plaintive cries of the Prophet Jeremias as he sat amid the ruins of Jerusalem, none is sadder than those three words, "*non est lex*." No law in the City, no order—what a picture this opens out before us, reminding us of that terrible description of Hell given us by God Himself, "*where no order but everlasting horror dwelleth*."[1]

Order, then, is necessary to our happiness. None are more sensible of this than children. Leave quite little ones in untidy rooms where they are free to get toys out one moment and throw them aside the next; where the whole place is littered about with things taken up to satisfy the whim of the moment; where no kind, firm voice is by to settle their little quarrels; where the strongest and the most selfish get all that is best, and the weak and the timid are ill-treated—what a miserable place such a nursery is sure to be! Great things have small beginnings, and it is kind of those who watch over us when we are quite little to insist upon order and obedience. Nay, they are bound to do it. God will punish them as He punished Heli[2] if they neglect this duty. They are strictly bound, not only to teach children to fear and love God, but to insist on obedience and reverence to themselves as holding His place. And they are bound to correct when necessary.

---

1   Job 10.
2   Eli, the High Priest, whose story is told in I Samuel 1-4.

By the Fourth Commandment, they are obliged to check the spirit of independence and want of respect for lawful authority which they may observe in children, and with kind but firm determination to require from them honour and respect. Frightful things will happen, both to the children and to the country, if this duty is neglected.

There are terrible words spoken by God Himself of those who refuse obedience to lawful superiors. "They have not rejected thee but Me," He said to Samuel,[1] when the people clamoured for a King. "He that despiseth you, despiseth Me," are our Lord's own words.[2] "Let every soul be subject to higher powers, for there is no power but from God. Therefore he that resisteth the power, resisteth the ordinance of God."[3] Can I, after this, think it a trifle to show my airs to my parents, to give offhand or impudent answers, to be sulky or obstinate?

We have seen what kind of a Leader He is Whom we are following, and through what kind of country He has to lead us on our journey Home. Like our troops in the late campaign we are fighting our way through a desert, *and the enemy is ourselves.* I do so hope we have got this last fact well into our minds. If in our talks we have given so much time to Afridis and Dervishes, to wars in America, and India, and Egypt, it has not been with the object of learning about earthly warfare, but solely with the view of coming to understand, by its means, the rules of the Heavenly. How to drill ourselves in *that* is our one business.

"Do you know, I think fighting the Afridis and the Dervishes is easier than fighting ourselves."

Perhaps you are right. Perhaps the little King of Spain has found out that to battle with oneself is not easy. The story in the papers of his gallant desire to fight the Americans, was

1   I Kings 8.
2   St. Luke 10.
3   Romans 13.

followed by one which showed him seizing his sister by the hair and only releasing her after tearing some out. No doubt the Queen Regent explained to His Majesty that it would be well to turn his arms in another direction, and overcome injustice and violence in himself before overcoming it across the water.

Go back to the frontispiece of your book. Standing upright with arms outstretched, in the church of the Benedictine monastery of Montserrat, you see a Spanish soldier, whose history you will, I hope, read some day. He is exchanging the warfare of this world and the reputation his valour has won, for the long and weary contest with self, which is to make him a valiant soldier of Christ. Years ago he held his vigil in the church, watching his armour before receiving knighthood. He will hold another vigil now and pray for grace and strength in the warfare on which he is entering. His armour he has parted with—all but the sword, so dear to a soldier's heart. That he has brought to the church and hung up on the pillar before the miraculous image of our Lady. It has served his country well and now it is to hang there quiet and forgotten. "Go into thy scabbard, rest and be still." Little he suspects the work that lies before him, little he thinks that after overcoming himself, he is to overcome multitudes and bring them happy captives to the Feet of Christ! That sword hung on the pillar is to be exchanged for "the sword of the spirit which is the word of God."[1] "How shall it be still when the Lord hath given it a charge and hath made an appointment for it!"[2] A Latin inscription cut in the pillar in memory of this vigil may be thus translated:

> The Blessed Ignatius Loyola here devoted himself to God and to the Virgin with much prayer and tears. Here, covering himself with sackcloth, as with spiritual armour, he passed the night. Hence he went forth in the year 1522 to form the Society of Jesus.

1 Ephes. 6.
2 Jerem. 47.

True to a soldier's instincts, the Saint made obedience the watchword and distinguishing badge of the Society which he founded. *Parati ad omnia!*—"Ready for all things"—the first novices used to sign themselves. Let us try and see obedience as he saw it, as all the Saints have seen it, what the example of the Saint of Saints has made it—a glorious virtue, one that calls for the exercise of that noble faith which is the glory of the children of the Church. Obedience is one form of that submission which is distinctive of a Catholic. We look to authority. This it is that marks us off from all who are not of the household of the faith. Obedience is the characteristic virtue of the children of God, and of the true soldiers of Christ. We must be proud of it then. Let us not be led astray by the silly talk of those who look upon submission to authority as something degrading, something beneath them. Let us get well into our heads that, just as far as we suffer ourselves to be affected by such notions, we are like Robert Clive—*out of sorts.* Whatever is the use of pretending to be what, neither in this life or the next, we can ever be—*independent!* The Saints in Heaven glory in their dependence. The just on earth glory in it. They know that if God did not keep His Hand upon them they would fall into all kinds of sin; that if He did not hold up their human nature itself, it would fall back into its first nothingness. Would it not be foolish, they say, for any one in such a position to try to look independent?

"Oh, I can bear to depend *on God;* it's not that, but it's knocking under *to others* I can't stand."

Well, then, do not knock under to any one but to God. Look straight to Him always; take your commands from Him.

"But isn't it hard not to think of the persons who tell us to do things, especially if they tell us to do what we don't like, or if they tell us in a nasty way?"

Of course it is hard. But this is just where our faith comes in and that excellent resolution of yours not to knock under to any one but God. Do not think of the person or of the ways that aggravate you. Look straight at Him Whom, in others, you obey—our Lord Himself. This is the only way of finding obedience tolerable, or even possible where it is at all difficult. But the habit of looking straight to God Himself makes all easy, even sweet.

"I don't see how we can think our Lord tells us to do things when the person who is telling us is not a bit like our Lord, or when we are told to do something which is no use or stupid."

Once more, rouse up your faith. Think how the faithful soldiers of King Alfred[1] knew their Sovereign in his disguise, and bent the knee before him who, to the dull eyes of others, was but a stupid blunderer. Remember that true obedience subjects us to God for His own sake and to others for His sake, not for their own. There will be mistakes at times. Our Lord has never promised that all who hold His place shall be infallible. There are occasions in which the soldier can see that "some one has blundered." But what of that? The world's outburst of admiration for the "Noble Six Hundred"[2] proves that, with all its silly twaddle about independence, it does not account this heroic obedience a blunder. Provided there is no sin in an order, but mistake only, or what I take to be such, there will be no mistake but high-minded generosity in obeying.

You know how many are the privileges of an ambassador residing in England. He pays no taxes, no customs-duties: lace,

1   The Anglo-Saxon King Alfred the Great (849-899) spent some time early in his reign hiding out in disguise from the occupying Vikings while gathering his forces to successfully repel them. Popular legend has it that during this time, he was asked by a peasant woman—in whose house he was staying—to watch some cakes she was baking; when he failed and let them burn, she chided him for his carelessness, unaware of his identity.
2   A reference to the famed Light Brigade, whose ill-fated charge against a well-fortified Russian artillery position at Balaclava was based on a miscommunicated order.

scent, cigars, tobacco—all come free to him, the post officials never raising the slightest query. He cannot be arrested. The precincts of the Embassy are as secure as if they were situated in another land. No judge in this country could try a case against him. Why all these privileges? He may be a very ordinary man. True, but he represents a sovereign—herein lies his dignity and the source of all his rights. Now, all who are lawfully set over us may say with St. Paul: "We are ambassadors."[1]

Among these ambassadors, parents hold the first rank. This is why God has laid upon us a strict command to love, reverence, and obey them. Notice particularly the word *reverence*. That seen to, the rest will follow. But it is just reverence in which children now-a-days are so woefully wanting. "It is true that there are some who love their parents and respect them to the full meaning of God's command. But how often do we not find even little children treating their parents with the most unbecoming familiarity, and behaving towards them in the most disrespectful manner? How often does it not happen that such children grow up to be anything but dutiful sons and daughters? They speak to their parents as though they were their equals; they calmly set aside all parental commands, and they are never satisfied unless they are following their own wills. They think little of discussing their parents with their friends and acquaintances, if they do not scornfully laugh at them behind their backs. Such children will never think of asking their parents' advice. They look upon them as 'out of date,' 'behind the age,' and they go where they will and mix with what company they desire, without ever consulting the wish of their parents...When they grow older, these will be the children to desert their parents, and in the case of old age or infirmity to leave them to hunger and want. This spirit of independence, this want of submission to authority, has been

---

1   2 Cor. 5.

generated in the nursery, and is not likely to grow less as the children advance in years."[1]

Some children, whose behaviour to their parents implies anything but honour, will tell you that they have enough of this in their hearts, but they cannot be always showing it— outward show goes for nothing. The probability is that such as these *never* show it for the good reason that there is none to show. Real, heartfelt honour, such as God requires, never fails to appear. Three things we are told cannot be hid—a fire, a cough, and love. We may add a fourth—a child's reverence for its parents, when there is real reverence in the heart.

As to outward manifestation being worthless, this is simple nonsense. Outward respect is the safeguard of inward reverence. Hence such ceremonies in the army as "trooping the colour," "presentation of colours," and "saluting."

"After the consecration, the major will hand the Queen's colour to the person presenting the colours, from whom the senior lieutenant will receive it, going down on the right knee…When the inspecting officer arrives in front of the centre of the battalion, at a distance of about 60 paces, he will be received with a salute, the men presenting arms, the band playing, and the drums beating. . . A soldier sitting when an officer approaches will rise, stand at attention, and salute. When walking, soldiers will salute an officer as they pass him, commencing their salute 4 paces before they come up to him, lowering the hand on the 4th pace after passing him." Such importance is attached to these "compliments," that directions are given as to the position of elbow, hand, wrist, thumb, little finger and finger-nails, as mounted officers salute with the sword in marching past the inspecting officer.

---

1   Bishop Hedley. (Editor's note: John Cuthbert Hedley, 1837-1915, was Bishop of Newport, England. He was well known for his sermons, and was quite influential in his day.)

Notice again the wording of God's commandment: "*Honour* thy father and thy mother." We should have thought the command would be "*Love*." But God knows that if the love is to be true and strong, showing itself by deeds—help in need, obedience, kindness, patience with peculiarities and faults— it must be founded on honour. The command is absolute: "Honour thy father and mother." It is not added, 'provided they be worthy of honour—good, kind, easy to please.' No, we are simply and without restriction bidden to honour them *because they are our parents.* This honour is to be shown in thought, word, and act. Our whole behaviour towards them, our way of speaking to or of them must be steeped in reverence, *because they are in God's place.*

There are boys and girls nowadays who think that the obligation to honour their parents ceases when they have left school. Blessed Thomas More did not so understand the commandment of God. It is related of him that when, as Lord Chancellor, he passed every morning, in his magisterial robes and surrounded by crowds, to his tribunal, he was accustomed to stop at a court hard by where his father was judge, and there on his knees ask the old man's blessing.

The late President of the United States always showed the most filial devotion for his mother. During her lifetime, no twenty-four hours were allowed to pass without some communication passing between her and her son. If he were at his home in Canton, Ohio, his daily call at his mother's little cottage was as certain as the dawn of day. Sickness alone prevented it, and then some message, written or verbal, would take its place. During the entire term of his Governorship of Ohio he sent a letter, no matter how brief, to his mother every day. Occasionally, under some tremendous pressure of work, his daily message would take the form of a telegram, but this resort he avoided as much as possible. At one time, during a serious disturbance in Ohio when the troops had been called out to prevent an anticipated lynching, Governor McKinley, for a period of ten days, scarcely slept. Yet every night, the very last thing before he allowed himself to snatch the briefest rest, he wrote a little note to his mother, knowing her great anxiety.

When, after the inauguration of her son as President, his mother returned to Canton, the daily letters were resumed. Every day there came to the Canton Post-office a White House envelope bearing some tender message to her from her "William at Washington." "William at Washington" was always the way that she referred to her President-son.

Just after President McKinley's inauguration, he had His relatives, who were in the city at a family dinner at the White House. It was a large company, and a very good dinner. His dear old mother was there, but she was not very talkative. She was too happy for words. But she kept a sharp eye on the dinner, and no detail of it escaped her. She was impressed by the quantity of cream served with the fruit and coffee, for she looked up at her son in her sweet, simple way, and said:

"William, you must keep a cow now."

Some of the younger members of the family party found it difficult to suppress a smile, but the President, with his usual tact and graciousness, replied:

"Yes, mother, we can afford to have a cow now, and as much cream as we want."

Love and reverence your parents—they are the best and truest friends you have on earth. It is only when the grave has closed above their venerated heads that you will realize their worth and understand how true the saying is, that a boy's best friend is his mother, aye, and a girl's too. Say and do nothing that will pain them. Check an offhand way of answering them; take refusals brightly when they cannot give you all you want; consult their wishes as to your occupations, friendships, reading, amusements, and cheerfully sacrifice your own wishes when they run counter to theirs.

We cannot practise heroic obedience every day of our lives. We do not stand every day on burning decks and feel the flames within our waving hair. But there is a bright sunny obedience amidst the troubles of everyday life, that falls little short of heroism.

A young Catholic lady had made it her resolution to be "a joy-giver." It sounds very sweet and delightful, but it means perfect self-sacrifice. She knew this. Yet she did not rush off to the bedside of our wounded soldiers, or to any romantic scene of action to find her work. She knew that in every home there is room for the heroic, that every true heart is a battlefield. Everywhere among her kinsfolk and acquaintance she would try to be a joy-giver, but first and foremost at *home*.

One evening she came down dressed for a ball, the expectation of many weeks. For some reason or other her father objected to the horses going out again that day. Her mother gently remonstrated—the girl was ready, it would be such a disappointment. But he saw reasons for remaining in opposition. There was a struggle we may be sure, but many conquests had made victory easier, and no sign of trouble appeared on his child's face. "It's all right," she said, brightly, and she rose and left the room. When, a quarter of an hour later, she appeared in her ordinary dress and took her place at the head of the tea table, there was nothing to tell of vexation or disappointment. Then and there she kept what to the day of her death she kept, in the face of difficulties and at the cost of continual self-sacrifice—how faithfully her parents, her friends, her poor, her works of zeal could testify—her resolution of being a joy-giver! This young lady was not a school girl. But she did not believe the commandment of cheerful obedience to parents had ceased to bind her because she was "out."[1]

The little Joy-giver at Nazareth running to and fro on errands for His Mother and His Foster-father is the Model for our home life. "Look at Me," He says, "and do as I do." If, when I find it hard to obey, I were to see Him obeying His Blessed Parents' least word or sign, and then looking at me with a smile and saying, "Won't you try?"—could I refuse?

"But our Lady and St. Joseph spoke nicely to Him, and if He had to do hard things He was not ordered about."

What do you call the savage words of the executioners, as He stood trembling by the Cross? "Lie down!" "Stretch out Your Hands! this one, the other!" Shall we be ever ordered about like that? spoken to like that?

Rouse up your faith when you find submission hard. Look, not at who he or she is whom you obey, but at Him for Whose sake you obey—Christ our Lord.

"But when people are nasty and disagreeable, I don't see how you can help looking."

Don't you? Listen.

One night—it was in the old feudal times—a lady knelt in her turreted chamber praying. Oh for a message from her absent lord! Oh for one word to know at least that he lived, that the wound at the siege of Acre[2] had not proved fatal! A page stood on the threshold. A travel-stained messenger was in the servants' hall, he said, with a missive for my lady. He was from

1 Young girls did not participate fully in society, attending balls or dinners, until they had reached a certain age, at which time they would "come out." This rite of passage afforded them a new level of freedom from constraint.
2 The siege of Acre was the first battle of the Third Crusade, lasting from August 1189 to July 1191.

the East. Was it her will that he should be— The page finished his sentence to himself, if he finished it at all. She had passed him like the wind. Past, fast down the narrow stairs and along the corridors and through the banqueting-room she sped, till she stood breathless in the servants' hall, holding out her eager hands for the roll. They watched her as she read. They saw the tears and the smiles that came and went heedless of all observers. Her lord was safe but a prisoner, and there were weighty matters touching his ransom that he had entrusted to her. She looked up to take counsel of the messenger, but he was gone.

"Did ever mortal eyes, dear lady, gaze on a countenance so foully scarred?"

"Nay, Marie, I marked it not. What was the messenger to me? This"—and she held up the crumpled roll—"This was all I sought and saw, *the word of my lord to me.*"

Help me, dear Lord, to show myself a true soldier in my obedience. Give me faith to see in all who are placed over me by Your will—in my parents especially—You and Your authority; to see in direction and advice a *word of my Lord to me*, and to obey promptly and cheerfully for Your sake.

XVIII.

DRILL

*I am a man having under me soldiers; and I say to this, Go, and he goeth,
and to another, Come, and he cometh. Do this, and he doeth it.*
(St. Matt 8, 9.)

IT is drill that makes the soldier. Gymnastics, firing exercise, target practice—all this comes in the daily parade, which occupies about four hours a day. After two months' service a recruit commences marching practice, beginning with about six miles, and ending after three months with ten, carrying his accoutrements and kit.

But drill is not confined to recruits. Every living thing in the service, whether in regimentals or not, must serve its apprenticeship. In military stables, horses have been known to pretend to be lame in order to avoid going to exercise. The German army dogs are trained to set up a prolonged howling when they find a dead body. If no one comes they take the dead man's cap or some small article, and with this in their teeth go on a hunt for their trainer, whom they lead to the spot. If the man is wounded he gives his cap to the dog and the same object is accomplished. "It is very necessary," says Lord Wolseley, "that oxen in South Africa should be accustomed to the language or voice of those who drive them. At the opening of a campaign teach your animals to eat the grain of the country. Horses and ponies will eat leaves when grass is not to be had, and can do hard work on bamboo leaves. Chopped straw is a good substitute for hay; horses have done work for some considerable time on the thatch taken off houses." "Camels scrunch thorns that would run any other beast's tongue through; their lips drop blood, but they never notice it."

Everything, you see, has to be trained, from recruits downwards.

"Are recruits, like us in class, all in different places, or are they—"

"Much of a muchness?"[1] Oh dear no! These young fellows, nearly all between seventeen and twenty, do not seem to give much trouble by inattention or laziness. Yet they vary very much in the amount of ardour they throw into their work. Sergeants will tell you that it is more trouble to "knock some into shape" than others. It is pleasant, by the way, to find that, whilst sergeant-instructors are required to be "clear, firm and concise" in giving their orders; they are also told to allow for the different capacity of recruits and to be patient.

From the outset, recruits are stimulated to exertion by the hope of promotion. "Recruits should be moved on from squad to squad, according to their merit, so that the quick, intelligent soldier may not be kept back by men of inferior capacity. To arrive at the first squad should be made an object of ambition to the young soldier."

In the education of a soldier, no points are considered too trifling to deserve attention. Everything down to the smallest detail is to be done in the way prescribed. There is a special drill for "piling arms," making way for an officer to pass through the line, "issuing and returning tools." Each digger must take up and put down his pick and shovel in the order laid down.

When troops travel by railway they have to enter the

1   A colloquial phrase meaning "much the same" "difficult to distinguish."

carriages in a fixed order. "Each man is to stow away under his seat his great coat or valise and to retain possession of his rifle. Silence must be maintained until the train moves off. No shouting is to be allowed, and no man is to put his head out of the window or leave the carriage except when ordered by his officer to do so."

"What little rubbishy rules! What can it matter *how* the men pile their arms or *how* they make way for an officer?"

"And why mayn't they put their heads out of the window; they might want to say good-bye to their friends, you know?"

Unsoldierly speeches both of them! Nothing that concerns the training of our troops is rubbishy. "Armies" says Lord Wolseley, "are held together by discipline, and discipline is essentially a matter of detail and attention to small things." "Volunteers are, speaking generally, more unruly than either the Line or the Militia…They should be under military law at least whilst they are out training. Then, perhaps, they might become a well-disciplined body. This would make them more respected." Thus writes one who signs himself proudly, "An Officer not of Volunteers."

You see, our soldiers pride themselves on this smartness in obeying orders and look down upon those who despise little things.

"The armies that are in Heaven followed Him."[1] Why is there talk of the armies in Heaven? Why are the inhabitants of that land, where there is no strife but everlasting peace, likened to an army? Because, in our mind, an army awakens thoughts of order, unity, obedience, loyalty.

The hopes of sergeant-instructors are built upon the teachableness of those they have to train. No one can *make* the recruit a smart soldier. There must be readiness, eagerness even. Teacher and learner must work together. Patience on

1   Apoc. 19.

one side, docility on the other, labour on both—this is the only road to success. We may see the striking result of discipline, docility, and drill in the Anglo-Egyptian Army, whose fortunes we have been following.

Egypt, as you know, is governed by a Turkish Viceroy, who acts nevertheless in all respects as a Sovereign, and holds undisturbed sway, provided he pays up the yearly subsidy to the Sultan. In 1881, before we came to Egypt at all, a religious teacher, Mohammed Ahmed, seeing that the people of the Soudan were smarting under the bad government of the Egyptian Viceroy or *Khedive*, proclaimed himself the *Mahdi*, or Mussulman Messiah. Followers gathered round his standard, and in 1882 he took El Obeid, the chief city of Kordofan.

Meantime, the oppression of the Egyptian Government, together with the horrors of the slave trade and the disturbances caused by the adventurer Arabi Pasha, had led England and France to interfere in the affairs of the country, and in 1882 the British Expedition, under Sir Garnet, now Lord Wolseley, resulted in the victory of Tel-el-Kebir.

"And then was Gordon[1] killed?"

Not till three years later, when Khartoum fell into the hands of the Mahdi. But we must not stop to speak of the gallant Gordon now, or how his death was avenged in 1898, when the place was re-taken by the Sirdar. Our business is with the Egyptian army.

"Why do they always call it the Anglo-Egyptian?"

We shall see in a moment. The old Turco-Egyptian army which Sir Garnet had in command at Tel-el-Kebir, was composed of such poor material and was so badly trained that it must have been a sad trial to such a general. It was all but knocked to pieces in that battle, and what remained of it was afterwards disbanded.

---

1   Major-General Charles George Gordon was in command of the Anglo-Egyptian forces in Sudan at the time of the Siege of Khartoum. See notes on page 143 for more information.

The Khedive saw that the only chance of turning the fellaheen, or natives of Egypt, into good soldiers was to make them over for training to British officers. The reorganization of the army was therefore undertaken by his order, Sir Evelyn Wood being the first Sirdar, or Commander-in-Chief. He had a difficult, all but hopeless task before him. Two armies led by English generals were cut to pieces by the Mahdi's forces, simply because the Egyptians threw down their weapons and ran.

But reward came at last. On Good Friday, 1898, at a place near Khartoum, called Atbara, a victory was gained which, to all appearances, will be the turning-point in the history of Africa. This victory teaches many useful lessons, and it is worth our while to consider it carefully from our point of view.

When the news reached England, the name of the successful general was received with acclamation everywhere. But soldiers saw more to applaud than the common folk. What Sir Herbert Kitchener deserved praise for, according to them, was not this one successful action, but the marvelous patience of his preparation, and the courage and perseverance with which he tackled unexampled difficulties. His greatest difficulty was his army. A victory won by British troops is comparatively easy, we are told, for once in action, the men are sure to fight well, and, unless overpowered by numbers, are pretty sure to win. Note this, young Britons, by the way. But Sir H. Kitchener's army was composed of what was, or at least what had been, the most unpromising material—blacks from the Soudan, and Egyptian peasants who had shown themselves so spiritless and cowardly. But they had now had sixteen years of training and—

"I feel an idea coming into my mind."

"And I do, too."

Drill, drill, drill from one year's end to another. Oh, how tired the trainers got! For the men did not seem to get on at all. They were so stupid. They could not be taught to ride or to hold their arms properly. Some would break the ranks and rush forward before getting the word of command. Others were afraid to advance when they did get it. And this, year after year! Poor Sir Herbert! But he did not give up. He did not expect too much of his beginners. "We shall have to drive it into those fellows," he said, on witnessing the first ridiculous attempts at soldiering made by the men. And it *was* driven in—into the timid Egyptians and into the utterly fearless blacks—untamed savages, man-eaters, as some of them had been. By labour and by patience the work was done. The blacks were taught not to break line and run forward; the Egyptians not to break line and run back. We know how both behaved at Atbara and Omdurman. How they won the admiration and praise of the whole force, and will henceforth be worthy to fight shoulder to shoulder with the bravest men in the British army.

"*Now* may we say what we have found out? If we want to do great things by-and-by, we must begin by doing little things now and practise a long time, as the blacks and the peasants did. And even if we *are* foolish or easily frightened, like the Egyptians, we can get to be brave by practice."

"*I* was thinking how Sir Herbert's men must have liked him for being so patient with them, and when they got into battle they would do their best, just to please him and win the victory for him."

"I want to know what kind of men the enemy were and what sort of a commander they had."

The enemy was the Arab Baggara tribe, the scourge of the Soudan. The Khalifa, successor of the Mahdi, belonged to this tribe. His followers, the Dervishes, about whom we have heard so much, were some of the most magnificent soldiers in the world. Their courage equalled that of the best European troops. Cavalry and infantry alike were men incapable of fear, absolutely obedient, and entirely reckless in the face of death. They were mown down line after line without halting.

"What kind of man was their general?"

The Dervish general was an Emir of the Khalifa's, named Mahmoud. He was—well, you shall judge for yourselves. Seeing that he was to be attacked, he "mounted his horse, inspected his lines, gave his orders, and then, having exhorted his men to fight to the death for their faith—the miserable creed of Mahomet—he retired to his tent and hid in a bomb-proof pit scooped out under his bed. "It was no use," he said afterwards, "to expose the person of the general during the fighting."

"The coward! He did not deserve to command such men!"

"No wonder his army was defeated!"

And utterly destroyed. Bravely as they fought, these warriors of the desert, they were no match for our brigades, inspired by the presence of their general, who with his own hands helped to tear up the thorny bushes that defended the enemy's position.

"I hope Mahmoud was found and killed."

He was taken prisoner and marched into Berber at the head of the prisoners, with his arms tied behind his back.

"Hurrah!"

"It seems to me that a battle depends more on the leader than on the men."

The two must work together. General Gatacre[1], a hard worker himself, set to work to make his men work. "No drink, constant marching, sleep every night in your boots," was the order. What wonder his men called him "General Backacher"! Yet they were devoted to him. You see, he trudged along by their side and shared every hardship with them. The whole army did its chief credit, as we have seen, when the hour of battle

1   Sir William Forbes Gatacre (1843-1906) was very strict but well-beloved by his men.

struck. The sudden unforeseen charges neither unnerved the Egyptians nor overexcited the blacks. The courage, discipline, and endurance shown by both have never perhaps been surpassed.

The dry air of the Soudan cracked the buglers' lips. "If it hurt them to bugle, they could stop," some one will say. What are we told? "At reveille you heard the ring of perpetual bugles. To keep the lips supple they were practising incessantly." Fancy, the minute the camp woke to life in the morning, as soon as the eyes were open—to begin to do *what hurt!* "Comfort," says the Commander-in-Chief, "must be disregarded when men take the field, as it is only a personal matter." In one place where the camp was pitched there was hardly a shelter in which a man could stand upright; impossible to be comfortable anywhere. It was nobody's fault—part of the ordinary hardships of a soldier's life in the desert, and nobody grumbled.

"The English officer will carry his pre-conceived notions of comfort into the field. . . We are too prone to overload ourselves with baggage. It is a saying abroad that '*chaque officier anglais a sa bassinoire.*'[1] This chaff comes home to us with only too much truth. Any officer who cannot make up his mind to live upon the same fare as his men had better remain at home with his mother. An attempt to carry about a table or chair during the active work of a campaign is ridiculous. Officers, like their men, must get their dinners sitting on their beds or on any large stone that may be at hand."

We imagine the soldiers whose endurance was so sorely taxed at Waterloo, arriving on the field at least warm and comfortable. What was the fact? "Many of the troops had fought desperately on the 16th, and retreated on the 17th from Quatre Bras to Waterloo under furious rain, and the whole army was soddened and chilled with sleeping unsheltered on

1 'Every English officer has his bed-warmer.'

the soaking ground. Many of the men, as they rose hungry and shivering from their sleeping-place in the mud, were stiff and cramped to such a degree that they could not stand upright." On the other hand, the Battle of Omdurman was fought under a sun so fierce that the metal parts of the guns burnt the soldiers' hands.

"Iced champagne in the middle of the desert would be an admirable medicine," says Lord Wolseley. But who looks for it? Do you suppose any one grumbles because it is not forthcoming?

Grumbling, as a rule, does not help much. During a certain regiment's stay at Aldershot, the orderly officer was going his rounds one dinner-time. On coming to an Irishman, he asked if there were any complaints. Paddy, after a pause, exclaimed: "If yez plaze, sorr, oi've got the thin of the soup." The officer, turning to the orderly sergeant, said, "Will you see that this man gets the thick of the coffee to-morrow morning."

"What are the chief hardships of military life?" a sergeant was asked. He looked puzzled.

"If you mean real solid hardships, I don't know of any. A man has a certain amount of unpleasantness to put up with of course, but we never look upon this as a hardship."

"But bivouacking in the open, sleeping on wet ground, without sufficient covering—by the way, what has a soldier in the way of bedding?"

"If in the field, usually an oil sheet and one blanket— sometimes not that. If suddenly called out to an engagement and bivouacking, you have, as we say, 'the ground for your bed and the sky for a blanket.' But we don't count such things hardships. Not even war. A man who loves the service considers that all this has to be done to gain the object in view. Some one must do it, and the soldier is the man because he is paid for it."

If the "*real, solid hardships*" of our life were asked for, what could we produce?

We have heroes, too, nearer home.

With blue but resolute hands, little Douglas was attacking his basin of bread and milk. Grandma, always anxious to instill gratitude for favours received, exclaimed impressively, from beneath her spectacles:

"How grateful Douglas ought to be for that good breakfast. What would he do if he had no nice bread and milk?"

"Do! *Do without*, grandma," he answered, stoutly.

To come now to ourselves. We are no exception to the rule. If we are to be got into shape we must be drilled. But to expect to get through our drill without any effort, or our fighting without any pain, is, to say the least, unreasonable. Why not make up our minds, once for all, that we will take trouble and bear pain. All who expect to make anything of their profession or trade do this. We are told of Gustave Doré that as a baby, he would crawl out of his crib into his mother's room, crying for a pencil, and go back to bed with it, happy. In his fifth year he made drawings of battles. He would beg his father's friends to cut his pencil for him, and to cut it at both ends that it might last longer. He had executed upwards of 40,000 drawings before he was thirty years old. Of his work in London, he wrote: "My innumerable engagements make my life an almost perpetual slavery." Paderewski[1] rarely devotes less than six hours daily to hard practice on the keyboard. He spends part of each day in gymnastic exercises, employing an apparatus designed and made by himself to keep the muscles of his arms strong and supple. "In fact," as he laughingly says, "I have to train quite as rigorously as if I made my living as a prize-fighter."

1 Ignacy Jan Paderewski was a famous pianist and composer who also served as Prime Minister of Poland in 1919.

"But we are not clever like that. We couldn't do those things no matter how we tried."

You are not asked to do for a Divine Leader and an incorruptible crown what men will do for a little earthly reward that will be gone directly. But you *are* asked to do something. And if you aspire to be at all chivalrous, you must do more than is of strict obligation. You must try—we must all try—to get some manliness into us, to put some generosity into our service.

No one wants to have babies for fellow-travellers. A man comes hurrying up to a full train just starting, looks into a carriage and sees an empty place. But—there is a baby in the compartment. He moves on quickly and squeezes in elsewhere. There are people who always travel with a life-size baby doll which they hold at the windows as people come up to choose their carriage. This device often secures them the compartment to themselves.

"What a shabby trick!"

"How selfish!"

"Any way it's clever."

And proves how general and well known the fear of babies is.

We have spoken of manly virtues. But please do not suppose that men have these all to themselves. Women come in for a large share. They, too, must put out the strength that is in them. The King cannot do without them. There are parts of the field where no help but theirs can reach. They must come forward, or His cause in that quarter will be lost. Children, too, have their appointed work, which no one else can do.

You know that the Military Religious Orders were the props of the Kingdom of Jerusalem during the ninety years of its existence, and that when the Crusades were over, the heroic knights of St. John were still the defence of Christendom, from their outposts of Rhodes and Malta beating back the enormous hosts of the infidel. But you may not know that those champions of the faith were helped by women and children. When the Turks laid siege to Rhodes, tiny hands were seen hurling sticks and stones upon the Janizaries. At the siege of Malta, women and children defended the trenches, rendering no small assistance to the garrison. And when the garrison had disappeared before the overpowering number of the assailants, the women in casque and cuirass[1] crowded to the ramparts to deceive the enemy by the appearance of troops, and feeble children worked the guns. A hundred years later the same indomitable courage was shown within the walls of Vienna. The first shot fired by the Turks into the city fell near a little child of three years old, who ran fearlessly up to it and extinguished it before it had time to burst.

Now, we are made of the same stuff as this little hero of three, the same as the Maltese children and the Rhodians. We have to fight in a different field, that is all; not with Janizaries, but with *ourselves*. Any child of three, by checking its temper, can prevent explosions, and save a whole house from being upset. But there must be effort, and vigorous effort.

In the Regulations for Infantry Drill issued by the War Office, we are struck by the energy of the terms employed. Arms are not to be "taken up" and "held," but *seized* and *grasped*. "*Seize* the rifle," "*seize* the scabbard." "Raise the left foot and beat it *smartly* on the ground." "*Grasp* the handle of the bayonet." "Open the pistol with a *smart jerk*," &c.

"Words of command are to be given sharply and quickly: *Rĭght—Fŏrm, Quĭck—Mărch*. For this reason: the way in which an order is carried out depends on the tone in which it is given. All force would be gone were the sergeant to say: "Turn to the Right," "March quickly."

---

1 Parts of a suit of armor. The casque was an iron helmet; the cuirass covered the torso.

One of our great educators believes the time is coming when all teachers will be required to speak to the class in tones of command. However this may be, the time has certainly come when we must speak *to ourselves* promptly, decisively, in a tone of command. We are called in the morning. It is foggy, miserable—Friday, moreover—we are inclined to turn over: *Advance!* Bed time comes—but there are just the last pages of a novel to finish: *Retire!* An angry retort is on the tip of my tongue: *Halt!* It got out, and here I am with flashing eyes, delivering volley after volley: *Cease Fire!*

"It isn't easy to speak *to ourselves* like that."

No, *March at ease!* is about the only word of command some of us seem to expect in our service. We must brace ourselves a bit, and overcome our fears and frights.

An imaginative child made his life a misery by nursing his fears. Nothing was too dreadful or too impossible for his poor little brain to lay hold of and turn into an instrument of torture. Night time naturally was his terror, for his bed was a rack. Outstretched there, he lay awake, hour after hour, conjecturing what might or might not be lying in wait underneath, or even beneath the mattress and pillow. He once heard some stories about cobras getting into houses. This served him for months. One night, long after he had been sent to bed, he made his appearance in the drawing-room and went with a scared look to his mother.

"Well, Frank, what now? You ought to have been asleep hours ago."

"Serpents, mother!"

"Nonsense, child. Serpents where?"

"Under my bed."

"My dear Frank, I've told you over and over again there are no serpents in London. They couldn't live over here to begin with; the thing's impossible."

"But what if there were!" he exclaimed piteously.

Two little sisters aged six and seven, went every autumn to stay with their grandfather and grandmother who lived at the sea-side in a big house, in a big square. It was in those old-fashioned days when town-criers took the place of daily papers, and proclaimed losses, news, and robberies, to all passers-by. Now the crier at M— was a black man, short, ugly, and deformed. He wore an old red coat with brass buttons, white trousers, and a chimney pot hat much battered and worse for wear. Often, on returning from their walk, the children saw him swinging his bell vigorously before commencing operations. And they were terrified of him. Dora, the elder of the two, was a sensible person, as she was bound to be, having passed her seventh birthday and come to the use of reason. She knew she was afraid of the black man, and she asked herself why. It seemed to her unreasonable to be so frightened of a poor man who did not want to do her any harm—frightened just because he was black and ugly. She would cure herself of that fear somehow. One day the little pair had been out for their usual walk and were on their way home. Dora was silent and thoughtful. At length she broke silence:

"Ellie, you know the black man."

"Oh, yes, we both know him, don't we?"

"*I'm going to kiss him*"

"Kiss him! What for? O Dora don't, don't. He will kill you, I'm sure he will."

"It's silly to be afraid of him just because he's black, which he can't help, you know. I'm going to kiss him to make myself not afraid. Will you come too?"

"If you do; but oh, please don't go, Dora, I'm so frightened."

"Then I'll go by myself. There he is!" And she was off like a shot across the square and on to the top of the steps where Sambo had just taken up his position. He stooped to lift his ponderous bell and—two arms flung round his neck held him fast till a kiss heard by trembling Ellie standing by, had been imprinted on the black cheek. It was well his assailant's eyes were closed, for in his surprise and terror the poor fellow rolled his eyes, threw out his arms, and looked so hideous as he shouted for help, that the sight might have proved too much for even Dora's courage. As it was, Ellie had the worst of it. The feat accomplished, Dora started off and made for the house at full speed. She was as white as a sheet and trembling from head to foot as she stood at the door. The effort had been almost too much for the brave little heart. But she had taken the bull by the horns and gained her point. Henceforth, there was no more fear of black men.

In one of our talks some one used the word "*can't*." No one, I hope, would use it now. Could we have the face to look up and say "*can't*" when we see who *can*?

I suppose we may take it for granted that if our Lord wants us to fight, we can fight, and that if He calls us to His service it is because He wants us. Now He does call us as we have seen. He calls us all, therefore all are qualified, "all are well appointed to march on to the war," We need not be giants in height or in strength—six feet to get into the Guards, and passed by the doctor to get in anywhere. Broad chests and brawny arms are not necessary in His army. Stout hearts He wants certainly, but if ours are weak we must not hold back on that account, for He can strengthen them. Men of any race can be trained into fine soldiers—civilized negroes from Jamaica and uncivilized negroes like the Soudanese; Red Indians, timid Egyptians, Chinese, Hindoos. Our King wants all—French and Germans; Poles, Irish, and Scotch; Spaniards, Americans, English—all. Of all He can make soldiers, and good soldiers.

All have fighting stuff in them if only they will bring it out and let Him guide it in the right direction. The Duke of Wellington paid a just tribute to the bravery of the French, when he called their cavalry "the finest in Europe." The Irish, we are told, are amongst the most resolute of earth's children, and will stay for ten minutes fighting, after any other troops in the world would have fallen back. History will tell of the splendid courage and daring displayed on both sides in the Spanish-American War.

As for ourselves, our histories and tale-books have so impressed upon us the superiority of the British soldier, that we take it for granted, and look upon ourselves quite naturally as the grandest fighting race in the world. And it must be allowed that, side by side with much that is ugly, there are in the English character, in a very marked degree, the qualities that go to make a good soldier—obedience, promptitude, pluck, thoroughness, dogged perseverance. We are naturally warlike. We have been so from the beginning and seem to be made that way. Other nations are content to take for their patron the Saint who converted them, but *we* must have a soldier even if we have to go to Cappadocia for him.[1] Let us turn this warlike material to account, and for a change, fight against *ourselves*. If it be true that, in all their wars, the British have won the splendid average of 82 per cent of their battles, *we* should be a crack regiment in the Church Militant.

"I could fight like anything against the devil and the world. But I do think it's rather hard to have to fight *against myself*."

Oh, dear, oh, dear, how often shall we have to say it! It is hard, of course it is hard. Who ever doubted it! You bring up the hardness again and again, just as escaped and rescued nuns are brought up after having been disposed of a hundred times. You shall have it all your own way, gain your cause completely

---

1   St. George, the patron saint of England, was believed to have been born in Cappadocia.

and without any more pleading—*it is hard*. It is disagreeable, distasteful, discomforting, disquieting, distressing, disturbing, disenchanting— all the *disses* you like, except five: It is *not* dishonourable, nor disloyal, nor disgracing, like the act of a deserter. It is not discouraging, for the King Himself is at our side, always ready to make good our losses. And it is not disappointing, for the prize is a crown.

Have you never discovered how difficulties are swept away by one brave effort? And how the Holy Spirit helps us the moment He sees us put our hand to the work and make some little attempt? He is coming to us with His Gifts and His Fruits; and He will look to us, as to His soldiers, to turn them to account, by waging war, first for our own souls, and afterwards for the souls of others. On the day of our Confirmation, we shall put on His uniform and be ready to start for the front. For *there* is the children's place. They are the most important corps in the Christian army now-a-days. The victory or defeat of either side depends on them. To them the leaders are looking.

You see, then, it is all stuff and nonsense to talk about "can't." We *can* well enough, like that King of whom it was said that, "he could if he would."[1] These are the days in which it is perfectly useless to say "can't," because nobody will believe you. Everybody knows that children can do everything now.

"But it seems so funny for *us* to be of any good, when we're not grown up."

Not at all funny. Nothing you do seems funny. It is not what you do but what you *do not do* that surprises people. Heretofore a Children's Crusade called forth a Pope's astonishment. But you may have your Crusade now, and carry it through successfully without attracting notice—if that is what you are afraid of. If you were to turn out first-rate Catholics, soldierly, with plenty of pluck, plenty of zeal for the colours, plenty of ardour in making

1   King Charles II of England.

recruits, no one would marvel at it. The days of marvels have not gone, it is true, but the power of marvelling has.

Are children to be precocious only as musicians, artists, winners of honours at public examinations? Have the days gone by when the Church, too, had her precocious children —Agnes and Pancratius, Maurus and Imelda, Aloysius, Stanislaus, Berchmans? No, thank God. Our own days and our own land have seen many examples of saintly lives among the young, lives not only noble and beautiful in themselves, but raising and strengthening and ennobling the lives of many.

Whenever extraordinary results are obtained by children, whether in the learning of this world or in the science of the Saints, it is evident that they must have begun their work very early, and put their heart into it from the first. "To begin young and cultivate patience and indomitable perseverance"—this is the advice for those who mean to excel.

How lucky we children are! The youth we have got: and the eagerness—well, if we have not got it already, it is to be had for the asking. One thing remains—to cultivate *patience* and indomitable *perseverance*. These grand virtues are like oaks: beautiful, strong, sheltering. The whole of our life must be overshadowed by them, and it is hard to say at what part they are most needed. We start with a good will. But when difficulties come and our bad nature crops up, we get tired; we think we have done enough; and looking round, we begin to notice others and to say—it is enough, surely, to be like the rest.

We must pray often for patience with difficulties and *with ourselves*. And for perseverance to courageously put ourselves through the drill that is to transform us from raw recruits into good soldiers, a credit to the Service and to our King.

XIX.

MARCHING

How long does this wicked multitude murmur against me?
(Numbers 14, 27.)

As WE followed, in paper after paper, the vast army that the Sirdar took across the desert in 1898, did we ever think of another and far greater multitude that long ago, 1,500 years before our Lord came, marched across Egypt to the desert, passing, it may be, at one part of the track, over the same sands and camping under the same sky? Marching is an important part of an army's work. Shall we watch these two hosts and see what we can learn from them? We will begin with the first.

"And the children of Israel went in through the midst of the sea dried up, for the water was as a wall on the right hand and on the left. And they saw the Egyptians dead upon the sea-shore, and the mighty hand that the Lord had used against them.[1]

And they came into the desert of Sin, and all the congregation of the children of Israel murmured against Moses and Aaron in the wilderness, and said to them: Would to God we had died in the land of Egypt, where we sat over the flesh-pots, and ate bread to the full. Why have you brought us to this desert, *that you might destroy all the multitude with famine?*

1   Exodus 14.

Why have you made us come up out of Egypt, and have brought us into this wretched place, which cannot be sowed, nor bringeth forth figs, nor vines, nor pomegranates, neither is there any water to drink?[1] And the Lord said to Moses: Behold I will rain bread from heaven for you, and you shall know that I am the Lord your God. And it was like coriander-seed white, and the taste thereof like to flour with honey.[2]

Then all the children of Israel encamped at Raphidim, where there was no water for the people to drink. So the people were thirsty for want of water, and murmured against Moses, saying: Why didst thou make us go forth out of Egypt, *to kill us, and our children, and our beasts with thirst?* And the Lord said to Moses: Thou shalt strike the rock and water shall come out of it that the people may drink.[3]

So they marched three days' journey and the cloud of the Lord was over them by day when they marched.[4] In the meantime there arose a murmuring of the people against the Lord, as it were repining at their fatigue. The children of Israel said: Who shall give us *flesh to eat?* We remember the fish that we ate in Egypt free-cost; the cucumbers come into our mind, and the melons, and the leeks, and the onions, and the garlic. Our soul is dry, our eyes behold nothing else but manna. Now Moses heard the people weeping by their families, every one at the door of his tent. And the wrath of the Lord was exceedingly enkindled; to Moses also the thing seemed insupportable.[5]

And Mary and Aaron spoke against Moses. And they said: Hath the Lord spoken by Moses only? Hath he not also spoken to us in like manner?

1   Numb. 20.
2   Exodus 16.
3   Exodus 17.
4   Numb. 10.
5   Numb. 11.

And Moses sent men to view the land of Canaan. And going forward as far as the tomb of the cluster of grapes, they cut off a branch with its cluster of grapes, which two men carried on a lever. They took also of the pomegranates and of the figs of that place. And came to Moses and Aaron and to all the assembly of the children of Israel. And speaking to them and to all the multitude, they showed them the fruit of the land. And said: The land in very deed floweth with milk and honey, as may be known by their fruits. But it hath very strong inhabitants. The people that we beheld are of a tall stature. We saw certain monsters of the giant kind; in comparison of whom we seemed like locusts. In the meanwhile Caleb, to still the murmuring of the people that rose against Moses, said: Let us go up and possess the land, for we shall be able to conquer it. But the others that had been with him said: No, we are not able to go up to this people, because they are stronger than we. And they spoke ill of the land which they had viewed.[1] Therefore the whole multitude crying wept that night, and all the children of Israel murmured against Moses and Aaron, saying: Would God that we died in Egypt and would God we may die in this vast wilderness, and that the Lord may not bring us into this land, lest we fall by the sword, and our wives and children be led away captives. Is it not better to return into Egypt? Let us appoint a captain, and let us return into Egypt. And all the multitude would have stoned Josue and Caleb, who had viewed the land."

"Well, I never knew they were as bad as that!"

"A whole army of grumblers!"

Is it wonderful that God was "exceedingly angry with them" at times, and punished them? For think—as Moses reminded them—Who He was against Whom they dared to murmur. "The Lord your God is the God of gods and the Lord

1   Numb. 13.

of lords, a great God and mighty and terrible." "Heaven is the Lord thy God's and the heaven of heavens, and the earth, and all things that are therein. And yet the Lord hath been closely joined to thy fathers, and loved them and chose their seed after them, that is to say, you out of all nations."[1]

Have you ever thought of the daily life of the Israelites in the desert? Has it ever struck you how like it is to our life, or to what our life ought to be? Its business was to march. Any kind of regular occupation carried on within itself by the travelling nation —any buying or selling, any studying or teaching, any working at trades, any washing or cooking within the tent homes—was of quite secondary importance to *the* work of the day, which was *to march*. This was the work of every one, of the little child as well as of its father and mother, of priests and people and the "mixed multitude without number that went up with them,"[2] of the youngest soldier in that huge army of 603,550 men, as well as of the great leader. Even the sick had to move on. To stop meant to be left behind to perish by hunger, or enemies, or wild beasts. Children grew up into men and women with no other idea than this—that the one business of life was *to march*. We can imagine the march of an army, but a whole nation on the march—can we imagine that? There were enemies to be fought; there was a hand to hand struggle with deadly foes that opposed their entry into the land of Promise. But, as a rule, the difficulties of the way did not lie in sharp, fierce conflicts, but in bearing day after day, month after month, year after year, the weariness and discomfort of that monotonous march. Now and again they came to a brighter tract of country, green grass and bubbling springs turning a patch of the stony wilderness into a garden of beauty. But the rest and refreshment was given to strengthen them for further

1   Deut. 10.
2   Exodus 12.

toil, not to tempt them to linger on the way. After a brief encampment, the order was given to strike their tents, and with the pillar of cloud or the pillar of fire at their head they were again on the move. On and on and on—how tired they must often have been—how footsore and heartsore! How they must have wondered at times if the journey would ever come to an end. The sick had to be carried, and they were suffering and cross. Their comrades on the road were disagreeable. They went too fast or too slow, or did not take their share of the baggage. The sun blazed down fiercely in the day-time, and at night the dews of the desert chilled them through and through.

Now, how did they bear all these troubles?

"They grumbled."

Yes, again and again. Did this grumbling do them any good? Did it lighten in the very least the troubles of the way? Did it bring them any nearer their journey's end? Or did it throw them back? If you look at a map of Egypt, you will see that in a few months, at most, they might have come out of the desert and entered into their own land. But because of this murmuring they were kept wandering about there for forty years. Sometimes they murmured against their leader. Why was he set over them? Why could they not do as they liked? Another time there arose a murmuring of the people against the Lord, *as it were repining at their fatigue.*[1]

Or the heavenly food rained down from heaven for them each morning did not suit them, though God took care that it should be pleasant to the taste of every one. What a ridiculous picture Moses draws of them: the people weeping by their families every one at the door of his tent, saying: "We remember the fish that we ate in Egypt free-cost; *the cucumbers come into our minds*, and the melons, and the leeks, and the onions, and the garlic."

1   Numb. 11.

"Nice things to cry about!"

"How greedy they were!"

"And how stupid to expect figs and melons whilst they were in the desert. Why couldn't they wait a little; they knew they would have plenty of nice things when they got to their own land!"

"But they couldn't wait for water, you know."

"Then they should have asked for it properly. God always gave them what they really wanted."

"And weren't all the men soldiers! Fancy soldiers crying all night because they couldn't have figs!"

"And because they were tired."

"It's not right to call them the *children* of Israel; children don't go on like that. They ought to have been called the *babies* of Israel."

Yet I have come across children, that set to work to grumble if things on the march were not quite to their liking—always crying out, "But it's hard," when our Lord asked them to bear some little pain or make some little effort to conquer themselves. Unfortunately, it is not necessary to be the children of *Israel* to be grumblers.

It was not the little ones who were the grumblers of the camp, though no doubt they chimed in, but grown men and women, the "*603,550 men able to go to war.*" One would have thought they would be ashamed of themselves to make such a fuss about their food. And notice how absurd this grumbling was: "*Our eyes behold nothing else but manna.*" What was the matter with the manna—was it dry or stale? No, it rained down fresh every day. Any trouble to get? No—lying thick round the tents ready for the morning meal, for *when the dew fell in the night upon the camp, the manna also fell with it.*"[1] Were they tired of the taste? No—it suited the taste of each. If they liked

1   Numb. 11.

flesh, and fish, and cucumbers, and onions, it tasted like flesh, and fish, and cucumbers, and onions. What on earth, then, was there to grumble at? It did not *look* like these things, the pouters said. "Our eyes *behold* nothing else but manna."

"*Nothing else but manna*"—the manna that never failed them once during forty years! They sat weeping and murmuring, with the heavenly food all around them, and before them the pillar of cloud that was their heavenly guide: *The Lord went before them to show the way by day in a pillar of a cloud and by night by a pillar of fire; that He might be the guide of their journey at both times. There never failed the pillar of the cloud by day, nor the pillar of fire by night before the people.*[1] *The cloud also of the Lord was over them by day when they marched.*[2] This was the people whose discontent and grumbling has passed into a proverb. If they wanted water—no prayer, but murmuring. If report came that strong enemies filled the land flowing with milk and honey— discouragement and grumbling.

Now, what rights had these wanderers in the desert that they should take such liberties with God, and show Him this hateful and persistent ingratitude? As the work of His Hands, they were His servants. They knew they were on a journey, and therefore must expect the inconveniences of travelling. They knew that when they reached their own land they would have an abundance of all their hearts could crave for. They knew, too, or ought to have known, that the God Who had delivered them so wonderfully out of the hands of their enemies, and adopted them for His people, and taken up His abode in the midst of them, Who led them, and fought for them, and cared for them so tenderly, would give them, even in the desert, all that was good for them to have—and still, so rooted in them was this detestable vice of grumbling, that they were not afraid

---

1   Exodus 13.
2   Numb. 10.

to say: "*The Lord hateth us, and therefore He has brought us out of the land of Egypt that He might deliver us into the hand of the Amorrhite and destroy us.* Whither shall we go up? The messengers have terrified our hearts, saying: The multitude is very great, and taller than we are. The cities are great and walled up to the sky."

In vain did Moses try with tender words to pacify them: "Fear not; neither be ye afraid of them. The Lord God, Who is your Leader Himself, will fight for you as He did in Egypt, in the sight of all. And in the wilderness, as thou hast seen, the Lord thy God hath carried thee, *as a man is wont to carry his little son*, all the way that you have come."[1]

No use: "The Lord hateth us, and therefore He hath brought us out of the land of Egypt that He might destroy us." Can we wonder that God was angry? The chastisements which their repeated murmurings drew down upon this people make us tremble. But ought we not rather to wonder that the Divine Patience was not utterly worn out; that it did not cast them off, but bore with them, and brought them at last to their journey's end, and put them in possession of the Land of Promise? This was not, however, till the worst among the murmurers had left their bones in the desert, a warning to all, of the chastisements, more terrible than any others we read of, with which God punishes this hateful sin.

Though murmuring is so unreasonable and so ungrateful, notice how catching it is. It spreads like the plague. Here was a whole nation of more than 600,000 infected by it. And would to God it were only to be found in that nation. But there is another nearer home that is stricken too, and so grievously, that it is rare to find one born and educated on its soil and glorying in the name of Briton, who does not bear about with him the plague-spot.

1   Deut. 1.

And this is curious—that instead of being ashamed of a defect which is very ugly and disfiguring, people rather plume themselves upon it. An Englishman's *right* is to grumble, they say. Who gave it them, I wonder? Who are we that we should fare better than our fellow-travellers all the world over, who have to make the best of their way home, putting up with all sorts of inconveniences on the road? If we are no better than our neighbours, why have we any more right to grumble than they? And *right* to grumble!—as if it were a privilege acquired at much cost and to be guarded jealously.

Let us try to check this miserable propensity in ourselves. It is anything but a quality to be proud of. It takes all the energy out of our souls, all generosity out of our service of God, all power of helping, by word and example and little acts of kindness, the numbers who are trudging on at our side, burdened, many of them, with loads far heavier than any we shall ever be called upon to bear.

"But people are so aggravating," we say; "no one with any spirit would put up with such ways." Stop! Does it show spirit to complain of everything that tries us? We saw one day a crest with this motto: "No one shall insult me with impunity." It sounded fine and spirited; we adopted it forthwith and gave it out as our own. But a little reflection later made us doubt the wisdom of this resolve. *Is* it spirited? Does it show pluck to be able to bear nothing that hurts? Where is the common-sense of applauding our *martyrs*, our *soldiers*, our poor for their patient endurance, whilst we plume *ourselves* on the impatience that will endure nothing?

Why must we fix our eyes so persistently on the little daily miseries and discomforts through which we are passing? Why can we not look, at least as often, at the blessings and "mercies that are new every morning"? If the Israelites had done this, what a different march theirs would have been, and how the blessings for which they showed themselves thankless would have been multiplied a hundred-fold! As God's chosen people, they had so much to be grateful for, that their hearts ought to have been overflowing always with joyful praise.

What a sight it must have been—that Arabian desert by night, when the camp was still, and the stars looked down through the clear Eastern heavens on the slumbering camp! "All the children of Israel by their troops, ensigns, and standards, and the houses of their kindreds round about the tabernacle of the covenant"[1] On the east the tents of Juda, his ensign a lion— an army of 74,600 men. "Next unto him they of the tribe of Issachar encamped"—54,000. Three tribes on each side of the immense quadrangle. In the centre, the Tabernacle with the tents of the Levites round. And over the Tabernacle, streaming up far into the dark sky, the pillar of white fire that told of the presence of the Lord with His people. Now and again the cry of a wild beast broke the stillness, but it did not frighten the Hebrew child that could see, through the looped-up entrance of the tent, the bright sentinel keeping watch over the camp, lighting up with soft radiance the thousands upon thousands of tents and guarding all from harm. *Behold He shall neither slumber nor sleep that keepeth Israel. The Lord watcheth over thee: the Lord is thy Protector. The Lord preserveth thee from all evil.*[2]

Was not that Divine Presence joy enough to sweeten every sorrow and silence every murmur! Is not a much nearer Presence enough to comfort us in our pilgrimage and fill our hearts always with joyful praise? If the march is hard and the way long, Jesus is with us sharing all our trouble. What nation ever had its God so near to it as we have ours? The Jew might not press within the Levite guard to lay his sorrows before the

---

1   Numb. 2.

2   Psalm 120.

Tabernacle. But from His Tabernacle on our altars, Jesus is ever saying to us: "Come to Me all you who labour." All day long the Holy of Holies is open to us. And when we wake at night we may turn our eyes towards the Tabernacle like the Hebrew child, and feel safe in the keeping of our God.

The *Imitation of Christ* tells us that, though our daily march is troublesome, it is very meritorious. And even its troubles are lightened by the example of our Lord and His Saints who are gone on before us. How short the journey is after all! How soon we shall be at Home! Children going home for the holidays do not worry about a stuffy carriage or a broiling walk from the station. The only thing that really puts them out is what hinders or stops them—missing a train, or losing their luggage.

And so on longer journeys. We do not make ourselves miserable because the room in the hotel is not quite as comfortable as it might be, nor do we spend our time heaping up ornaments on the mantel-piece and gim-cracks all about the room. What is the use, when we are only staying one night? We can wait till we get home to be comfortable, and have everything pretty all about us.

Think what the Eleven felt as they stood gazing up into the open heavens on Ascension Day, when the cloud had hidden their Master from their sight.

> The silver cloud hath sailed away,
> The skies are blue and free,
> The path that vision took is now
> Sunshine and vacancy.

No trace remained of Him. And still they gazed and gazed, striving to follow, at least with their eyes, Him Who had carried up with Him into Heaven their hearts, their desires, all they loved, all they hoped for. They had seen Him ascending in His glory to take possession of His throne at the right Hand of the Father, and to prepare a place for them. How could they help that steadfast, longing gaze after Him which made the Angels say, "Ye men of Galilee, why stand you looking up into Heaven!"

When we have looked long into the sky on a glorious day in June, our eyes are dazed with the brightness, and looking down upon the earth again, all is confused and dull. Thus was it with the Apostles as they came slowly down the slopes of Olivet that day. What was there worth looking at in this world, after what they had seen! How dull and weary it all looked! In losing Jesus, they had lost all that made life bright to them. Dull indeed it would be, till that day in the far future when they were to see Him again. Was there anything to cheer them? Yes, there was His Real, though veiled, Presence on the altar. There was the smile of Mary and her motherly protecting care. There were the souls of men crying out to them for the good tidings which they were to take over the world.

It was work for their Master that must be their comfort now. All that they could do they would do for Him. And when He called, they would go to Him with joy, no matter by what road. Think how free their hearts were always, how calmly they passed through the pains and pleasures of this life, like pilgrims hastening Home.

This name of pilgrim was very dear to them, as we see from their writings. They want us all to think and feel as pilgrims, and look at all we see passing by us, as pilgrims look, as we look from the carriage window upon bright, or grand, or gloomy scenery, through which the rushing train is carrying us. "*Strangers and pilgrims,*" St. Peter calls us.[1] "*Pilgrims and strangers on earth,*"[2] St. Paul says, "*for we have not here a lasting city, but we seek one that is to come.*"[3]

1   I St. Peter 2.
2   Hebrews 11.
3   Hebrews 13.

In the midst of his heavy trials, holy Job cheered himself by this thought: "*Behold, short years pass away and I am walking in a path by which I shall not return.*"[1] If we have to go back by the difficult and dangerous path over which we have come, the journey is discouraging, but we can easily brace ourselves to get over the ground *once*.

The Church is always trying to lift up our hearts above the cares and pleasures and troubles of this passing world, to the lasting City we are nearing. "Sursum corda,"[2] is her daily admonition to us every morning; though we always answer, as to a quite unnecessary reminder, "Habemus"—*we have* them lifted up.

And when the day is done and she gathers us round her once more for the evening Benediction, and raises her Lord above our heads, as if to force our eyes and hearts to lift themselves to Him, there is the plaintive sadness of exile in her song, reminding us that we are not at Home yet, but on the way.

> Qui vitam sine termino,
> Nobis donet in patria.

"Are we coming to the second army now?"

"Was it a grumbler, too?"

There was *some* grumbling, of course, because it was the *Anglo*-Egyptian army on the march. But the grumbling did not amount to much. The brave fellows bore their hardships gallantly. Their long marches—98 miles in three days, made under a burning sun—were broken by short halts only. Hundreds went all but barefoot, for the soles of their shoes peeled off, and there was next to nothing between their feet and the hot, blistering sand.

"How the children of Israel would have grumbled!"

"But *their* shoes didn't wear out."

---

1 Job 16.
2 "Lift up your hearts"

Many of the men went to sleep while marching; others
dropped with weariness and want of sleep. "One subaltern with
baggage in the rear-guard, fell off his camel without noticing it,
and went on peacefully slumbering on the sand. He woke up
some time in the dead of the night, and, of course, had not the
vaguest idea where the army had gone to, or in what direction
he ought to follow it. He had hung his helmet and belt on the
camel, which padded on composedly, only too glad to be rid
of him. He was picked up later by a man who was looking for
somebody else. Those who dropped down asleep went on as
soon as they woke, and overtook their regiments."

"I call that splendid."

"And I'm so glad our English soldiers are not grumblers."

Don't come to conclusions too fast. The march to
Omdurman speaks well for the military spirit of the Sirdar's
force. Yet the testimony of the Commander-in-Chief, who
ought to know, is not altogether satisfactory in this respect, as
regards the army generally.

"Soldiers, particularly old soldiers, are naturally
grumblers. The self-abnegation which is necessary on service,
finds a safety-valve in a 'good growl.' The tendency should be
checked in young officers, for if they grumble, the privates will
follow in a chorus that will soon grow too loud. Partial delays
and mistakes are inevitable, entailing more or less discomfort
upon all ranks—but these petty inconveniences are necessarily
attendant upon our lot as soldiers, and they should be accepted
cheerfully. Grumbling about the delay and finding fault with
the arrangements made, is not the way to further the interests
of the service or the ends aimed at, but it is a certain method
for causing disorder."

A soldier's duties, as we have seen, are far from being
confined to fighting. Marching comes next in importance, as
Lord Wolseley clearly shows:

"The fitness of troops for the great final struggle, when they at last meet the enemy, must ever depend greatly upon the manner in which their marches have been arranged. Take great heed that everything has been thought of and provided for beforehand. Let me see two armies on the march, and I believe I could tell you the respective fighting value of each. No military quality is so frequently tested as that of marching." Notice—*military quality*—the tedious daily march is as much a soldier's work as the fierce encounter that comes from time to time. "Marches are means to an end, that end being a battle which has for its object the destruction of your enemy's army. . .

"There is one general principle which applies to every description of march. The greatest harmony of movement should exist between the columns; all working together, not as independent units, but as intelligent portions of one machine, all being ready to concentrate when required.

"At the opening of a campaign, it is essential that you should begin to practise your men in marching as soon as possible. Give them plenty of drill and route marching. Begin by short marches of six or seven miles, gradually increasing this length until your men are in good marching condition. The army has its ordinary rate of marching, its *quick time* and *the double*. Except in case of necessity the men should not be hurried on the march; they are to be instructed that they are never to step out beyond regular step; still less to double unless by word of command. Forced marches should be avoided as much as possible."

Some *of us* step out with tremendous vigour when starting—after a retreat perhaps. They are going to do this and this and that, and be Saints at Christmas, or next Easter at latest. They will hear daily Mass of course, go to Confession and Communion every week, make a meditation every day and two visits to the

Blessed Sacrament. They will make the nine First Fridays, be enrolled in eight confraternities, put on six scapulars, and find time somehow to say our Lady's Office. The church linen is badly cared for. They will take charge of it, and play the organ, and superintend the choir; take a catechism class on Sundays, and make arrangements for visiting the prisons—that all the men and women may be got to their Easter duties. Then there will be the homes of the poor to see to. What a blessed reformation there will have been in the neighbourhood by this time next year! It may even reach the ears of Government and—who knows—the Sirdar may request them to undertake the Soudan!

Perhaps we are not old enough as yet to effect all this good. But there is home. We had better begin with the conversion of our parents, whom we are "bound to assist in their wants both spiritual and temporal," the catechism says. They have the first claim upon us. We will get them to make a retreat and a general confession. Whilst they are away, we will look after the servants, instruct them and make them go to their duties, *convert them* in fact. Our cousins are not half as good as they ought to be; we had better take them in hand next. We shall meet them at dances, and tennis, and parties, and can talk to them there. They won't like it—the boys especially —but it must be done! By this time the holidays will be nearly over, and we must find time to tell the old Irish cabman to go to his duties, which he has probably neglected for years. What a transformation in six weeks! Why home, to say nothing of the rest of the world, will be a different place when we come back to school!

Now this is stepping out with a vengeance. Will it last? No. We shall be pulled up by father and mother long before we have seen them off to their retreat, and be told to keep in our place and mind our own business. This will quench our zeal, and we shall have no heart to see to cook's conversion, or the cousins'.

Suppose we had set to work rather differently, begun with *one* conversion, contented ourselves with *one*—there is every probability home *would* be a different place during the holidays. Suppose we were to take our *own* conversion thoroughly in hand, reform our own careless habits of prayer and spiritual duties, our own sharp way of speaking that causes explosions right and left, to the great discomfort—not to say danger—of all around?

This reserving of our fire for expenditure on the enemy at home is strongly to be recommended. Take, for example, some practical form of charity. Special kindness to those who have to suffer from our faults, is an excellent practice, and opens out a magnificent field of work. The only difficulty is to see where the limit comes. For who is there who has not to suffer from us in one shape or another—who at home, for instance?

"Well, I'm sure cook hasn't much to suffer from *me* in the holidays. I never see her to speak to."

Exactly. That is just the kind of proof I wanted to bring. We may take it for granted, then, that the only people who do not suffer from us are those whom we never see or speak to. Now, what can we do for the others?

We are getting near the end of our talks and must try to make them lead up to something. The something is ourselves. In war-fare the road is always *to the enemy*—all guns are pointed *there*. Our enemy is *self*. In some form or other the attack must be there. When there has been a good long course of victory in that direction, it will be time enough to think of extending our conquests elsewhere. We need not fear others will suffer by waiting whilst we drill. Father and mother, cook and cousins will be all the better for every improvement visible in us, and thus our praiseworthy desires will have their effect—home *will* be a different place.

It does not follow from this that all other good desires—at this time of Confirmation for instance—are to be set aside as useless. It is quite right to want to help others. Many of those who have done most good among their fellow-men and women, have had this noble desire from childhood, and found it a stimulus to exertion in the work of self-training and self-mastery. But this must come first. You must be strong if you are to pull up a run-away horse; a good swimmer if you are to save a drowning man; have gone through a course of training if you are to be of any use in a street accident.

Still more does this truth—that self-training must precede any other—hold good with respect to the higher works of mercy. Look at the lives of those who have done great and lasting good in the world, and you will see where their zeal began. They did not pour themselves out upon a number of external works till they had accomplished, or taken fairly in hand, a greater work at home; for they knew that the measure of success they might hope to achieve later, by influencing the minds and lives of others, must depend on the results obtained first within their own hearts.

We may put as much vigour as we like into our spiritual marching. Yet too much "stepping out" is not encouraged, even here. The reason is that what is violent never lasts. We have a long journey before us and must not tire ourselves out at starting. One good practical resolution, with a minor one to back it up, will often be better than half a dozen more showy ones. To rise when I am called in the morning, and put a halfpenny into the poor-box when I don't—may make more difference in my life, and therefore be a wiser resolution than to squeeze our Lady's Office into a full day.

A word about halts. These are matters of great importance, concerning which very precise directions are given.

"As a general rule, long halts are not to be advocated when the men are in good condition. Whether at the halt or on the march, be always on the alert, always looking out…Always act on the assumption that the enemy is watching you and may possibly pounce upon you from a village, or defile, or hollow way…After a march the men are to occupy themselves in putting their arms and appointments in complete order."

We notice here three things: halts are not to be too long; nor unguarded; nor idly spent. Rest and recreation are a necessary part of our lives, but they are to be a regular break in the midst of regular work: the brightening, not the business of our lives. At recreation, our minds may be unbent, but we must never be wholly off our guard. The Russians, being halted and off their guard, could not withstand the charge of the Heavy Brigade at Balaclava,[1] though the assailants were so few. Lastly, resting is not idling. You would be much surprised, I fancy, to see what is expected from soldiers at the halt. All are to put their arms and appointments in order. But the poor cooks! In the Sirdar's army they had to march like the rest, but with this difference, that when the tremendous distance was got over and there came the welcome order "Halt!" they—tired, perspiring, hungry and thirsty, had to stand out in the broiling sun preparing dinner for their comrades. To sacrifice themselves for others was part of their business—they did not grumble. Often enough, charity requires that in times of recreation, our rest and ease, our likes and dislikes, should be sacrificed for the sake of others!

An army marching during the night has special instructions. Danger may lurk in the darkness; there must be caution and vigilance. Speed is lessened. "It is not safe to allow for a force of 1,000 men making good more than one mile per hour at night, over an undulating and roadless country…

---

1   A battle that took place in 1854 during the Crimean War.

Guides who know the country well by daylight are not to be depended upon for night operations, unless they have been accustomed to pass over the ground in the dark. Night changes the appearance of even the most familiar objects and magnifies the importance of all obstacles…Men expecting to be attacked have often their ears and nerves so strained that they imagine they hear noises, troops marching," &c.

"I don't quite know what all that means about marching in the dark."

Perhaps not; you will know some day.

We are told that "an officer able to ascertain his bearings by a knowledge of the stars has a great advantage over others… The moon and stars, if in the required direction, may be used as aids, or points to march on…The only star the bearing of which is practically fixed is the pole-star, which always bears true north."

"We all know who that is."

"Yes—why should our Lady be only Star of the Sea? I'm sure the soldier wants her quite as much, especially at night. It must be bad enough going to battle in the day-time, but I should be horribly afraid of marching in the dark."

Look at the Star, then, when you are sad or troubled.

> Hail! thus cry we from afar,
> Hail to thee our guiding star!
> Hail! for we thy children are.
>> Holy Mary, pray for us.
>
> Amongst women, pure and bright,
> Amongst women, holiest sight,
> Amongst women, star of light,
>> Holy Mary, pray for us.

"Following her you shall not go astray," St. Bernard says, "under her protection you shall be safe."

342

And that reminds me of a capital precaution to be observed by an army at night: "The watch-word should be one difficult for the enemy to pronounce." Now, which of you will find a watch-word difficult for *our* enemy to pronounce?

"Jesus!"

"Mary!"

XX.

COMRADESHIP

Bear ye one another's burdens.
(Galat. 6, 2.)

THE glorious and decisive victory that closed the desert campaign of 1898, was bought, as victory is always bought, at the price of hardship and pain. It could not be otherwise. War is war, and when forethought and organization have done their best, an army must suffer. Now what do you think helped most, on the march and in the fight to support and cheer our soldiers?

"I think it was the bravery of the men which made them not care for hardships and wounds, and that kind of thing."

"*I* think it was the example of the General and the way in which they all helped and defended one another and carried each other out of battle, as we have seen in pictures."

I believe you are right. It was the share-and-share alike spirit that kept them all up, officers and men. If the poor fellows did go, many of them, all but barefoot, they were cared for as well as might be under the circumstances. On the march to Atbara every available camel was burdened with a man who wanted neither "strength nor courage to march on—only boots. General Gatacre had half-a-dozen chargers; every one was carrying a barefooted soldier; while the General trudged with his men. All the mounted officers did the same."

This *esprit-de-corps* kept up the military spirit—that is, the cheerfulness and courage of the force. With these two c's an army can do and bear anything. Hence the care of Commanders to promote brightness by every possible means, and to keep out of sight whatever would have a depressing effect upon the men.

No despairing army ever won a victory. Of the brave Machabees, we are told that "they fought with cheerfulness the battle of Israel." [1] It is hope that puts ways and means into the brain, and courage into the heart; that makes the arm strong, and the hand steady, and the aim true. A glumpy soldier going up and down with his "Alas! Alas! Alas!" does no end of mischief in the camp. The army must have its scarlet to make it *look* bright, and its band and its cheering to make it *feel* bright.

"People say scarlet is a bad colour, because the enemy can see it so well."

There are military experts who say just the contrary. Scarlet is more conspicuous than grey, but when the sun shines on the troops it blurs the sight, and is consequently more difficult to hit. In our warfare, the more scarlet there is about us the better. Our enemy cannot aim at cheerfulness, it disconcerts him and his shots fall harmlessly around.

Which of us does not feel his heart beat high with pride and patriotism as a military band strikes up a march? The crash of cymbals and the blare of trombones have done more to keep up armies than a thousand national wrongs, or the hope of glory to be won on battlefields.

"Whenever it is possible, have music to march to," says Lord Wolseley. "If the band is broken up, the drums and bugles should play together. Nothing is more martial in sound, and

---

1   I Mach. 3.

the men march a hundred per cent better to it than in silence. If you have nothing else, get your men to sing by companies. During long-night marches in India at the beginning of the mutiny, I found that with singing we got on admirably. Whilst when we marched in silence, as men will do after the first half-mile at night, they almost went to sleep, lagged behind, stumbled and fell. The moment a song was struck up the men stepped out briskly."

"A ringing cheer is inseparable from charging—I do not believe it possible to get a line in action to charge in silence—and, were it possible, the general who would deprive himself of the moral assistance it gives the assailants must be ignorant of human nature. It encourages and lends nerve and confidence to an assailant; its very clamour makes men feel their strength as they realize the numbers that are charging with them. Nothing serves more to strike terror into a force that is charged than a loud ringing cheer bespeaking confidence."

We have an immense advantage over *our* enemy here. In many things we are no match for him, but in some he is nowhere beside us. Whoever heard of a troop of devils coming on to the assault singing! No song or cheer is ever heard in their dismal camp. Cheerfulness and humility—two powerful weapons in our hands—are altogether unknown to them, and as they cannot handle them themselves they try to wrench them out of our grasp.

We may well cheer as we realize the numbers that are charging with us. Not only is the fight going on all over the battlefield of the Church Militant, but the Church Triumphant is looking on and helping. What should our Lord's soldiers be sad about? We are "all well appointed," splendidly equipped, splendidly led. And we march in such splendid company!—martyrs, confessors, virgins, high and low, learned and simple, old and young—followers of the same Leader, on the warpath with ourselves. All with Him in view, all encouraged by His example and cheery words, all with their feet in His footprints, all trusting in His strength and looking to His reward.

"But those people are not like us. They kept good somehow, but we don't, we are always breaking our resolutions."

And what if we are! They will mend surely. When your tire gets punctured, you do not give it up as a hopeless case, but you get down and mend it and spin on again. As to thinking that other people never break their resolutions, we could not make a more mischievous mistake. The Saints did not lie in their cradles with tiny halos round their heads. They had inclinations like ours to fight against, and they did not always fight successfully. It was only by degrees that they got rid of bad habits.

Cheerfulness, then, is a necessary part of our spiritual warfare. The standing shoulder to shoulder is another.

"In my opinion," writes the chaplain to the Household troops, "soldiers are an exceedingly fine class of men. You would be amazed if you knew how self-sacrificing they can be." They will clean the accoutrements of a man on duty and get him ready for parade next day. If a man feels ill on the march but thinks he is able to keep up, his comrades will help him by carrying his rifle or equipment

Lord Wolseley says: "When an army bivouacks in the open country, cavalry picket their horses"—that is, fasten them to a stake—"and each man sleeps in front of his own horse. When troops bivouack in the immediate presence of an enemy and a night attack is possible, the men must remain accoutred, the horses saddled and harnessed. The men with horses must sleep as best they can, taking it in turn to lie down whilst the comrade holds the two horses.

"A staff-officer should remain behind with the rear-guard

until it marches, to direct in the collection of the baggage. No more disagreeable duty can fall to the lot of an officer or soldier than this. It is most fatiguing to march in the dusty wake of an army, but it is on such occasions that officers show their true mettle. Any man can be cheerful and zealous with an advanced guard or even with the rear guard during a retreat, but it is only those who have the keenest professional feeling who can throw all their energies into every little duty, irrespective of its being agreeable or otherwise."

"War," it is well said, "brings out the best and worst qualities of human nature." Among the best is surely the soldier's love of the home he has left behind, and devotedness to the comrades enlisted in the same service with himself.

The bravest soldier can have a tender heart.

"At Waterloo, early in the morning after the fight, Mr. Hulme woke the Duke still grim, unwashed and smoke-blackened, and read the list of his principal officers—name after name—dead or dying, until the hot tears ran like those of a woman down the iron-visage of the great soldier."

"From my experience," says a sergeant, "I should say soldiers are rather tender-hearted. I have seen great strapping men—who have fought with the utmost recklessness and looked death in the face a score of times—standing by the side of the wounded crying like children." When a soldier sees his comrade wounded, he feels almost as if the injury had been done to himself. That soldiers are ready to die for one another is such a simple truth, and is proved so repeatedly in every campaign, that it would be waste of time to do more than notice it.

May we not well learn a lesson or two from our brave redcoats! And this one in particular—that it is not because a fellow-soldier attracts by his personal qualities, that he is to be kindly treated, helped, defended. But because he is *in the Service,* fighting under the same banner, under the same Leader, for the same cause. The foundation of our comradeship is respect for one another, because—as St. Paul says: "*You are Christ's.*"[1] Only cruel Cain could ask: "Am I my brother's keeper?"[2]

"But *we* cannot die for one another, can we, nor cry when we see people wounded?"

Some people are wonderfully clever in discovering what they *can't* do for others, and quite overlook what they *can* do. We have all to care for one another, defend and help one another. This we may do in many ways—by amusing little brothers and sisters at home, by helping to entertain visitors; by cheering the poor, the old, the sick, who have none to visit them.

We might deny ourselves a little gimcrack now and then to put its price into the poor-box or the offertory plate. I am afraid we are too much inclined to make our pity for others a matter of words only, and because we cannot do everything, we do nothing.

One thing we can all do, we can try to *think* kindly of those about us. How many mistakes we have all made through misunderstanding one another! A general officer tells the following story of himself:

In the midst of battle he was trying to check the flight of some panic-stricken men. One of these came stumbling along, not heeding a word that was said to him. Indignant and impatient, the officer, as he came near this man, leaned from his horse and touching him with his sword, said sharply, "Go back, sir!"

The man, looking up with an expression of anguish and despair on his face that said as plainly as words, "I am looking

1   I Cor. 3.
2   Genesis 4.

for a place to die," opened his tunic and showed a big, gaping wound in his breast. Then he dropped to the ground.

The officer instantly dismounted from his horse, but almost as he raised the man's head to his arm the poor fellow breathed his last.

"Oh, how sorry the officer would be! I think I'm more sorry for him than for the poor man."

"I'm sure he wouldn't have spoken like that if he had *known* what a bad wound the other had."

It may often happen that sharp words of ours fall upon a heart already smarting with some hidden sorrow. Should not this thought keep us from ever speaking unkindly?

To lighten another's burden is not difficult and is often the best means of lightening our own. Let us show readiness to lend a helping hand here, to carry a bit of baggage there, to set aside our own plans and conveniences in order to serve the general good. Here we must quicken our pace, for we have the young and the light-hearted by our side. Presently we shall have to fall back for the aged and the tired, who cannot get on so fast. Do you understand?

"Yes, we mustn't always be thinking of what *we* like, because perhaps other people don't like it at all. Some people want the window open in the train and some want it shut, and they can't both be satisfied, you know."

And have you noticed how much brighter as well as pleasanter those are who are ready to accommodate themselves to the taste of others?

Accommodating—this is what some of us are not. We cannot manage to suit ourselves to people and things that we come across. Hence there are collisions.

On a fine Saturday afternoon there are probably over a million men and women riding their bicycles on the roads of the United Kingdom. Of these, a certain number will come to grief, some by a breakage in the frame of the machine, or an unseen defect in the road, some by a side-slip on a soft piece of sand. But by far the greater number of accidents will be caused by collisions. Cyclists are continually being ridden into by other cyclists, or driven down by carts which will not keep their own side, or knocked over by old ladies rushing across the road. Or they hurt themselves under cart wheels, or, losing control of the machine down-hill, ride into brick walls, or collide with foot-passengers, or run over dogs.

But cyclists are not the only travellers whose mishaps are mainly due to collision. Most of the accidents which fill the newspapers have the same cause. This being the case, what living creatures will be least liable to accidents of any kind?

"Birds."

Yes; for speed and security combined, birds come first among travellers. The reason is that, whereas all crawlers on the earth's surface have to move along the same level and thus come in each other's way, birds have the whole of the free air in which to travel, at any height they choose. Each takes its own path without fear of finding anything to check, much less block its way. At a height of 400 feet, there are no obstructions whatever.

It is their freedom in this respect which makes the high rate of bird-speed possible. Collision can occur only among birds themselves when flocks are travelling together. As the direction is the same, the risk is very slight. Yet the birds take most careful precautions to prevent danger by maintaining regular distances, an even speed, and often a kind of military order. Such disasters are, therefore, rare.

But we need not go to living things to see the care with which collisions are to be prevented. Look at *f* and *i* when they come together in print. Instead of getting into each other's way, as they would do without a little friendly accommodation, they meet each other's needs admirably—*f* dotting *i* and *i* crossing *f*—*fi*.

"*We* don't knock up against each other."

I am glad to hear it. Your family must be an exceptionally happy one to be altogether free from collisions. You must be extremely careful, all of you, to show tact in dealing with one another—not insisting upon everybody seeing through your spectacles and thinking with your brains—careful to dexterously turn aside awkward subjects as they arise. But some people are wonderfully skilful in this way.

We were talking just now about birds. They possess in an extraordinary degree that wonderful homing instinct, the secret of which men are trying to discover. They find their way back to their homes however long, or new, or obstructed the road may be. Over vast stretches of sea and land, over mountains, over rivers, now across a trackless country, now through busy cities, the power of that wonderful instinct—the attraction of home—guides them in safety.

"I wish *we* had it."

It would be a convenience, no doubt. To be guided unerringly through the mazes of London to our own doorstep, would save time and trouble. But we have tongues to ask our way, and this, like other little bits of trouble, may be good for us—who knows?

Yet there is a Homing instinct we may well covet—not the bird's, but the Saint's. Troubles and difficulties beset their path. They looked beyond them—Home was beyond. Pleasures enticed them this way and that, but could not tempt them from the straight path that led to Home. Even the dropping off the path of those who had trod the way by their side, did not overwhelm them with "overmuch sorrow" for they were only gone on before and were waiting for them at

Home. And so the very loneliness of the road urged them to quicken their pace. If the sun shone brightly on their path, Home was still brighter, and they would not loiter. If the path was dark and dreary, what matter: soon—very soon—they would be at Home.

Beautiful Homing instinct of the Saints! would that we had more of it. It is a gift worth praying for and—which is much to our present purpose—it is a soldier's instinct.

"Do soldiers, as a rule, retain their home affections?" a sergeant-major was asked.

"You would think so if you saw some of the youngsters poring over a letter from home," was the answer. "Many of them send a portion of their pay to their parents, and a greater number go home on leave as often as they can afford it. In some cases they go when they can't afford it, when they have just sufficient money to pay their fare home and nothing whatever to bring them back. They write to their regiments for warrants, and the money is stopped out of their pay."

Of one campaign we are told: "Not letters only, but photographs of the scenery and beautiful Indian shawls and table-cloths find their way across the sea to the village; socks, too, for little brothers at home, guernseys, vests, stockings, and shawls, knitted by rough but loving hands among the wild mountains of the Khyber, attest the warmth of soldier-lads' affection. 'Ah, he's more comfort to me than all the t'other childern put together,' said one mother, as she related how two pounds sterling had reached her from the camp at Lundi Kotal; 'he never writes, doesn't Harry, wi'out puttin' summat in his letters.'"

The thought of home cheers the soldier while the fight lasts. And it is his first thought in the hour of victory. "They'll be talking about us at home," a young soldier was heard to say at Omdurman when the last shot was fired.

"Stand fast, 95th!" said Wellington at Waterloo. "What will they say in England!"

"*Stand fast!*" This is our Leader's word to us now. He is giving us the glory and the privileges of knighthood. He is giving us, with His Holy Spirit, Charity, Joy, Peace, Patience—just the equipment a soldier needs. And now He says to us: "*Stand fast!*"

O my Lord and my Leader, help me! Help me to stand fast to the end. I do not ask for an easy life in Your service. I ask this only—to be faithful to You, to satisfy You, to give You cause to be proud of me. Keep me at Your side always. Never let me be separated from You. "Wherever Thou shalt be, Lord my King, in life or in death, there let Thy servant be."[1]

Our talks have come to an end, and we must take leave of one another. Later perhaps we may come together again, to consider more at leisure our new dignity and what it involves—for according to the old adage, "*Noblesse oblige.*"[2] We may want to examine in detail our knightly duties, and to place our knighthood itself under a high Patronage. You know it was quite the idea of Chivalry to *dedicate* feats of arms to some noble dame even while loyalty to the Leader inspired them.

"I know the noble Lady we shall choose!"

"The one the Spanish Knight chose, when he hung his sword on the pillar beside her altar."

Suppose we commend one another before parting to that Soldier-Saint, that fighting after his example as Soldiers of Christ and Knights of our Lady here on earth, we may deserve to be crowned with him in Heaven!

---

1   2 Kings 15.
2   "Nobility obliges."

Additional titles available from

St. Augustine Academy Press
Books for the Traditional Catholic

Titles by Mother Mary Loyola:

Blessed are they that Mourn
Confession and Communion
Coram Sanctissimo (Before the Most Holy)
First Communion
First Confession
Forgive us our Trespasses
Hail! Full of Grace
Heavenwards
Home for Good
Jesus of Nazareth: The Story of His Life Written for Children
Questions on First Communion
The Child of God: What comes of our Baptism
The Children's Charter
The Little Children's Prayer Book
The Soldier of Christ: Talks before Confirmation
Trust
Welcome! Holy Communion Before and After
With the Church

Titles by Father Lasance:

The Catholic Girl's Guide
The Young Man's Guide

Tales of the Saints:

A Child's Book of Saints by William Canton
A Child's Book of Warriors by William Canton
Legends & Stories of Italy by Amy Steedman
Mary, Help of Christians by Rev. Bonaventure Hammer
Page, Esquire and Knight by Marion Florence Lansing
The Book of Saints and Heroes by Leonora Lang
Saint Patrick: Apostle of Ireland
The Story of St. Elizabeth of Hungary by William Canton

Check our Website for more:

www.staugustineacademypress.com